Akash Kapur is the author of *India Becoming: A Portrait of Life in Modern India* and the editor of an anthology, *Auroville: Dream and Reality*. He is the former Letter from India columnist for the *New York Times*, the recipient of a Whiting Grant, and has written for various leading publications in the UK, USA and India. He grew up in Auroville and returned there to live with his family after being educated in the USA and UK, where he received a doctorate from Oxford University as a Rhodes Scholar.

Praise for *Better to Have Gone*

'A forensic reconstruction of two deaths set against the background of a tropical utopia. It is beautifully written and structured, deeply moving, and realised in wise, thoughtful, chiselled prose. It tells an extraordinary tale of a paradise lost, and of the dangers of utopian naivety: what happens when dreams collide with harsh reality. Like *In Cold Blood*, it is that rarity: a genuine non-fiction classic.' **William Dalrymple, author of *The Anarchy***

'Akash Kapur's *Better to Have Gone* is a troubling and moving account of lives gone wrong in the search for an eastern Utopia.' **Damon Galgut, *Wall Street Journal*, Writers' Favourite Books of 2021**

'This beautifully written account … is fascinating in describing the efforts of people … to carve out a sustainable community in such a forbidding environment. But it becomes more fascinating still when it begins to explore the contradictions between idealism and real life.' **Mick Brown, *Sunday Telegraph***

'A haunting, heartbreaking story, deeply researched and lucidly told, with an almost painful emotional honesty … I kept wanting to read *Better to Have Gone* because I found it so gripping; I kept wanting not to read it because I found it so upsetting. *Better to Have Gone* ends with an unexpected lightness, even transcendence, as Kapur helps us see what Auroville has given him, gives him still, despite the pain.' **Amy Waldman, *New York Times***

'Using the framework of a personal historical quest, Akash Kapur gives us a gripping morality tale, phosphorescent and unsettling, of the cruelty that accompanies utopia.' **Jeet Thayil, Booker Prize shortlisted author of** *Narcopolis*

'Spellbinding and otherworldly, *Better to Have Gone* is an exquisite literary achievement. With graceful, luminous prose, Akash Kapur's intimate account of utopian Auroville is entrancing, devastating and unforgettable. Above all, this book is a hauntingly beautiful love story, composed by a writer in full command of his craft.' **Gilbert King, Pulitzer Prize–winning author of** *Devil in the Grove*

'Haunting and elegant ... The beauty of Mr Kapur's story lies in our conviction, by the end, that he and his wife have found most of the answers they were looking for.' **Tunku Varadarajan,** *Wall Street Journal*

'Akash Kapur has written a trenchant, nuanced account of the longing for a perfect world. Working from personal experience and a writer's profound curiosity, he takes us deep into the heart of an intentional community's ambitions and failures. This is an important work about the eternal human desire for utopia, and about the dystopia that always lurks within these dreams.' **Vikram Chandra, author of** *Sacred Games*

'Kapur's account of the trajectories of his main characters is gripping ... [he] has a fine understanding of the fundamentally flawed, even cankered, nature of any utopia. The author's cool, clean style, and his admirable refusal to judge any of his characters' words and actions ... give the book a quiet cumulative power.' **Neel Mukherjee,** *Financial Times*

'Kapur weaves together memoir, history and ethnography to tell a story of the desire for utopia and the cruelties committed in its name ... told with a native son's fondness, fury, stubborn loyalty, exasperated amusement ... the story is suspensefully structured, and I consumed it with a febrile intensity ... It is a complicated offering, this book, and the artefact of a great love.' **Parul Sehgal,** *New York Times*

'In this compulsively readable account, Akash Kapur ... unravels a mystery whose players are yogis and hippies, Tamil villagers and a disaffected son of the American elite. Kapur's great achievement is to narrate a personal tragedy with such generosity and insight that it becomes a love story – one that doesn't shy from the passionate idealism or devastating failures of sixties utopianism.' **Nell Freudenberger, author of *Lost and Wanted* and *The Newlyweds***

'*Better to Have Gone* tells the extraordinary true story of an "aspiring utopia" named Auroville, "The City of Dawn", established near Pondicherry in southeast India in 1968. A riveting account of human aspiration and folly taken to extremes.' **Dan Cryer, *Boston Globe***

'A riveting memoir of a search for utopia ... Kapur is a terrific storyteller ... his writing compels you to follow him as he digs deeper.' **Alison Arieff, *San Francisco Chronicle***

'This gripping, magical, deeply moving book is a story of stubborn, self-sacrificing idealism – both its beauty and its cost. Akash Kapur set out to understand the visionary lives and terrible deaths of his wife's parents in Auroville, the South Indian utopian community where he and she grew up ... It is exhilarating to read about a place and time where utopia seemed not just possible but close.' **Larissa MacFarquhar, author of *Strangers Drowning: Impossible Idealism, Drastic Choices, and the Urge to Help***

'An enlightening look at how a well-meaning utopian community in India became complicated by reality. In a propulsive narrative, [Kapur] chronicles the story of John Walker and Diane Maes, the parents of his wife, Auralice, who left their homes in the waning days of the hippie movement for South India's idealistic "planned city" Auroville ... Expect the unexpected in this riveting story.' ***Publishers Weekly***

ALSO BY AKASH KAPUR

India Becoming: A Portrait of Life in Modern India

Auroville: Dream and Reality (editor)

BETTER TO HAVE GONE

Love, Death, and the Quest for
Utopia in Auroville

AKASH KAPUR

SCRIBNER

LONDON NEW YORK SYDNEY TORONTO NEW DELHI

First published in the United States by Scribner, an imprint of
Simon & Schuster, Inc., 2021
First published in Great Britain by Scribner, an imprint of
Simon & Schuster UK Ltd, 2021
This edition published in Great Britain by Scribner, an imprint of
Simon & Schuster UK Ltd, 2022

1 3 5 7 9 10 8 6 4 2

Simon & Schuster UK Ltd
1st Floor
222 Gray's Inn Road
London WC1X 8HB

www.simonandschuster.co.uk
www.simonandschuster.com.au
www.simonandschuster.co.in

Simon & Schuster Australia, Sydney
Simon & Schuster India, New Delhi

A CIP catalogue record for this book is available from the British Library

Paperback ISBN: 978-1-3985-0677-0
eBook ISBN: 978-1-3985-0676-3

Interior design by Wendy Blum
Printed in the UK by CPI Group (UK) Ltd, Croydon, CR0 4YY

Diane, John, Gillian,
Auralice (always)

If there is a sense of the real, then there must also be something that one could call a sense of the possible....The possible embraces not only the dreams of high-strung individuals but also the still dormant designs of God. A possible experience or a possible truth is not equal to real experience and real truth minus the value of reality, but possesses—at least, in the view of its adherents—something exceedingly divine, a fire, a flight, a will to build and a conscious utopianism that does not shun reality but instead treats it as a mission and invention.

—Robert Musil, *The Man Without Qualities*

CONTENTS

Contents

BETTER TO
HAVE GONE

PROLOGUE

Unfinished Business

IN THE WINTER OF 2004, I moved with my wife, Auralice, to a town called Auroville. Situated in South India, Auroville is an intentional community on a plateau overlooking the Bay of Bengal. It was founded in 1968 with the ambitious goals of encouraging human unity and fostering evolution. Some people think of Auroville as a utopia, but the people who live there, including my wife and me, reject this label. Utopia is a place that's perfect and that doesn't exist. Auroville is real, and highly—humanly—imperfect. I guess it would be more appropriate to say that Auroville is an aspiring utopia.

People typically move to places such as Auroville, have moved throughout the ages, because they're searching for something new. Maybe they're tired of their lives, maybe they feel alienated by the way the world is. They sell the house, pack their bags, travel to a faraway destination, and hope for a fresh start. But for Auralice and me, our move represented something different. We weren't lunging toward the future; we were taking a step back, into the past.

Auralice and I grew up in Auroville. We spent our early years there, in a magical, denuded terrain, a flat desert that felt very remote, both physically and psychologically. We knew each other as kids, and then we went our separate ways in the world—the real world, as we called it—and built lives. Now, more than a decade later, we found ourselves leaving those lives, dismantling the identities we had so assiduously constructed, and moving back to the landscape of our childhoods.

We were living in Brooklyn. We had rented a one-bedroom apartment on Atlantic Avenue, in a prewar building with a brick façade and protruding metal fire escapes. Atlantic was noisy and a little dirty; its honking trucks reminded me of India, but I liked it there. We took the subway into the city, we worked at jobs, we spent our paychecks on the usual things—clothes and technology, books—and we tried new restaurants on weekends. We had lots of friends; we led good, *normal* lives.

People asked us why we were leaving all of that, and we didn't have a coherent answer. Sometimes we told them we were homesick. Sometimes we just said we wanted to try something new (though, of course, it wasn't actually new for us). We said things about America being the past and Asia the future. Also, we were horrified by the war in Iraq. I remember riding the subway one day, looking at a photo spread in the *New York Times*, American soldiers in green combat fatigues amid the orange glow of a dust storm, and I thought, so clearly, I don't want to be part of this.

These were all real reasons, and they strike me now, each, as valid reasons. But there was something else. My wife had a history in Auroville. Her mother and adoptive father both died there when she was fourteen years old. She left soon after, moved to New York to start a new life with a new family. She (and I) never understood those deaths. They loomed huge in our lives, hers especially, and also in the collective consciousness of our town. Over time, they had become part of an emerging mythology. But it was never clear what had happened; the deaths remained shrouded, inscrutable tragedies that hovered over my wife, and then eventually over me, too. Looking back, I know that's the real reason we returned to Auroville: we had unfinished business there.

October of 1986 and a man lies dying in a hut at the edge of a canyon. His name is John Anthony Walker. He's on a mattress on a cement floor, and by his side sits a woman wrapped in a shawl, a yellow cat in her lap, and she cries. Her name is Diane Maes. This has been going on for months. All through the summer, first in the brutal South Indian heat, and then into the monsoon, with dark clouds blowing in and promising respite, the man's condition has worsened. What is it that ails him? What is it that has brought him—brought them both—to this point?

Once their lives were full of promise. They are part of a great adventure, this quest to build a new world called Auroville. They arrived here like so many idealists and romantics, filled with aspiration and optimism, and they have worked hard, held their faith diligently. John, the intelligent, privileged scion of a wealthy American East Coast family. Diane, the beautiful, spiritually inclined dropout from Belgium. Both have been determined, alongside hundreds of others who have left families, friends, homes, and possessions behind, to come to this flat patch of land in India and remake human society. But now John lies ill on a cracked concrete floor, and Diane cries.

On October 13, it rains. Parched soil comes to life. Streams cut into red earth, flow toward the canyon, join to form rivers that replenish the ocean. Roots are exposed, trees and shrubs overturned. The frogs are a cacophony; snakes emerge to feast on them. A drizzle turns into a downpour. Diane scribbles an urgent note to a person she thinks might be able to save them, a Frenchman named Bernard. "Where is the force for us?" she writes desperately. John dies early the next morning. Diane dies the same afternoon.

This is the story we knew; this is the history Auralice carried with her when she left for America as a fourteen-year-old girl, to move in with John's family.

The mystery and sense of secrecy were always nagging. But you get on with life, you push the questions away. Over time, they subside, or at least lose their urgency.

Then one evening I was browsing through a drawer at the apartment of John's relatives (Auralice's new family) in New York, and I stumbled upon a stack of overflowing green folders. They were filled with letters and postcards, pages from diaries, and wrinkled old photographs. These were John's surviving papers, preserved by his sister, Gillian, now Auralice's adoptive mother.

Those folders opened worlds for me. For the first time, I was able to go beyond the myths of John and Diane, to see them as human beings—a man and a woman who had dreamed, who had loved, and for whom things had gone horribly wrong. The folders also brought me back to the Auroville of my youth: a place I had cherished dearly, a vista of eroded red canyons and dusty fields that seemed full of possibility. But there were fault lines below that idyll, conflicts and divisions of which Auralice and I had been only dimly aware. John's papers helped us better understand the social tumult of our childhoods; and they allowed us to see, too, how that tumult was implicated in what happened to him and Diane.

I stayed up practically all night reading (and, later, there would be many more sleepless nights). It was raining outside and at one point I heard a loud fight on the sidewalk, full of cursing and violent threats, but I hardly noticed. I didn't know it then, but my immersion in John's papers was the start of a journey, for both Auralice and me. My name is on the cover of this book, but we have undertaken this project together, every step of the way. We have tracked down old friends of John's and Diane's, their former lovers, family members, fellow travelers in Auroville, scores of them on six continents. We have read and inhaled the dust of old letters, diaries, crumbling, typewritten meeting reports, often in ill-lit archives. We have lived with this book for more than a decade, and the experience has changed how we see ourselves and our community; and changed, also, our feelings about the very idea of utopia and the search for perfection. There was much more to this story than we ever knew. Those deaths were far more complicated than we could have imagined.

So Auralice and I moved back to Auroville in early 2004. I came first, right after the New Year, and then Auralice boxed our belongings in New York and traveled a couple of months later. We'd been away almost two decades (though we'd made brief visits in that time), and it was strange being back, familiar yet also jarring. My parents and many of our friends still lived in Auroville. They had changed, we had, too, and so had our community. The once-desolate plateau was now a thriving township of about three and half thousand people from fifty-nine countries. The desert of our youths was a vibrant forest. Over the years, Aurovilians had dug irrigation trenches, built dams, drilled wells, and planted more than three million trees. The results of all this labor were dramatic, and inspiring. Auroville was arguably the most successful reforestation effort in India, and a global model for environmental conservation.

We settled into this newly greened topography. We built a house, got a dog, bought a motorcycle, and had two sons, one of whom we gave the middle name John Anthony. Sometimes as we walked around town, people looked at Auralice and I felt they were gazing in wonder, as if incredulous that she had built a family, a life, despite her history. They came up to us with stories, memories of John and Diane, different (and often contradictory) versions of their deaths. Once, a woman approached me and expressed concern for the well-being of our children. She spewed a theory about bad karma, of a curse still emanating from that hut by the canyon. I was abrupt and suggested she keep her superstitions to herself. But I had trouble sleeping that night.

One day, about two years after returning, Auralice asked me if I would accompany her to the canyon. She hadn't previously expressed a desire to go; she'd hardly spoken about John's and Diane's deaths. This would be her first visit since she left Auroville some twenty years earlier, her first time at the house where she'd lived as a girl. She said she wanted to find their grave, which she had never seen.

We went by motorcycle on a sunny afternoon. We drove through the flat land of Auroville, now scattered with apartment buildings, schools, cultural centers, and restaurants. We took a dirt track that went over a stone bridge, and then the track ran out and we parked near a forest. I had spent time around here as a boy, and I knew we were close to where John and Diane lived. But the area was unrecognizable; the foliage had grown so thick we couldn't even see the canyon anymore.

We pushed our way through bramble and thorns, and first we found the hut. All that remained of it was a shell in the forest: a couple of mossy walls, crumbling plaster and brick, blackened as if charred by fire. A few feet on, we stumbled over their grave. It was just an indentation in the earth—no marker, not even a clearing. Mosquitoes buzzed in the air, a mongoose pawed nervously at the earth. A powdery termite mound stood over it all, tall but crumbling.

We crouched on the ground and took the scene in. There was nothing there to signify John's and Diane's deaths, and certainly nothing of their lives. We closed our eyes and tried to summon something we could hold on to—a sound or a smell, at least a feeling, anything more than memory. Auralice started to cry. "I miss them so much," she said. I noticed a trickle of blood on her leg, a vertical line running down her calf; probably a scratch from the surrounding bramble.

"I miss them so much," she said again. And I wondered: What really happened here?

PART I

Let's make heaven on earth, my friends
instead of waiting till later.

—Heinrich Heine

The only lies for which we are truly
punished are those we tell ourselves.

—V. S. Naipaul, *In a Free State*

DREAMERS

John

IT BEGINS LIKE THIS. A young man, born into privilege, his life a steady ascent from the town houses of Georgetown to the halls of Harvard, every door open to him, his family a bastion of the East Coast establishment. His father is the director of the National Gallery of Art in Washington, a mentor to Jackie Kennedy, and a regular visitor at the White House. The family's social circle—Isaiah Berlin, Dylan Thomas, T. S. Eliot, Paul Mellon, Joe Alsop—unlocking worlds and opportunities.

Cocktail parties with crystal chandeliers and monogrammed silverware. Weekends in Dumbarton Oaks, an elegant estate at the highest point of Georgetown, where his father is on the board. Swimming in the marble-edged pool, Schubert concerts at night, tea under the loggia, playing hide-and-seek with his sister, Gillian, amid the wisteria and fountains in the Italian gardens.

Summers crossing the Atlantic, to his mother's childhood home in England, and an ancestral castle in Scotland. First class on the *Queen Mary*, John and Gillian excited kids, running around, exploring the boiler room and lower levels. The war has just ended and sometimes they see troops on the ships, in hammocks strung across decks. Once they bump into Fred Astaire and Ginger Rogers; of course they ask for autographs.

John Anthony Drummond Walker, born June 30, 1942. He is tall (six feet two inches) and angular, with a long, pensive face, handsome in a reticent, unreachable way. Everyone says he has his father's easy charm; he leads a gilded life. And yet: He has always felt a twinge of dissatisfaction, a constant if barely articulated restlessness, like an itch. It will propel him from place to place, quest to quest, cause to cause. Always searching, always moving—never, it seems, quite arriving.

His father, John Walker III, is a man of substance, part of a Georgetown clique that dominates political and cultural life in the capital in the postwar years. He is the first curator of the National Gallery, joining the institution when it is founded in 1937, and soon he is its director. He walks with a limp from a childhood case of polio, but he is handsome and imposing, and through charisma, connections, and persistence, he builds the fledgling gallery into one of the preeminent cultural organizations of the world. He comes from old Pittsburgh money—his grandfather was part of a circle of wealthy Scotch industrialists, a partner to Andrew Carnegie—and travels in rich, cultured circles. This helps Walker Sr. acquire for the gallery, and for the country, a string of notable artists: Cézanne, da Vinci, Picasso, Rembrandt, Titian, Raphael, van Gogh.

John's mother, Lady Margaret Drummond, is the daughter of Sir Eric Drummond—the sixteenth Earl of Perth, the first secretary-general of the League of Nations, later the British ambassador to Rome. They are lineal descendants from Mary, Queen of Scots, and two Catholic saints and martyrs, including Thomas More, the patron saint of utopia. Her marriage to Walker Sr., held at St. Andrew's church in Rome, is the subject of international newspaper headlines; the pope sends a telegram with benedictions.

John grows up with tales of his family's esteemed lineage. He carries these tales with him wherever he goes, ambivalently and often grudgingly, a pedigree to live up to. As a child, he reads his mother's gold-edged copy of *A Book of English Martyrs*, which includes sections on his ancestors. "Not disloyalty, not treason, but conscience was their true offence," proclaims the preface. John is taught that his forefathers ended up in the Tower of London for their Catholic convictions. When push comes to shove, he is told, one must be ready to die for one's beliefs. Perhaps this offers some insight into what comes later.

A rich, privileged life; and a fun life, too. While there will always be a certain austerity to John, an element of renunciation and self-abnegation, he is a man of multitudes, and he also contains a strong streak of hedonism. He parties at Harvard, dancing on tables at the Casablanca, a bohemian hangout, and sipping daiquiris and cheap Italian wine (Orvieto white, $1.20 a bottle) while talking literature at the *Harvard Advocate*. He belongs to a circle of off-campus rich kids that drink and smoke with glamorous women and men (it's a very gay scene, ahead of its time). The socialite Edie Sedgwick—one of Andy Warhol's Superstars, an icon of the sixties—is a close friend, and a regular at their parties. John drinks with classmates on the top floor of the A.D., a student club, and they rain glasses on passersby below. Later, the police will make them get on their knees and clean the brick sidewalk with toothbrushes.

The prince of Lichtenstein visits Cambridge while John is at Harvard. The prince's father has a formidable art collection. It includes Leonardo da Vinci's *Ginevra de' Benci*, one of the only Leonardos in the world still in a private collection. John's father is eager to get his hands on the painting; a self-respecting national gallery must have a Leonardo. He has heard that the royal family might be amenable to selling, and he seeks to cultivate the young prince ("Baby Lichtenstein," he calls him). He asks John to meet the prince in Cambridge and opens an expense account for his son at the Club Henry IV, an upscale French restaurant in Harvard Square. John takes maximum advantage, racking up bills on escargots, coq au vin, steak, and imported wine. One lunch with the prince amounts to $124; his father is flummoxed, but all is later forgiven when the *Ginevra* is acquired—at a rumored price of more than $5 million, the highest ever paid for a painting—making it the only Leonardo in the Americas.

Around the same time, John's father presides over a courtly evening at the National Gallery, attended, among others, by President Kennedy, Vice President Johnson, their wives, Secretary of State Dean Rusk, and nearly every member of Congress. Walker Sr. has worked for months in partnership with Jackie Kennedy and André Malraux, the French minister of culture, to set up an American viewing of the *Mona Lisa*. The four-century-old painting has been transported in its own ship cabin across the Atlantic, and Walker Sr. unveils it in a columned rotunda on the second floor of the Gallery. The ceremony cements his position at the heart of Washington's power structure.

John is going in a different direction. He attends a lecture at MIT by Aldous Huxley, the English author and philosopher who has just published his utopian novel, *Island*, in which psychedelics and Eastern mysticism combine to create an ideal society. John listens to Huxley, and something in him stirs. Shortly afterward, he gets mixed up in the Timothy Leary–Richard Alpert drug experiments at Harvard and takes LSD for the first time. The stirring becomes a shaking. John's world—that safe, establishment cocoon of his father's—loses its foundations. He is depressed and aimless; his sister visits him in Cambridge and finds his apartment disordered, its condition, she feels, reflecting John's state of mind.

The first in a series of dropouts and incomplete assignments in life ensues. He takes time off from college and heads to Portsmouth Abbey, a Catholic Benedictine monastery and boarding school in Rhode Island, where he was a student before Harvard. He spends a year in retreat, meditating and wandering the expansive campus that slopes into Narragansett Bay, attending prayers in the vaulting wooden cathedral. He is searching, seeking new horizons; and so, during the same period, is American Catholicism, which is opening itself to Eastern religion. John discovers Buddhism, he reads Thomas Merton, and grows close to Aelred Graham, a member of the Portsmouth community. He helps Graham build a Zen garden outside the monastery. Every morning, Graham takes his clothes off in a ground-floor, glass-fronted room and performs elaborate yoga poses. One time the cleaning man walks in and finds an undressed Graham in a headstand. "Well, he seems to see the world upside down," the cleaner later remarks. He's onto something: it's the early sixties, and soon everything will be upside down.

Diane

In Belgium, in the town of Sint-Niklaas, a warren of winding streets and attached homes, a baby girl, Diane Maes, is born on May 23, 1950. She will grow into a vibrant, vivacious woman, and she, too, will feel a constant restlessness. But Diane's restlessness is less vague. There is no ambivalence in her; she is blessed with clarity and single-mindedness, a gift of faith that will long elude John. Diane knows what she wants. She wants to escape her town, get away from its provinciality and the clutches of her controlling mother.

Small-town life in East Flanders is idyllic, or deadly boring—it depends on your perspective. Farmers' markets on weekends in the town square, the largest in Belgium. A few steps away, a green park and a castle, with a wide moat. Like most families in the region, hers is devoutly Catholic. Every Sunday they attend the Church of Our Lady, with its colorful murals and towering gold statue. One time when Diane is fourteen, she visits a local country market and enters a dance contest. She's on a wooden stage, laughing, loud music playing, and she does the twist; she wins a prize, a lamp. Happy days. She's slightly built with high cheekbones and cherry lips that open up to straight white teeth, and a girlish, joyful giggle. She has dreamy gray-blue eyes, and a habit of punctuating her sentences with *"Weet ge? Weet ge?"* (You know? You know?) Sometimes she puts her arm on people's shoulders when she says that, leans in to them. Men melt; Diane is magnetic.

Her father is a housepainter. He spends much of his time on the road, at construction sites across the country. He is a big, popular man, nicknamed Tarzan. One day he visits an astrologer. When he returns home, he tells his family, "Look at me, I am a man as strong as a tree but I won't live long." As his wife turns toward him, he seems to vanish. That night in bed she touches her husband and his body is cold. Soon after, he travels for a job. His wife gives him money for a train ticket and tells him to be careful. He drinks and gambles the money away, and a friend offers him a ride home. Maybe the friend also has been drinking. A train hits their car at a crossing and Diane's father is killed. One of his eyes falls out; it is later found on the floor of the car.

Life gets harder for the family. Diane, her sister, and their mother must now rely on government welfare money, monthly checks that are conditional on the girls continuing their educations. Diane enrolls in an arts institute in Antwerp. She's an indifferent student, bored and distracted. She meets a man. He's five years older, tall and good-looking, with a long beard and flowing brown hair. He's a hippie. He has traveled overland to India, Turkey, Afghanistan. He's written about it in a local newspaper; he tells such stories! Diane wants to run away with him but her mother steps in. Diane is just sixteen, and besides, the family needs the government checks that arrive for her education.

Diane's mother puts her in a Catholic reform school, and her world constricts further. She feels trapped by the rules, the formality, and the hierarchy. She will harbor a lifelong suspicion, terror even, of institutions, and she comes to abhor organized religion. One day she steals the flowers from church. Her family is aghast. Later, they will wonder if this was the reason for all her troubles.

Bernard

In Paris, on a snowy October 30, 1923, a boy is born. Bernard Enginger is the son of Maurice, a chemical engineer, and Marie-Louise, a housewife. Bernard is the second of eight children. He spends his young years between Paris and Saint-Pierre-Quiberon, the family's ancestral village in Brittany. He, too, feels constrained by the smallness of his world: the pettiness of commerce and religion, the strictures of bourgeois propriety. He is happiest in the summers, when the family vacations in Brittany and he can sail alone on the Atlantic. Out on the waters, Bernard is free. As soon as he returns to land, he feels imprisoned. Even as a boy, he is possessed by doubts and questions, a sense of existential vacancy.

He is strong-willed and a little wild. As a child, he sets fire to a closet at home. One night he cuts the electrical wires with a pair of scissors and plunges the family into darkness. He butts heads with his father, who accuses Bernard of having no religion. When the Nazis invade France, Bernard is determined to join the French Resistance; his father warns him that he will be expelled from the family. Undissuaded, Bernard joins Turma-Vengeance, one of the largest and most active wings of the Resistance. He surveys military installations on the Atlantic coast, carries messages between cells, and transports weapons and explosives.

One day Bernard is sent on a mission to Bordeaux. A spy has infiltrated Turma-Vengeance and he must warn his colleagues. But he is betrayed by another spy—they are everywhere, these spies: this will feed a lifelong suspiciousness—and, on Boulevard Pasteur, in Bordeaux, a black car from the Kriminalpolizei screeches to a halt, two men with pistols jump out, and they arrest him. Bernard spends the next several months being moved from prison to prison, often in solitary confinement, interrogated and brutally tortured by the Gestapo. Later, he will say that his life begins only when he is tortured; it is his first real moment of existence.

The Nazis plunge Bernard's head into a sink of water, and they almost drown him. They do other things, too, gruesome things about which he will never be able to speak. But Bernard remains unbroken. The Nazis call his parents in; they warn the father that unless he gets his son to talk, Bernard will be executed. The father asks Bernard's torturers if they would try to convince their own children to betray their companions. Bernard is put on a train for the concentration camp of Buchenwald, and from there he's sent to Mauthausen, in Austria. Mauthausen has a reputation as one of the toughest concentration camps. Bernard works in the granite quarries; half his fellow prisoners die.

After liberation, Bernard makes his way back to the family home, in the sixth arrondissement of Paris. His mother's hair has turned white during his absence. He is barely recovered from typhus, and he weighs just fifty-five pounds. Europe rebuilds, France begins unpicking the tangle of defeat and collaboration. Life goes on—but not for Bernard. For him, the period after liberation is worse than the camps themselves. Everything is broken; he feels hollow, and he contemplates suicide. Finally, a cousin who has been appointed the governor of Pondicherry, a French colony in South India, steps in and offers him a job as his secretary. Bernard leaps at the opportunity: a chance to get away, to start anew.

On the way to Pondicherry, he stops in Egypt and, in a hotel in Luxor, bumps into the French writer André Gide. Bernard has long admired Gide's work; he credits it with keeping him alive in the concentration camps. He writes Gide a letter, saying, "*J'ai soif. Tous les jeunes ont soif avec moi*" (I am thirsty. All the young people share my thirst). To Bernard's surprise and joy, Gide replies. He writes that he sympathizes with Bernard's impatience; he advises him to avoid all ideologies and institutions, to resist the temptations of religion and isms. He adds, "*Le monde ne sera sauvé, s'il peut l'être, que par des insoumis*" (The world will be saved, if it can be, only by rebels).

J'ai soif. All these dreamers, all these searchers. John, Diane, Bernard: all rebels in their own way, each trying to fill a distinctive gap in their soul, each looking in a different place. Who can foretell how their lives will intersect? Who can predict that they will meet on the same arid patch of earth in India? They will be joined by hundreds and then thousands of others. So many around the world are propelled by the same thirst, the same vague longing for something different, something more meaningful—a deeper way of living.

Where does this urge come from? You could say it's the human condition. We all want better, we're all always imagining fresh starts and alternative lives. Everyone is at heart a utopian. But maybe it's easier to follow our dreams at certain times than at others. There's something about the era in which these people are living. Some moments in time are simply more epochal: they offer more scaffolding for our ideals, and for our fantasies of reinvention.

Auroville will be founded in 1968. Really, though, it emerges from the rubble of the Second World War. In the wake of that nihilism, anything seems possible—anything, as long as it's not the same. The dreamers who spill out across the world are dismayed with humanity and society, utterly lacking faith in existing institutions and traditions. This is primarily a Western phenomenon; it's no coincidence that there's a heightened interest around this period in Eastern religions and cultures. The spiritualism of the East offers a salve against the broken materialism of the West.

The 1950s see an initial wave of postwar communes and intentional projects. In Japan, the Yamagishi movement lives by a credo of anticonsumerism and egalitarianism. In Israel, the kibbutzim swell with an influx of refugees. In 1955, the preacher Jim Jones creates the Peoples Temple in Indiana, rooted in a combination of Christianity and Marxism (this community will culminate more than two decades later with the deaths by suicide of over nine hundred people in the Jonestown Massacre: the line between utopia and dystopia is often thin). Things really take off in the 1960s, when all the restiveness coalesces into the countercultural and hippie movements. Thousands of experiments in alternative living emerge across the planet. The sixties are the golden age of utopia. More than ten thousand communities, with at least 750,000 members, come up in the world during the decade. Auroville emerges at the tail end of this efflorescence—though it will, ultimately, outgrow and outlive many earlier projects.

Many years later, a man who lives in Auroville, an American friend of John and Diane's, will put it to me like this: "Auroville couldn't have happened without the sixties. It was just such a creature of its time. We brought everything with us—all the good stuff, all the baggage. Hope, faith, love, free love, drugs, all the sloppiness, all the energy and good vibes."

We're sitting in his garden having coffee when he says this. He's telling me stories of the pioneer days, how they'd all landed in Auroville and etched this town out of a wasteland. He dropped out of college in Boston when he got a high draft number. He lived for a time in Haight-Ashbury, in San Francisco, where everything—food, rent, clothes, marijuana—was free. When he first heard about Auroville, it was just a notion, an idea about change like so many others in the air. Now here we are in the twenty-first century, almost fifty years later, and the idea is materialized. "Most of all, we were young," the man says. "We were so young and innocent. We were naïve; I don't think anything could have happened without that naïveté."

The sixties. All that hope, all that youthful confidence—and the darkness right around the corner. John leaves the Portsmouth monastery after about a year, and returns to Harvard. He decides he's not cut out to be a monk after all, but he's still searching for a cause. He contemplates Scientology, Zen Buddhism, maybe a job as a forest ranger. In his final year at Harvard, 1965, he visits William Alfred, an English literature professor and a well-known poet and playwright. What should I do with my life? John asks. Alfred advises him, If you want to know life, real life, join the army.

So John enlists and he's sent to the Schofield Barracks, in Oahu, Hawaii, where he joins the recently reactivated Eleventh Infantry Brigade. He's the only person in his group to have graduated from college; people call him "the professor." His head is shaven, he trains hard, and he earns admiration after holding a plank position for five minutes (the first man in five thousand, he later claims, that his trainer has ever seen doing that). He barracks in a cream-colored stucco building, with machine-gun-bullet holes preserved from air raids during the Pearl Harbor attacks. The accommodation is stark, but John is

John, and he finds his comforts. He rents a house by Waimea Bay, overlooking turquoise waters crowded with surfers chasing massive waves. He buys a silver Mercedes SLR 300 and a horse he never rides. He drinks Brandy Alexanders and frequents the local antique stores, spending lavishly on expensive vases.

Vietnam bubbles below the surface. Body bags on TV, protesters in the streets. Everyone knows that the Eleventh Infantry will be deployed, and John is one of the men in his unit tasked with manning the phones at night, awaiting orders to ship overseas. But the date keeps getting pushed off, and then, when the unit does finally leave, in a convoy of buses for the airport in December of 1967, it's too close to John's discharge date. So he stays behind and misses combat—and much more. The Eleventh Infantry will go on to be centrally implicated in the My Lai massacre.

By the time John is discharged, he's thoroughly disillusioned—with the army, with the war and its massacres, with his government. Martin Luther King Jr.'s assassination, in the spring of 1968, only deepens John's sense of alienation. But soon he's presented with a new cause. Using his father's connections, he secures a position on Bobby Kennedy's presidential campaign. He's reinvigorated with a fresh sense of purpose, and he joins an advance team that scouts and sets up venues on the West Coast. He is with the campaign during the low of its primary loss in Oregon, in May of 1968, and he is in the Ambassador Hotel in Los Angeles a week later, when Kennedy bounces back and wins California. "My thanks to all of you, and now it's on to Chicago and let's win there," Kennedy says to an adoring crowd, John among them. Kennedy raises his right hand and gently, as if hesitantly, pushes back his hair.

A few minutes later, shots ring out in the kitchen. Kennedy is dead, and John is shattered. Another aborted quest. Once again, he is adrift.

Diane is eighteen, out of reform school, and she's living in an attic on a quiet street in Antwerp with a man named Philippe. She starts frequenting the cafés in town. Travelers from around the world gather in those cafés, drinking, smoking, philosophizing. Diane and her friends have a sense that they are living in a moment. They refer to "the something" they feel all around them—*something is happening, something more exists, something is within reach.*

They are hungry for experience, and people in the cafés talk about India—its spirituality, its mysticism—and so Diane and Philippe decide to travel there. They set off in winter, hitchhiking through snow, an arduous journey that takes them through Sweden, Germany, Yugoslavia, Turkey, and Iran. They arrive in Lahore, in Pakistan, and check into the Hotel Shahid, a three-story lodge with rooftop shacks where travelers trade stories from the road. They meet a young woman; she is small and nervous and she seems sad. She tells them she has been in a wonderful place, a serene ashram, or spiritual retreat, located in the South Indian town of Pondicherry. But then—she doesn't say why—she was asked to leave. She talks about the purity of the ashram and says she would love to go back.

Diane and Philippe head for Pondicherry. They stay in a guesthouse by the sea, a modest place that caters for visitors to the ashram. They meditate, meet fellow pilgrims and seekers, and attend evening talks on spirituality and religion. They spend about two months in town, and during this time, they hear about a new project being built outside Pondicherry, a planned city named Auroville. They gather that this project is somehow connected to the ashram, but they don't get too many details. They see a few signs around about it, and they notice vans and buses—motorized vehicles are a rare sight in Pondicherry—with *Auroville* painted on their sides. They meet a woman who has been out to the land. She speaks of an empty terrain, with just a few impoverished villagers living in thatch huts. Soon, she says, this bleak place will be brought to life, transformed into a model society.

Diane and Philippe never make it to Auroville. They leave Pondicherry and continue their travels. But something sticks in their minds. Later, after Diane returns to India to be part of this adventure, she tells a friend that the journey back was inevitable—it was like following "a golden bridge."

A few years before Diane and Philippe visit the ashram, an elderly French-woman sits in a room on the second floor of a colonial-era mansion in Pondicherry. The woman has a gentle, benevolent face, and a long neck that cranes slightly forward. She sits facing an array of windows, overlooking a courtyard dominated by a large copperpod tree. Perhaps the tree is flowering, an explosion of yellow; striped squirrels crawl its branches, their high-pitched chirps piercing the silence.

The woman leans over a desk and writes a document. She calls it "A Dream":

> There should be somewhere on earth a place which no nation could claim as its own, where all human beings of goodwill who have a sincere aspiration could live freely as citizens of the world and obey one single authority, that of the supreme truth; a place of peace, concord and harmony where all the fighting instincts of man would be used exclusively to conquer the causes of his sufferings and miseries, to surmount his weaknesses and ignorance . . . ; a place where the needs of the spirit and the concern for progress would take precedence over the satisfaction of desires and passions, the search for pleasure and material enjoyment.
>
> Beauty in all its artistic forms, painting, sculpture, music, literature, would be equally accessible to all; the ability to share in the joy it brings would be limited only by the capacities of each one and not by social and financial position. For in this ideal place money would no longer be the sovereign lord; individual worth would have a far greater importance than that of material wealth and social standing.

Call this dream utopian if you will; it is utopian. The ideal world can never exist; it's always one step ahead of itself, in an overleaping ambition, a grasping aspiration that exceeds its ability to manifest. Still, so many great advances begin that way, with a vision of the seemingly unattainable. "We *act* only under the fascination of the impossible," writes E. M. Cioran, the Romanian philosopher of utopia. I want to stay with the dream for now. I want to follow its potential and see how long I can hold on to it; and see, too, if I can rescue it from what comes later.

The dream becomes Auroville. The nascent town's formal inauguration takes place on February 28, 1968, in a makeshift amphitheater on a denuded plateau. According to local legend, the region was once a forest. Centuries earlier, someone said or did something to insult a holy man, and he condemned the land to barrenness. It hardly ever rains now, and when it does, water runs off the plateau, carrying away topsoil and saplings, perpetuating a cycle of erosion and desiccation. What remains is moonscape: vacant, panoramic, the earth packed hard, and red from iron oxide in the soil. A fitting tabula rasa for the new world.

The buildup to Auroville's inauguration is frantic. Some five hundred workers, mostly from surrounding villages, dig and saw and sweat in eight-hour shifts around the clock. The amphitheater is excavated, five miles of road are pounded into the earth, and a mile of water pipes is laid. A parking lot with space for three hundred vehicles is established. Delicate, not always entirely harmonious, negotiations take place with landowners and village authorities.

Somehow, it all comes together. On the appointed day, buses and cars emerge in clouds of dust on the horizon, and farmers and fishermen stream in by foot and bicycle, and on bullock carts. Beginning at five in the morning, some five thousand people converge on the amphitheater. Governments and aid agencies from around the world send representatives and messages of support. The president of India promises the country's backing. The Soviet Union, after some hesitation over the community's spiritual goals (Is it a religion?), expresses an interest in helping build the new town. UNESCO, from its offices in Paris, pledges to "promote the development of Auroville as an important international cultural programme."

The crowd gathers, and the sun rises higher. Only a select few—VIPs, the elderly—have shade covering. At 10:30 a.m., a gong sounds and a voice rings out. It belongs to that elderly Frenchwoman and is broadcast from her room in Pondicherry. "Greetings from Auroville to all men of goodwill," she proclaims in French, in a voice that is at once frail and powerful. "Are invited to Auroville all those who thirst for progress and aspire to a higher and truer life." She continues with what will be known as the Charter of Auroville, the closest the community has to a constitution.

The Charter is read aloud in sixteen languages. Young men and women from 124 countries and 23 Indian states file into the amphitheater, carrying samples of soil from their respective parts of the world. Many are dressed in white, some in their national costumes, and they carry placards bearing the names of their countries and states. They make their way to the center of the amphitheater, ascend a small mound, and place their earth in a sculpted marble urn. The earth is mixed, and the urn sealed—a symbolic enactment of human unity.

The audience sits through all of this in almost perfect silence. Shivers run along their spines, and tears down their cheeks. Even in the searing heat, attendees feel goose bumps. One man will later compare the occasion to a comet landing in the middle of the desert. Another will speak of being present at the making of history, a turning point for humankind. There is a sense that something tremendous is happening—though it isn't clear, just yet, what precisely that is.

The ceremony is completed shortly before noon. The crowd disperses, and the cars and buses kick up dust again on their return journeys. Speakers and broadcasting equipment are dismantled and packed away. Soon the land is empty once more, and a hot afternoon breeze blows in; now the hard work begins.

THE CHARTER OF AUROVILLE

Auroville belongs to nobody in particular. Auroville belongs to humanity as a whole. But, to live in Auroville, one must be a willing servitor of the Divine Consciousness.

Auroville will be the place of an unending education, of constant progress, and a youth that never ages.

Auroville wants to be the bridge between the past and the future. Taking advantage of all discoveries from without and from within, Auroville will boldly spring towards future realisations.

Auroville will be a site of material and spiritual researches for a living embodiment of an actual human unity.

THE FOUNDERS

The Mother

THE ELDERLY FRENCHWOMAN'S NAME is Blanche Rachel Mirra Alfassa, but everyone calls her the Mother. She was born in Paris on February 21, 1878, to Jewish parents of Turkish and Egyptian origin. She grew up in a cultured world, interacting with writers such as Anatole France and Émile Zola, and the artists Rodin and Matisse.

Her parents were atheists, but during her youth she began having supernatural experiences. At thirteen, she had a recurring feeling of stepping outside herself at night and sailing through the streets of Paris, healing the sick and wounded. She had repeated visions of a barefoot man dressed in white robes. She knew little about India—at that point—but she gave a name to the man: Krishna. In her early twenties, she read the Bhagavad Gita, an ancient Indian text, and a world of Eastern spirituality opened for her. "I rushed headlong into it, like a cyclone," she later said of the Gita.

The Mother's first visit to India takes place in 1914. Her husband, Paul Richard, a French clergyman turned lawyer, has political ambitions, and he's interested in standing for election from Pondicherry for the French House of Representatives. They arrive in Pondicherry, one of five French colonial settlements on the subcontinent, after a long journey by ship and train. They find a lethargic, provincial outpost, described by one observer as a "dead city . . . like a backwater of the sea, a stagnant place."

The town is divided in two. On the east, bordering the shimmering Bay of Bengal, sits La Ville Blanche, or White Town—a spacious area of high-ceilinged villas and wide boulevards with names like Rue Dumas, Rue Labourdonnais, Rue Dupleix, and Rue Suffren. This sun-battered equatorial Riviera is where the colonial masters live. On the west, separated from White Town by a fetid open canal, is Black Town—a denser, more crowded maze of bazaars and tile-roofed structures, home to the local Tamil population. The town has a tumultuous past that belies its sleepy appearance. Over the years, control of Pondicherry has passed back and forth between the British and French in a series of bloody battles, echoes of great-power rivalries in distant Europe.

Richard has been to Pondicherry before. He returned to France from that earlier visit and told his wife of meeting a great Indian yogi, or sage, a man who appeared to possess a distinct spiritual knowledge. Richard speaks highly of the man, and Alfassa, always eager for mystical experience, is eager to meet him. The afternoon of the day she arrives, still dressed in her winter clothes, she sets out in search of him from the Hotel de L'Europe, an art-deco building that is the only decent lodging in the area.

She walks the empty streets, through the dried-out city park, at its center a large archway built by Napoléon III. She passes in front of the Government Palace, a pillared structure that is the seat of French administration, and she arrives at a walled mansion at 41 Rue François Martin. She pushes open a gate and crosses a courtyard, follows a winding staircase with a curved wooden banister. A man stands at the top of the stairs. He is slender and dressed in white robes, and he has a long beard. His head is held high, in profile, and as he turns toward Alfassa, she recognizes him. This is the man she has been seeing all these years, the one she calls Krishna.

Later, Alfassa will write that she immediately recognized the significance of the moment. She is convinced that this is no ordinary man, and no ordinary encounter. It sets the stage for a long-lasting spiritual partnership that will result, among other achievements, in the creation of Auroville. March

30, 1914, from Alfassa's diary: "It matters little that there are thousands of beings plunged in the densest ignorance. He whom we saw yesterday is on Earth; his presence is enough to prove that a day will come when darkness shall be transformed into light, and Thy reign shall indeed be established upon Earth."

Sri Aurobindo

The man at the top of the stairs is Aurobindo Ackroyd Ghose, and he is known as Sri Aurobindo.[*] He's a Cambridge-educated former freedom fighter who has escaped the British and sought refuge in French India. In Pondicherry, accompanied by a small group of followers, he has renounced his revolutionary past and turned inward, to spiritualism. His reputation has spread; people have heard that there is a great sage in South India, a holy man pushing the limits of

---

[*]   *Sri* is an honorific, often used before the names of spiritual masters.

31

conventional mysticism. Sri Aurobindo is seeking, in his formulation, "a new system of yoga."*

He lives a spartan, solitary existence. His daily sadhana, or spiritual practice, consists of meditation, reading, writing, fasting, and pacing within the confines of his room. Not until the arrival of Alfassa does the full import of Sri Aurobindo's work become apparent. She leaves Pondicherry after the first visit with her husband, but returns a few years later and decides to stay without him. She becomes an integral part of the ashram coalescing around Sri Aurobindo. A sense builds that she's a first among equals when it comes to his disciples, a collaborator in the search for a new yoga.

In 1926, Sri Aurobindo retreats to his chambers to devote himself to spiritual pursuits. He appoints Alfassa—whom he designates the Mother—to serve as his conduit to the outside world. She passes instructions from the master to his growing band of disciples, and she takes over the practical responsibilities of running the Sri Aurobindo Ashram (as it is now known). Among other responsibilities, she takes on the jobs of fundraising, dealing with authorities, and feeding and housing disciples. The Mother proves herself an adept administrator. Under her guidance, the Ashram grows rapidly—from some one hundred members in 1931 to more than twelve hundred in 1959, making it one of the largest such communities in India.

While the Mother becomes the public face of the Ashram, Sri Aurobindo withdraws ever deeper. Hunched over his desk writing, pacing relentlessly into the nights, he's like a scientist in his laboratory, searching for some kind of alchemy. His new system of yoga emerges gradually through his writings, a learned, prodigious corpus that includes vast tomes with titles such as *The Life Divine*, *The Synthesis of Yoga*, and *The Human Cycle*; and spiritual poems,

---

* Yoga, in the context of Sri Aurobindo's philosophy, and this book, has a more expansive meaning than the practice of breathing or stretching exercises. The term derives from ancient Indian tradition and refers to an integrated pursuit of physical, spiritual, and psychological perfection, with the overall aim of cultivating a higher awareness and consciousness. In this sense, yoga is an ethical or spiritual discipline similar in some respects to those practiced for centuries in the Far East and in ancient Greece and Rome.

the most notable of which, *Savitri*, is a twenty-four-thousand-line reworking of an ancient Indian myth. Sri Aurobindo's new system comes to be known as the Integral Yoga, for the way in which it fuses disparate aspects of traditional practice. It is complex, multistranded, a bold reworking of ancient Indian thought. The Integral Yoga will form the philosophical underpinning for Auroville.

Two aspects of this yoga are important to highlight in order to understand Auroville, and what ultimately happens with John and Diane. The first is a reconceptualization of typical yogic practices, which extol asceticism and withdrawal from the world. Sri Aurobindo, by contrast, emphasizes the importance of engaging with the material world. "All life is yoga," he writes in the epigraph to one of his books. He is determined to infuse everyday existence, regular labor and quotidian habits, with the sincerity and integrity of spirituality. This idea will prove central to the Aurovilian experience, and in particular to the task of building a new city. Auroville's founders will consider their daily exertions on the land to be infused with divine sanctity; their labors represent an attempt to materialize a spiritual consciousness.

A second key strand of the Integral Yoga is evolutionary. "Man is a transitional being; he is not final," Sri Aurobindo writes. One of the main purposes of his yoga is to hasten the natural process of evolution, to push beyond human limits (physical and mental) and bring about a more advanced supramental being. This being will not simply emerge on its own. It must be willed into existence, through a conscious process of self-cultivation and spiritual rigor. Sri Aurobindo is himself pursuing this undertaking while in seclusion; as part of his yoga, he seeks the transformation of his own body and consciousness. Humankind, he writes, "must discover and release the spiritual godhead within him." Elsewhere, he adds that "evolution is not finished. . . . As man emerged from the animal, so out of man the superman emerges."

The evolutionary strand, like the first one, will be at the heart of the Auroville experience. This new city is intended as a cradle for the supramental being. As the Mother later puts it, Auroville will be "a place where the embryo or seed of the future supramental world might be created."

Bernard

None of this—the Integral Yoga, the supramental being, a divine consciousness, evolutionary transformation—none of this means anything to Bernard as he sails from Egypt to Bombay in early 1946, then catches a train to Pondicherry. Bernard isn't on a spiritual search; he isn't looking for a guru or an ashram. His journey East is an escape from his personal ghosts, and from the wreckage of history.

He arrives in town, twenty-two years old, still broken from the concentration camps. He's gaunt, with a blank look and a sunken face that accentuates penetrating blue eyes. He's short and slightly built, but he has a certain coiled energy, and he develops a reputation as a man in a hurry—never walking, always running, someone who takes stairs four at a time. He settles into a room at the Government Palace and assumes his duties as secretary to the governor: organizing receptions and dinners, writing correspondence, accompanying the governor's wife as she moves around the area. He is diligent and earns praise for his work, but he finds many of his tasks tedious. He soothes his boredom and anxiety by chain-smoking Charminar cigarettes, and with opium.

As always, he gravitates to the ocean. In the late afternoons, he can be found walking Pondicherry's Cours Chabrol, a wide promenade that curves along the coast, passing by a French First World War memorial, a whitewashed lighthouse, and a statue of Joan of Arc. It's the only paved road in town, busy with men and women in shorts on their daily strolls. At the northern end of the promenade are some tennis courts where the Mother plays on most days ("as if she was playing with the whole universe," a devotee will later recall. "Every ball was as it were the universe and she was beating the universe as it were with her racket"). Sometimes Bernard watches the Mother play, and then he walks to a low wall facing the ocean and sits on it with one leg crossed over the other; he lights a cigarette and stares out at the horizon, the wind blowing through his thinning hair.

Inevitably, he hears rumors about the great yogi and his French companion. There's a discernible buzz in Pondicherry, a sense that important spiritual endeavors are being undertaken behind the high walls of the Ashram. Bernard keeps his distance; he remembers André Gide's warnings about ideologies and institutions, and he is skeptical of what sounds to him like another religion. But then he reads Sri Aurobindo and finds himself drawn to the formidable intellect. One day he comes across that phrase: "Man is a transitional being." This notion—the idea that there can be more, that man can surpass himself into something finer—speaks profoundly to Bernard. He is so disillusioned by what he's seen in the war.

He decides he'd like to meet this philosopher. But it isn't easy. Sri Aurobindo has been secluded for some twenty years. Only on four days a year does he grant a darshan, or audience, to his followers. On a hot April afternoon, Bernard ascends a narrow staircase to partake of one such darshan. He stands in a line with other devotees and then he's ushered into a room where he sees two figures, Sri Aurobindo and the Mother, seated on a low sofa. A leopard skin is draped over the sofa. She's dressed in a silk sari and an embroidered cap sequined with pearls and precious stones; Sri Aurobindo wears a white dhoti, thrown over his shoulder like a Greek toga.

Bernard files through the room, pauses for a moment in front of the sofa, and, as he has been told to do, folds his hands in a gesture of respect. The whole thing lasts three or four seconds, but it's life changing. In Sri Aurobindo's gaze, Bernard feels a sense of wholeness, of being at home, that he has only ever experienced in his boat on the open ocean, off the coast of Brittany. He comes away from that brief audience convinced that Sri Aurobindo is far more than just a philosopher; something much deeper, something monumental and unfathomable, is going on. Bernard will later tell someone that in Sri Aurobindo he feels a sense of "immensity, infinity," as though he is traversing millennia. And it isn't just Sri Aurobindo. The Mother looks at Bernard, too, smiles, and he senses something equally powerful. No one has ever looked upon him with so much love. He later says that the Mother hands him a "saber filled with love"; it pierces directly into his heart.

Sri Aurobindo dies on December 5, 1950, aged seventy-eight. He is placed in a rosewood coffin laid in an elevated marble structure under the yellow-flowering copperpod tree, in the central courtyard of the Ashram. His distressed followers gather around the grave, which comes to be known as the Samadhi (a samadhi refers to the tomb of a holy man). They sit amid a bed of jasmine and marigold flowers, and they wonder what will happen to the Ashram—and to them—now that the master is gone.

A consolatory message goes out. It says that the mantle has been passed to the Mother, and that she will now administer the Ashram. This is an unusual arrangement (a seventy-two-year-old Frenchwoman running an Indian spiritual community), but the Mother is a tireless manager, up most days from before daybreak until past midnight, and under her leadership the Ashram thrives. It comes to include a school, a laundry service, a bakery, a paper factory, a printing press, several farms, and a sports ground where the Mother gives French classes in the evenings. These activities occupy a growing swathe of prime real estate in Pondicherry. The Ashram's buildings are marked by a blue-gray paint that spreads like a splash across White Town.

Bernard watches from the sidelines—alternately skeptical and inspired, studying Sri Aurobindo's books, considering his next move. One day in February of 1954, he makes his way along Pondicherry's beach, navigating between wood and metal debris, remnants of the city's pier that has recently been destroyed by a cyclone. He crouches behind a fishing catamaran, as if hiding from the choice he knows he's about to make. He has decided to join the Ashram, and he's terrified. The rebel in Bernard fears imprisonment. Is he cut out to be a divine warrior? Can he give himself to Sri Aurobindo's teachings and the Mother's guidance? Can he really follow their yoga?

There's still time to take a train out of here, he thinks; or maybe, he further reflects, just put a bullet in his head. He smokes a cigarette and tells himself (wrongly, it turns out), "Well, my dear fellow, you realize that this is your last cigarette. You're about to enter an ashram."

There is so much to do, so much to build. The Mother is familiar with Bernard's previous employment as the governor's secretary, and she immediately sets him to work translating Sri Aurobindo's writings into French and helping with her correspondence. Bernard writes his own books, too, including a novel about a gold prospector seeking enlightenment in India, and an introduction to Sri Aurobindo's life and philosophy. These works showcase a powerful, dramatic literary style; they are full of sweeping proclamations and hungry quests for truth (or Truth, as Bernard often puts it).

Gradually, Bernard sheds his hesitations about joining the Ashram. He surrenders to the Mother both psychologically and materially, referring to himself as her child and donating to her a monthly pension of around 2,500 francs ($700) that he receives for his time in the French Resistance. In 1957, the Mother gives him a new name, Satprem, which she says indicates "the one who loves truly." One day the Mother tells Satprem, "We are going to do something together." They start meeting at regular intervals for recorded conversations, the contents of which include ruminations on the Mother's life, and observations on daily events in Pondicherry and the world. The conversations also contain an account of the Mother's personal yoga, and in particular of her efforts to undertake within her own body the evolutionary progress envisioned by Sri Aurobindo. One historian will later describe these interactions between the Mother and Satprem as "ECG recordings of the very heart of the Ashram."

Around this time, the Mother starts having troubles with her body. She speaks of these, too, with Satprem, but she doesn't reveal many details. She's eighty years old in 1958, and she refers vaguely to a pain on her left side, maybe related to her heart, and of other ailments. Soon she curtails her activities, playing her last game of tennis, withdrawing from most administrative responsibilities, and retiring to her upstairs room in the Ashram. People say that the Mother is resting; she says she's working, fending off occult attacks and trying to spur an inner transformation that would allow her to transcend physical limitations.

Satprem travels some three hundred miles south, to the coastal town of Rameswaram, where he meets with a Brahmin priest who goes by the title Guruji.[*] The priest comes from a long line of holy men, and Satprem knows that the Mother has often spoken highly of his spiritual abilities. Satprem visits Guruji at a temple the priest maintains on a hill and asks whether he can do anything about the Mother's condition. Guruji confirms that she is a victim of occult forces, and he performs a secret rite on her behalf for eleven days. Satprem writes to the Mother that the priest is "luminous and good," and that he derives his abilities "directly from the Divine." He adds that no dark forces are capable of resisting Guruji's powers.

The Mother's health improves, and Satprem returns to Pondicherry, where they resume their conversations. Now, in the wake of her health crisis, the Mother's pursuit of a way to surmount the body's limitations intensifies. She goes deeper into her yoga, and Satprem is enraptured. He feels as if he's being taken on a fantastic supernatural journey; he doubles down on his commitment to her. He offers himself as a "more perfect instrument" for all her purposes, and he asks the Mother to help him grow and make him more sincere. His tone is often plaintive, almost suppliant; he implores the Mother to let him be her "sword of light."

For some time now, the Mother has had the idea of building an "Ideal City"—a geographic base for the Integral Yoga, where men and women from around the world could live together and practice Sri Aurobindo's philosophy. The project has almost come together a couple of times, but it never quite materialized. In 1965, even as she continues with her inner work, the Mother embarks upon what will prove to be her most audacious venture in the material world. Shortly after a conference on human unity held in Pondicherry,

---

[*]   A guru is an intellectual and spiritual teacher. *Ji* is a suffix that denotes respect.

she announces her decision to create a new township. She assigns a recently constituted body of businessmen and devotees, the Committee for the Yoga (CFY), to be the project's legal holder. She names this town Auroville, after the French word for dawn (*aurore*); clearly, this City of Dawn also contains a reference to Sri Aurobindo.

The purpose of Auroville, the Mother tells Satprem during one of their conversations, is to be a city where people from around the world will live in peace and harmony. She envisages Auroville as a "Tower of Babel in reverse," and she emphasizes its central role in manifesting Sri Aurobindo's yoga. "Humanity is not the last rung of terrestrial creation," she writes in a note about her planned city. "Evolution continues and man will be surpassed.... For those who are satisfied with the world as it is, Auroville obviously has no raison d'être."

Events move quickly after that 1964 conference. The CFY purchases around ninety acres of land to the north of Pondicherry. The Mother writes to a French architect of some renown, the modernist Roger Anger, and invites him to join the project as chief architect. Roger travels to India and, together with the Mother, develops a swirling, futuristic master plan that will come to be known

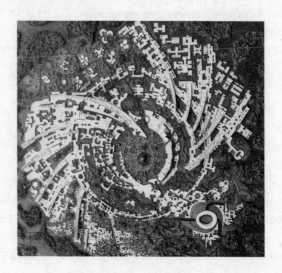

as the Galaxy. The Galaxy is divided into four zones—industrial, cultural, residential, and international—and at its center is a park containing a large spherical meditation space that will be called the Matrimandir, or the Mother's Temple. The whole thing is meticulously conceived by a team of planners, a refined concept that befits a bold project such as Auroville. Like most models—like virtually all planned cities—the Galaxy will have trouble adapting to reality. Things get messy as soon as people start moving in, disrupting the planners' well-laid schematics with humanity's chronic propensity to extemporize.

There is some debate about where Auroville should be located. Roger is dissatisfied with the CFY's first land purchase; building there, he tells the Mother, would mean that the town would be bifurcated by a highway. He shows her a map of an alternative location, a plateau around five miles north of Pondicherry known as the Red Hill, historically a staging ground for colonial military operations. The Mother gives her assent to the new location and points to a place on the map. Roger goes out in a jeep, driving through a couple of underdeveloped agricultural villages, and finds himself on barren, empty land. There is almost nothing on this Red Hill—nothing, except at the precise spot the Mother has indicated on the map. There, at the crossroad of unpaved tracks, ancient pilgrimage routes, Roger finds a sprawling banyan tree, one of the only patches of green on the plateau. This tree—which comes to be known simply as the Banyan Tree—will be the geographical center of the City of Dawn.

John

In the summer of 1968, Auroville has been formally inaugurated, and America is in turmoil amid a string of assassinations and rising opposition to the Vietnam War. Still recovering from Kennedy's death, John is wandering the West Coast, bouncing between places and emotions. At a gathering with a crew of rich friends in Bolinas, California, he consumes six different vintages of wine, prompting him to crow in a letter to his father that "at life as an art form I am no small cheese." Shortly thereafter he's in Los Angeles, in a gloomier mood, looking out of a hotel window onto an abandoned factory as the man next door coughs and spits and calls God through the night. John thinks the man won't make it. He closes his window and wonders about the heater in the corner of his room: Will it leak gas and kill him tonight, too?

Eventually, he floats back East. He takes refuge in his family's country home on Fishers Island, an enclave off the coast of Connecticut. Fishers Island is bucolic, a thin stretch of oak and maple forests, clapboard homes, and hidden ponds. John goes for walks in the forests and along rocky beaches; he swims in the waters, which remain icy even in summer. He reads Heidegger and Aristotle, a *Daedalus* special issue about utopia, and books on Zen and Hindu philosophy.

"Before you have studied Zen, mountains are mountains and rivers are rivers," he writes in a lined notebook, paraphrasing a well-known proverb. "While you are studying it, mountains are no longer mountains and rivers are no longer rivers; but once you have enlightenment mountains are once again mountains and rivers, rivers."

One windy Sunday afternoon in November, John climbs to the top of the house and sits on a sloped shingled roof above a narrow island. He clutches a handheld radio and watches as ferries cut through the rippled water, their foghorns bringing to his mind a chant of "Om, Om, Om." Nixon has just been elected president; his antipathy to the civil rights and antiwar movement fills John with despair. He tunes in to WBAI, a nonprofit New York station, and listens to a talk by Baba Ram Dass, the American spiritual teacher who will later write the New Age classic *Be Here Now.* John has a history with this man. Ram Dass was formerly Richard Alpert, one of the Harvard psychology professors who conducted the LSD experiments that so entangled John in college. But on this Sunday afternoon, with seagulls overhead and a turbulent Atlantic below, Ram Dass offers John something of a lifeline.

Ram Dass talks about his time as a Harvard professor, his expensive Mercedes-Benz and his holidays in the Caribbean. He explains that it all began to feel superficial, and that he dropped out of civilization and wandered the world till he ended up in India. There, Ram Dass met a guru, the first genuinely enlightened person he'd ever known, and he learned about renunciation.

His is a version of renunciation that no doubt appeals to John. "You can stay at the Hilton, as long as you'd be just as happy in a hut," Ram Dass says. John believes in sacrifice, he wants to find a more authentic way of living. He's also a rich young man who likes his creature comforts.

Soon after that broadcast, John has a long, boozy encounter with a friend at Le Pavillon, one of New York's finest French restaurants, on Fifty-Fifth Street and Fifth Avenue. They meet in the morning for tea; tea spills over into lunch and a sequence of expensive wines, and then lunch into dinner. John tells his friend what he's heard on the radio, and she tells him about a man she knows who's traveled to India and is now part of a new utopian project. Almost immediately after that encounter, John books a flight to Bombay. He sends a letter to his parents apologizing for his impulsiveness.

"For a long time I have felt the need to immerse myself in a tight, somewhat abstemious discipline," he writes:

> The more I have thought upon going to India—which, having little else to do, I do constantly—the more excited I have become. It is a long time since I have felt so hopeful about the future. I really feel that this trip answers a deeply felt need in me. I realize that in the contemporary socio-economic value system, I am traipsing after a fantasy. Yet in the contemporary argot, it is my thing, which excuses a multitude of things. It would be interesting to see whether it is possible to build a utopia. Historically they apparently don't succeed, but emotively I long to find one that might.

John Walker III

Does the search for utopia—or simply, *the search*—run in families? Forty-eight years before John sets out for Auroville, his father is a freshly graduated fine arts major from Harvard, searching for his path through the world. He wins a

$1,000 art competition in college and uses the money to travel to Italy. Before leaving, he writes a letter to his grandfather that contains remarkable resonances with the one John will later send to his parents. "I feel that I am starting on the greatest adventure of my life—my discovery of Europe," Walker Sr. writes. "How I have dreamt of that continent, and how perfect it has seemed in my dreams! Perhaps I should not have risked the disappointment. It is often a good thing not to visit one's utopia. But mine is too tangible, the temptation too great."

In Italy, Walker Sr. finds his life's passions: he meets and marries his wife, he converts to Catholicism, and he cultivates a love for and expertise in Renaissance art. I wonder how much he tells John about these discoveries. He's closed off, in many ways emotionally distant. But sons have a way of knowing without being told, and I think that, John's ambivalence toward his family legacy notwithstanding, he has probably learned something from his father about taking risks and living life differently. It's so hard to avoid the shadows of our fathers; even in running away, we run in their footsteps.

Diane

In 1968, Diane and Philippe are traveling back to Belgium from Pondicherry, and they pass through Nepal. One night they're playing cards in a guesthouse in the countryside. The owner of the place, a Mr. Singh, is getting drunk and stoned, and he's increasingly belligerent. Diane finds herself alone with her host and he tries to sexually molest her. She scratches his arms in defense and draws blood. Philippe hears her screams and races into the room and kicks Mr. Singh in the stomach. Mr. Singh is enraged. They run out and Mr. Singh chases them with a gang of laborers and two vicious dogs. "I will kill you! I will kill you!" he screams into the Himalayan darkness.

Diane and Philippe hide in the back of a truck, but soon the men find them and draw knives and begin throwing stones. Surrounded and afraid for their lives, Diane and Philippe hurl themselves off the side of a ravine. The fall is steep, but it's miraculously broken by a bush, and they just manage to cling to that bush, cold and trembling through the night. By morning the men have dispersed, and Diane and Philippe know they are lucky to have escaped with their lives. Later, when they talk about the experience, they are surprised to find that they were both praying to the Mother the whole time.

Neither of them met the Mother or even saw her while they were in Pondicherry. What is it that makes them call out to her in the night? What is it that makes them turn to her in their moment of peril? Back in Antwerp after her travels in Asia, Diane feels a familiar sense of anomie. She struggles to get into the rhythm of life: paying rent, making ends meet, visiting her mother in her small house in her small town. It all feels so inane. She's brought a green sari back from Pondicherry as a gift for her mother; it's a memento from a place that means so much to Diane, but her mother cuts it up and makes shirts out of the cloth.

Diane is afflicted by Tolstoy's definition of boredom—"the desire for desires"—and perhaps it is this urge to feel something, to live with intensity, that leads her to separate from Philippe and get together with another man, a Belgian named Guido Graft, whose child she is soon carrying. Diane is determined to give birth to the baby in Pondicherry, in the Mother's light. She and Guido have hardly any money, and the trip will be arduous, especially as she's pregnant. But they are bountiful with faith—Diane will always be rich that way—and they travel overland, and they arrive safely in Pondicherry shortly after Auroville's inauguration.

One sunny morning Guido and a very pregnant Diane walk into the Indian Coffee House, a popular hangout on Jawaharlal Nehru Street, the city's main commercial avenue. Harried waiters in stained white uniforms and elaborate red turbans make their way between cane furniture, serving coffee, scrambled eggs, and dosas to Pondicherry's growing population of expatriates. Guido and Diane meet an American woman who lives in Auroville, and they tell her that they've just arrived in town. Guido is wearing a frayed lungi and looks as if he hasn't bathed in a few days. Diane is glowing in a white Oaxacan wedding dress with a colorful embroidered edge.

They say they've run out of funds, and that they're staying in a cockroach-infested lodge in Pondicherry's bazaar. The American woman tells them they should meet the Mother and ask her permission to join Auroville. Soon they are going up a carpeted stairway to the Mother's room, where they find her in an upholstered wooden chair. They get on their knees, and Diane feels everything rotten or resistant in her dissolving—"like snow under the sun," she later writes to a friend. The Mother doesn't say anything at that meeting, but after a few days, an attendant tells them that they've been accepted into Auroville. Diane is ecstatic. She is convinced that this new city is "the promised land," a refuge for all the troubled souls of Europe, the lost people living in that "cold, indifferent money-mass." Those who live in Auroville, she writes to her friend, will be capable of moving mountains.

Satprem (Formerly Bernard)

Week after week, month after month, he visits the Mother for their recorded conversations. He visits in her room on the top floor of the Ashram, the verdant smell of Muguet de Mai, a perfume from Provence, in the air. She sits in a rosewood chair under a standing lamp, and he sits on a golden wool carpet at her feet, which are enveloped in white socks and resting on a satin pillow on a wooden stool. Sometimes she holds his hand, and sometimes he rests his head in her lap. A great love has grown between them. She is his mother, his teacher, his spiritual guide; he is her scribe, her intimate disciple. The Mother, he later confides to someone, "is a grand novel of adventure and love."

He comes on Mondays and Wednesdays, at ten in the morning. Their discussions are unstructured, sometimes casual, other times theoretical or pedagogical. The Mother is sharing the experience of her yoga with Satprem, but gradually it becomes clear that she is also initiating him, showing him the way. Satprem reads to her from his work. His book on Sri Aurobindo is progressing and the Mother praises it. Once when Satprem reads her a draft she tells him his writing is like a miracle; it's as though it has emerged from a more perfect future. The Mother gets tears in her eyes and presses her hands to her face; Satprem lays his head on her knees.

One day he's downcast, depressed, as he often is, and the Mother asks him if he is aware of his cells. She tells Satprem that if he focuses on his cells, he will make amazing discoveries. Her health is still fragile, and her voice is weak, but it seems to contain universes. At last, after almost a decade of conversation, Satprem begins to understand what the Mother is really doing and what she has been trying to teach him.

The Mother unspools her grand project. She is developing her own system of yoga, an extension but also an adaptation of Sri Aurobindo's. She says she has come to understand that attaining the next evolutionary rung will require whole-scale physical transformation of the body. This work, she adds, begins at the smallest corporeal unit. She is working to change "the consciousness of the cells." She is formulating a "yoga of the body," or "yoga of the cells," as she alternately calls it. Her body, she tells Satprem, is now a stage upon which the evolutionary future of humankind will be decided.

It is a momentous yoga. Satprem knows he is blessed, the recipient of so much light. He believes that the Mother is working toward a formula that will unlock all of human potentiality. But already, in these early days, there are clouds. He comes to doubt other Ashramites and becomes convinced that his sessions with the Mother are being eavesdropped upon, perhaps secretly recorded. He thinks that people are jealous of their relationship, and that they are working against him and the Mother, resisting the cellular transformation.

He has nightmares several times a week, dreams that he's fleeing vicious enemies as he clutches transcripts of their discussions. The flair and drama evident in his literary style takes full flight. He slings extravagant insults, calling his perceived adversaries rats and cockroaches, and comparing them to primates who, he says, have historically resisted the evolution to a higher species. He will complain of an "old beast defending itself, with all its claws out." This anxious, febrile state will take over; it comes to dominate everything.

John

In late 1968, John is in the living room at Fishers Island. The walls are yellow and he's sitting on a couch with green-and-white jungle upholstery. He's about to embark on his life; he's a pampered young man, and he knows so little of the world. He leans over a table and scribbles an enthusiastic note to himself:

> This should be the moment when 26 spent years gather to a decision. Walk or sit as you will but do not stand irresolutely. Do I have the least chance of success to achieve the finality of answer that I seek? No. So the decision is to eschew a guaranteed comfort for an occasional flash of ecstasy. And the equipment I possess—a capacity to suffer? For discipline? Negligible. And I will cause suffering—needless— in others. God, direct my steps.

49

He writes this eighteen years, to the month, before he dies in Auroville. I find it in Gillian's green folders, stuffed between handwritten letters and typed diary entries. I want to stand in front of John and block his path. I want to hold him by the shoulders, shake him, and say: "Stop!"

FORECOMERS

IT TAKES A COUPLE OF years after returning to Auroville for Auralice and me to realize what we've gotten ourselves into. I suppose we start to understand around the time I discover Gillian's green folders, on a summer visit to New York. The letters and diaries contained in those folders open a door onto a place that we thought was safely compartmentalized; they thrust the past into the present. Really, though, the full weight of Auralice's biography begins to sink in after we visit John and Diane's dilapidated hut and grave, by the canyon.

Not long after that visit, Auralice comes home one rainy morning from dropping our kids off at school, and she asks if we can go for a walk. "What, in this rain?" I reply, and she says there's something she needs to talk about. So we go, under a single umbrella, past a few neighbors' places, and then into a forest of acacia and palmyra that runs behind the house we've recently built ourselves. We follow a dirt path, the path gradually becoming soft, turning into a bog of mud, fallen leaves, and branches. The bog is sticky; it sucks the sandals off our feet.

We make our way to a dam, an earthen wall constructed decades ago to keep the water from flowing off the plateau. This dam is our refuge: we come to it whenever we feel overwhelmed or confused, or simply disoriented by all the discrepancies between our lives in New York and the ones we're building in Auroville. We sit on our haunches, and Auralice is silent. She has these silences; I've learned to live with them. Then she tells me about a morning she recently spent at one of our son's classrooms. His teacher asked if she would come speak to the students, share with them what it was like to grow up in Auroville. So Auralice told the kids some stories about the old days, leaving a lot out, especially about her own biography, because she wanted to keep things light. After the talk, the kids asked why she had decided to return to Auroville; her answer, as always when we are asked this question, was somewhat muddled. She told them that people don't always make conscious choices, that life carries us in directions.

The teacher interjected. She suggested that the reason we'd returned was for the dream. "It's so beautiful that you have this place to hold on to, you must have come back because even after all those years away, you were still drawn to the ideals," the teacher said. She spoke about her own journey: how she was living what felt like a materialistic and rote existence, how Auroville pulled her in with its promise of a new beginning. She was eternally grateful.

"It all seemed so simple for her," Auralice tells me now as we sit on the dam under a neem tree. "She's new here and she doesn't have any history. She doesn't *know* any history." Auralice doesn't say this in a judgmental or critical way; it's more out of bewilderment, and some envy. We who have been around longer know that this town is more complicated. We are familiar with the dream, and, yes, we're attracted to it. But we also know the shadows.

"Do you think we made a mistake in coming back?" Auralice asks me, not for the first time. "I barely made it away, I hardly survived. What are we doing bringing our kids up here?"

There are no easy answers to these questions. Life takes you in a direction, and then you're in a place. We sit on that dam and we take in the forest, take in the life the rains have brought forth in it. A kingfisher explodes in a burst of blue; five pond herons float above the water, like white sails. A scorpion advances with its tail raised menacingly—or is it defensively?—through the bog. I remind Auralice that it was for all of this, too, that we returned: the lush teeming land, the regenerated forest, the geography of our youths that we are now introducing, with pleasure and some astonishment, to our children. There are many versions of Auroville, many layers to its history.

It's the summer of 1968. Auroville is just a few months old, and it's burning under the onslaught of a terrible drought. The earth is parched. Forlorn cows and goats roam the plateau, looking for a spot of green. Lines of red ants traverse the sand, dismantling corpses of geckos or insects, occasionally bigger prey, maybe a rodent or calf succumbed to dehydration.

Memories of Auroville's inauguration are still vivid, but the land upon which the City of Dawn must emerge remains empty. In Pondicherry, the planners plan. In an office across the street from the Ashram, they display a papier-mâché model of the Galaxy. They offer a soaring vision, replete with skyscrapers, moving sidewalks, monorails, an airport, a world trade center, and sports facilities to host Olympic Games. The planners send out fundraising brochures to aid organizations and governments around the world. They estimate that the Mother's new city will house some fifty thousand people—fifty thousand idealized beings—and that the project will require $8 billion. Thus far, $13 million have been raised.

But who will actually build this city? Who will brave the harsh elements, forsake the electricity and piped water of town, and settle the land? In June of 1968 two bicyclists make their way slowly along the Red Hill. There are no roads, hardly any tracks, and no water save what they carry in a couple of bottles tucked into cotton shoulder bags. There's no shelter except for the meager shadows offered by sporadic outgrowths of palmyra trees. The cyclists, an American man and woman, Robert and Deborah Lawlor, push their way through puddles of sand. They have left Pondicherry at dawn and are dressed in thin cotton; an hour or two into the ride, and they are drenched with sweat.

Deborah is a ballet dancer from California, and Robert an artist from New York. They've been living on the Lower East Side of Manhattan, near the Williamsburg Bridge, in a loft dominated by a large sand-casting box and Styrofoam sculptures that hang from the ceiling. Deborah is twenty-eight, and he's twenty-nine. She's fresh-faced with an oval chin; he's handsome in a rugged, frontier kind of way, with dewy eyes and olive skin. They will go down in history as the first people to live in Auroville—"Adam and Eve," as Deborah will later put it.

They have been staying in a hut outside Pondicherry, on a farm run by the Ashram. Robert arrived first, in 1965, then he returned to America to get Deborah. When he came to Pondicherry, he heard about the Mother and, like many, was initially skeptical. "The Mother?" he wondered. "What's that, some kind of Freudian thing?" A few encounters later, and again like many, he's now a convert. All he wants is to do the Mother's work.

Robert and Deborah have heard a lot of talk about Auroville. They don't know much about what's actually going on, but they're idealistic artists, and the project intrigues them. So they've decided to go out to the Red Hill. They're just looking around, sniffing things out, like prospectors. They pass through the villages outside Auroville, where kids chase after them yelling *"Vellakaran! Vellakaran!"* (White man! White man!), and then they leave the thatch huts and narrow alleys behind and they're out in the open, facing an endless horizon. They come upon a canyon—a gash in the red earth, like a wound. The rains have sculpted this canyon over the centuries, cutting ever deeper.

The canyon is forbidding: some fifty feet deep and a hundred across, bone-dry, sun bleached, so that streaks of yellow limestone have emerged in the red laterite. As everywhere in Auroville, the vegetation is sparse. Those austere palmyras, a few shrubs that cling to the loose earth of the canyon walls, and some low cashew plants whose leaves turn black from chafing when the wind is strong.

Something in the starkness inspires Robert and Deborah. Robert feels that the whole area has a certain charge, the "ingredients of a grand adventure." They are undaunted by the difficult conditions. They figure if they can survive on the Lower East Side of Manhattan, they can survive anywhere. They return to Pondicherry and send the Mother a note, asking if they can settle by the canyon. She sends a handwritten message in reply: "With my blessings." They meet with her and ask what they should call this place. "There are some people who become aware of things a bit sooner than others," the Mother says. She names their outpost—the first Aurovilian settlement—Forecomers.

Life for these early Aurovilians is all about survival: shelter, water, food. The Mother tells Robert and Deborah to construct a hexagonal, cone-shaped hut, which they do, using mud for the walls and woven palmyra leaves for the roof. "A new house for a new consciousness," the Mother will later say of architecture in Auroville. The hut is intended to combine traditional village construction materials with a more futuristic Western design; Robert names it the Experimental Hut.

Their new home sits on a ridge above the canyon. The sanctuary it provides is at best partial. Mosquitoes invade at dusk, and termites chew at the casuarina frame. At night, large rats climb up the hut's legs and nibble at the calluses on its sleeping inhabitants' feet. Calluses are essential in this forbidding environment, where the ground is burning and footwear has been discarded as a civilizational frill. Robert affixes smooth metal cups on the hut's frame to keep the rats out.

There are no wells or substantial water bodies on the plateau. Every two or three days, Robert and Deborah have to cycle to a well four miles away and fill a metal drum with a hundred liters of water. They balance the drum on their back bicycle carriers, then they push their cycles—now too heavy to ride—through the sand. Drinking water is rationed; they bathe every other day, or less.

They live like this—clutching to what one Aurovilian later calls "the thread of simplicity"—for several months. Then one day a water diviner comes out and picks a spot for a well. A team of bullocks is assembled from a local village, and a long drill bit attached to the animals' backs. The bullocks are weighed down with sandbags, to add pressure on the bit, and they go around and around all day, the drill cutting a little deeper into the earth with each circle, sandbags added at intervals to increase pressure. The bullocks advance in this way until they find a subterranean stream. But then the well collapses and they must start all over again. This happens several times.

Robert and Deborah refuse to be disheartened. "All life is yoga," Sri Aurobindo has taught. These obstacles are part of the great work. "Those who would come to Auroville must understand that it is not a sanctuary but a battlefield," Robert writes to a friend in America. "They must come ready to don the armor of the knight and be capable of giving up the concepts of time and self in the fury of the clash."

And there are other challenges: dysentery, pneumonia, thieves, cobras, vipers, and the long black-and-white-banded kraits, whose venom kills over excruciating hours, by suffocation. Once Robert is bitten by a spider and the poison creeps up his arm, a sinister red line running to his armpit. He sees a doctor, who tells him the condition is serious, he needs penicillin before the poison (or infection) reaches his heart. Robert refuses the medical advice; he asks someone to inform the Mother and, on her instructions, lies in bed and focuses on a photo of her. His arm swells and the red line advances and he is weak with fever. He keeps staring at the Mother's photo, then he falls asleep, and when he awakens, the wound is open, poison pours out, and the line recedes and he's cured. This episode goes around and becomes part of local lore. Nothing is impossible, all doors can yield if you just believe enough. Robert tells everyone the story, and later, after John dies, Robert will wonder if he told the story to him, too; Robert feels a twinge of guilt.

There are periods of progress, and moments of sublimity. They finally complete their well, and they start planting: cauliflower, carrots, millet, peanuts, watermelon, lentils, all of which they douse in a homebrew of tobacco and chilis to keep insects away. Two new people—an American named Francis, a Canadian named Gary—join Forecomers. Together they build more structures, including a communal dining room, which they paint blue, a white meditation hut, and a bathroom with a rainbow-striped door and an open-to-air squatting toilet that has exhilarating views. They lay a twenty-three-square-foot cement floor to dry crops, then they add a basketball hoop and backboard. The board soon blows away, carried into the canyon, but they continue to use the floor to dry crops. In the evenings they lie shirtless on the hot cement and the floor is touched by the sun and they feel the heat below them and the breeze of an advancing night above and they gaze up at the stars and the vastness of the skies reminds them of everything that's possible here, all that they are going to achieve.

"Distance disappears into rest and one's life slips away like a soiled garment and one lies there for a moment naked, smiling, and for a trace of a moment, knowing," Robert writes to friends in America. These early Aurovilians are poets—their *life* is poetry. And this moment—the very beginning, pregnant with potential, unburdened by the complications that will inevitably surface— is utopia's finest hour, when the dream remains unsullied. Robert continues, "I agree, Auroville is 'incomprehensible,' 'impossible,' and 'ridiculous.' Nonetheless I know of nothing beautiful that is not also almost all three of these things: a painting, the growth of a flower, a relationship with another person—all are 'impossible.' I hope I can continue here, and pray for the strength that is needed."

In New York, Robert had traveled in cultured, artistic circles. Among his friends was a painter named Judith. Judith was also friendly with John; it was she who first told him about Robert's time in India, at that expensive wine-fueled encounter at Le Pavillon. Robert's experiences in the Ashram and Auroville thus open the way for John's journey.

John arrives in Pondicherry in late 1969. He takes a train from Bombay, via the city of Madras, and checks himself into a guesthouse owned by a Punjabi Ashramite named G. N. Goyle. The New Guest House (everyone just calls it Goyle's Guest House) is a simple but stylish place, located in a French-era villa with a blue gate, its compound wall overflowing with bright pink bougainvillea. John moves into a room in the back. He spends his initial days acclimatizing—wandering the grid of Pondicherry's White Town, taking in the French architecture, and the quiet, car-free streets. It's his first time in India, and he's predictably shocked by the poverty. He sees malnourished babies with distended bellies, rickshaw drivers with swollen elephantiasis legs pedaling their customers around, and leprous beggars thrusting their discolored stumps as they plead, *"Missi, missi, s'il plait,"* in pidgin French.

In the afternoons he wanders down to the beach, where he smokes hashish under the sun, sitting on the sand among wooden fishing boats. Later he can often be found with other expatriates at the Continental Hotel, at a table scattered with ashtrays and empty bottles of beer. He makes new friends, many connected with the Ashram and Auroville, and he regales them with stories of his life in America. They are impressed by John's obviously entitled background and his cultivated, aristocratic accent, which one man will compare to William F. Buckley's. Word gets around (incorrectly) that John Walker is a beneficiary of the family fortune behind Johnnie Walker whiskey. It is at the Continental, too, that John first acquires a reputation for generosity; his tips are so large, it is said, that waiters get into fistfights in the kitchen for the right to serve him.

He goes out to Forecomers in November of 1969. It is, as far as I can tell, his first visit to Auroville. He hires a driver and an Ambassador car, and they go through the boulevards of White Town and then the congested streets of Black Town, clogged with pedestrians, cycles, and bullock carts. Things open up again at the outskirts of Pondicherry, near the Jawaharlal Institute of Postgraduate Medical Education and Research (JIPMER), a monolith of a public hospital. Three miles or so after the hospital, they take a right turn, off the tarred road and onto a dirt track that leads through the village of Edyanchavadi. The village is a sleepy settlement of thatch huts arranged around a murky *kulam*, or pond, where farmers and their families bathe and clean laundry. Groups of men sit under trees gambling, and cattle roam the alleys, their horns adorned with brass bells.

Soon they're out of the village and in Auroville, though there's nothing on the land to signify that—nothing to suggest that they are anywhere at all. The road gets thinner and muddier (it rained the day before), and then John sees a canyon at a distance, and standing in front of the canyon a white man leaning over the ground, working on a bamboo construction. Robert is barefoot and shirtless; he's in a loincloth, a turban on his head to protect him from the sun.

"How's Judith?" Robert asks John, inquiring about their mutual friend, and he invites John to join the community lunch. Robert introduces John to Francis, the young American who has recently joined Forecomers, and John tells Francis that he's graduated from Harvard. "Oh, Hahvad," Francis says sarcastically, and he asks John where he should invest his money. "Gold," John replies earnestly. Francis has no gold, little money, and he notices that John is well-dressed and that he's come out with a hired car. John wears leather sandals, long pants, a full-sleeved shirt, and an embroidered blue vest with satin lining. He looks like someone from the city.

Lunch is basic, vegetables and brown rice planted by the community. They sit on the floor of the dining room, and Robert and Deborah tell John about all the challenges in building Auroville. Money is tight—the entire community of Forecomers is living off Deborah's allowance of $100 a month—and needs are endless. They speak of possibly approaching Oxfam for money, or maybe some other organizations where John's family has connections. Robert will remember a "childlike innocence" to John. He is touched by John's enthusiasm, but John also strikes him as callow.

After lunch, they go for a walk in the canyon. Robert tells John about their efforts to revitalize the earth, about how he and the others are building bunds and check dams to keep water on the plateau. He shows John the site of one particularly ambitious recent effort, the leftovers of a nineteen-foot-high-by-sixty-foot-wide mud dam. Some seventy people, including a team of paid labor, worked on the project for forty days. They dug earth, compacted it into walls, and then clad the walls with heavy slabs of granite. There was a downpour the very night they inaugurated the dam, and early in the morning, Robert heard a roar from his bed. He went exploring, and all that remained of the dam was rubble strewn across the canyon floor, and a few shards of painted clay pots that Deborah had placed on the structure to commemorate its opening.

Robert tells this story with a touch of irony, even humor. He speaks of surrendering the ego, of listening to the land and respecting whatever it has to teach. Maybe, he says, it wasn't time yet, maybe they needed to learn more from the desert. He knows that building Auroville could never be easy. "If it works, then it didn't have enough imagination," he likes to say. Out of such humble, quixotic efforts are born Auroville's environmental rejuvenation.

John goes back to Pondicherry, spends the night in his room at Goyle's Guest House. It's more comfortable in the city: hot water, a fan, dinner on white linen. But Auroville is on his mind now, and he keeps thinking of Forecomers. He remembers the austerity of the land, its emptiness and silence. There wasn't even a bird in the canyon. He registered the silence not as an absence or a void, but as plenitude. There is depth in Auroville, he feels, and opportunity in its emptiness. "I know that I must now definitively give myself up and be like a page absolutely blank," he writes in his journal. "I must be no one here—essential, backgroundless seeker."

He sends a letter to the Mother, asking if he can be admitted to her world. She receives him the day before Diwali, the Indian festival of lights. Firecrackers echo as John ascends the staircase to her room. Soon he, too, is on his knees in front of her, and later someone tells him that he's been accepted into Auroville. "Vague fear that I cannot contain this," John writes in his journal. "That it will broach my sanity. The answer of course is to have faith in the Mother—which, extraordinary statement, comes to me quite naturally."

Before visiting the Mother, John plays a Bach violin concerto on a record player in his room. He throws the I Ching and the numbers come up 2, 5, and 6, signifying *decay*. "Into trouble," he writes.

Signs of life start appearing all over the Red Hill. They come up in clusters of homes known as communities, like little fortified settlements spread across the land. Many of these communities have exalted names: Certitude, Fraternity, Transformation, Revelation, Aspiration, New Creation. On the eastern side of Auroville, a community called Auromodele emerges in a huddle of concrete structures intended as prototypes for the city. Some people compare these low, saucer-shaped buildings to spaceships (and others, less charitably, to Smurf homes). Next door, in the community of Aspiration, a more rustic gathering of thatch huts comes together on a stretch of land that slopes toward the ocean. These huts have detachable windows, flaps that open to the elements, and they are set close to the ground, with low white walls. Although they are modest, inspired by village huts, they are comfortable and ecologically fashionable. One visitor to Auroville will describe them as "Club Med chic."

On the western border of Auroville, off the tar road that leads from JIPMER hospital, a community called Hope is built. It's set amid cashew bushes and swaying coconut trees, whose fruit drop periodically with a thud. The community consists of a handful of "capsules": detachable thatch constructions raised above the ground on granite pillars, sometimes accessed by rope-and-bamboo ladders. One day Diane and Guido move into Hope. They arrive with their newborn child, a boy that the Mother has named Aurolouis. He is the nineteenth baby born in Auroville, blond haired and brown eyed, with a perpetual dribble from his nose. Like all parents in this new world, Diane is filled with anticipation for his future. "I wish I could tell you in words what a paradise it is here," she writes to a friend from Belgium. "Everything is beautiful and money is no problem. If the Mother feels you're spiritually ready for her plans, she will take care of all your needs."

But despite Diane's optimism, she and Guido are having trouble. He's become interested in pursuing a more traditional Hindu ascetic path, and he's taken a vow of *sannyasa*, which requires giving up physical intimacy. Guido is now spending time down south with Guruji, the Brahmin priest who helped the Mother with her illness. As Guido's absences increase, Diane grows close to another man, a handsome, curly-haired American named Larry. They can be seen riding around together on his bicycle, Larry shirtless and his torso glistening with sweat while Diane sits on the back carrier laughing, holding him by the waist.

"I've always been very changeable, sometimes I wonder why I can't live a normal life," Diane writes to her friend. "But of course that's a stupid question. Auroville is the richest place for me. I love this earth very much and Mother said if we work on it with love, incredible things can happen. I often feel very young, like a small girl of four. A few days ago I found a silver hair in my sewing kit and I thought it must be the hair of a fairy."

She writes to her friend, too, of a recent visit she made to Pondicherry.

She went on August 15, which is Sri Aurobindo's birthday and also India's Independence Day. She stood with a crowd of four thousand people in a street behind the Ashram, waiting for the Mother to emerge from her room. When the Mother came out, she stood on a balcony and raised her hand and Diane saw a blue light, like a halo. She tells her friend that four thousand people felt the Mother's divine power raining down on them, and they stood in the street and cried. On a wall beneath the balcony a signboard contained a call to action that Diane is determined to live up to: *The world is preparing for a great change. Will you help?*

Auroville grows steadily during these early years. In 1970, the community has around 100 residents; by 1974, this number will have grown to 322. They come from all over the world, with the largest contingents arriving from India (81 in 1974), America (59), France (47), Germany (41), and Great Britain (14). In late 1969, a small health center is opened near the village of Kuilapalayam. December of a year later, and Auroville's first school is inaugurated, many of its students and teachers bused in from the Ashram in Pondicherry. The Mother names it Last School, because in the future, education will break out of the four walls of classrooms and take place in everyday life (she also foresees an After School, a Super School, and a No School). New wells are dug, roads are laid, and some communities get electricity, though supply remains highly erratic. Slowly, inexorably, civilization makes its incursions.

Auroville's green work starts taking off around this time, too. It begins out of necessity, almost inadvertently, less from some grand ecological design than as a response to the inhospitable conditions. Globally, there is little green consciousness. The inaugural Earth Day is held only in 1970; not until 1972 does the United Nations convene a landmark conference in Stockholm, the first time governments come together to discuss the environment. Developing countries, including India, are at best reluctant participants, fearing that a focus on ecology will come at the expense of economic growth. Prime Minister Indira Gandhi famously stands up in Stockholm and says that poverty is the worst form of pollution.

So Auroville's green workers are accidental ecologists, in many ways forerunners of the global environmental movement. They plant because they need shade and food to survive, and they bund because nothing can be done on this land if the water runoff isn't halted. They are amateurs, informed by common sense and persistence rather than scientific knowledge. Because there are no seeds on the plateau, they must travel to nearby forests, places where the land is more fertile, to jump-start their efforts. They go by bus and spend days walking around with just a flask of water, maybe some peanut brittle for sustenance. They wear leaves on their heads to shield them from the sun, and they study the forests, trying to understand what grows, and when and how it grows. In the droppings of monkeys, pangolin, loris, and other wild animals, they forage for seeds, which they store in paper bags. Back in Auroville, they spread the seeds out and attempt to identify them, then set out to re-create the ecological matrices they've just seen.

"What you're trying to do is slow down," one Australian man, an early planter, will later explain to me. "You've come from Paris, or wherever, and things have been pretty fast. Now you need to slow down and learn to see. The first thing to do in the forest is look. Which plant is which, and then see if it's got flowers, seeds, maybe there are little seedlings on the ground. Look at the other plants that grow alongside it. Slowly, you will start to understand the forest. You have to remember, there were no books on it at the time, there was no information. Now it's called restoration ecology; that's what we were teaching ourselves to do."

Some of the seeds make their way to Forecomers, where Auroville's first nursery has been established. Every day a group of Ashram youth comes from Pondicherry; they sit on the ground while the girls nick seeds with fifty nail clippers imported from America, to let in moisture, and the boys stuff clear plastic bags with compost. Sometimes a German man shows up and plays classical Indian music on his bamboo flute, to encourage the plants. Then, about a month before the monsoon, the residents of Forecomers head along the canyon, accompanied by hired local villagers. They dig pits and place the bags with compost and seeds inside, fill the pits and build low earthen ridges, protective lips to keep the rains out. Despite these efforts, the monsoon sweeps away about half of what they've planted, thousands of seeds. The survivors emerge gingerly, hesitatingly—first as saplings, then gradually growing into forests.

As Auroville—and its forests—expands, so do tensions between those who direct the project from Pondicherry and those who live on the soil. Although Roger Anger's master plan includes a greenbelt of several thousand acres, the core of his envisioned Galaxy is a dense urban agglomeration. For many of Auroville's planners, the forests sprouting up, sporadically and haphazardly, are inconvenient facts on the ground. It's becoming clear that Auroville's planters aren't following the program—that their trees, as one woman will later put it to me, are "growing without permission."

In a letter home, John refers to a dichotomy between the "organicists" of Auroville and the "constructionalists" of Pondicherry. The latter, he says, believe in blueprints and systems. Comparing them to the technocratic managers of modernist totems such as Brasília or Chandigarh—very much utopian projects themselves—he writes that the constructionalists seek to raise funds, quickly put up buildings, and worry about people later. The organicists, on the other hand, work the land and "hold that Auroville must be allowed to grow naturally, like a tree in a forest." John's sympathies are clear: "Give each Aurovilian a watering can and lo and behold around him will grow up the city."

In 1970, in one of the first stabs at a governance framework for the community, the Mother forms an eight-person Comité Administratif d'Auroville (CAA). Not one of these administrators actually lives on the plateau; they are from the Ashram or the CFY, which remains the project's legal titleholder (although distinct legal entities, the CFY and the Ashram have a significant membership overlap). The members of the new committee are older, tradition-bound, and predominantly Indian. The gaps separating them from Auroville's hippies and rebels, many of whom have been forged by Western street protests of the 1960s, are huge.

The administrators look down on the hippies, and the hippies are equally disdainful of the administrators. Aurovilians wear hardly any clothes; their hair is matted, they have oozing sores on their legs, and their digestive systems are riddled with worms, amoebas, giardia, and other parasites that enter through the cracks of their bare feet. The planners wear starched white shirts and tight khaki shorts. They are meticulously talcumed, comb their hair with coconut oil, and bathe with sandalwood soap after their forays onto the sweaty plateau. In a 1971 article on Auroville from the *New York Times*, M. P. Pandit, a senior member of the Ashram, is quoted as saying, "We have a hard time in keeping out the hippies. We do not want them because they are not serious about anything."

People in Pondicherry are scandalized when an Aurovilian shows up drunk at the Ashram sports ground, and again when another person throws a punch at the entrance to the Ashram after he's denied entry. One Aurovilian man will recall several people working together on a building, all dressed in loincloths, when an administrator from Pondicherry pulls up in a car. The administrator shouts out that the American consul general is coming to Auroville, and he asks the hippies to put some clothes on. They ignore him and keep working—"all our lovely buttocks on display," the man will tell me later, still gleeful after many years.

In mid-1971, these tensions converge on a community of organicists called Silence. The community consists of about ten people, including Diane and her new friend Larry, who have moved out of Hope. John has also been spending time in Silence; this is possibly where he and Diane meet. He comes out regularly to Auroville now, bearing gifts from town: apples and oranges, cold coffee, chicken, and—everyone's favorite—thermoses of vanilla ice cream that he carries in a Harvard shoulder bag. People have started referring to him as Ice Cream John.

John's new friends in Silence plant the land, smoke pot, play the guitar, and throw parties under the stars. They live together in a communal hut, and they use the fields as toilets. It's rumored that the planners refer to their community as the "slums of Auroville." One day Roger Anger shows up with an engineer in an air-conditioned Jeep. The chief architect gathers the residents of Silence and tells them that he's had to make some changes to his master plan. The Galaxy, he says, has been rotated by fifty degrees; they're now living on the site of an intended public building, a concrete behemoth that will house an auditorium, a restaurant, and various exhibition spaces. The building is forecast to cost more than ten million rupees (around $1.3 million). Roger tells the residents of Silence that they will have to dismantle their hut and make way for the city.

"But where should we live? Where do you want us to go?" the residents ask Roger, whose shirt is open at the collar, revealing a gold chain. "I don't care where you go," Roger says. "You can move to Forecomers, or you can just all go back to San Francisco." His contempt for these unruly specimens who have infiltrated the Galaxy is apparent, as is his disdain for the trees they've planted—which, he now says, are blocking the views of the building that needs to come up.

So the organicists of Silence go looking for a new home. After wandering around for a few weeks, they settle on a plot of Aurovilian land located on the northwest of the plateau, outside a village called Kottakarai. The village is a jumble of mud roads and some ninety-five huts, dominated by a brightly painted turreted temple dedicated to the goddess Mariamman, who is believed to protect from chicken pox. A notion grows in the Aurovilians' minds that they'd like to set up a new kind of community. They want closer ties with their Tamil neighbors than have thus far characterized the largely fleeting intercultural relationship. In pursuit of this goal, they give a distinctly less exalted, and more regional, name to their community: they call it, simply, Kottakarai.

The most important project, the work that is geographically, psychologically, and spiritually at the heart of Auroville, is the Matrimandir, the Mother's Temple. The Mother's original concept for this structure was humble. Speaking to Satprem in 1965, she envisioned a small building with a single meditation room. But her—and Roger's—ambitions grow. By the early 1970s, the Matrimandir is conceived of as a massive sphere, 118 feet across and 97 feet high, encrusted with gold-plated disks and containing a large marble-lined meditation space known as the Inner Chamber. The structure will be near the center of Auroville, adjacent to the Banyan Tree and the amphitheater where the community's inauguration took place.

Aurovilians are deeply invested in this building, which they consider a physical embodiment of their community's spiritual goals. The Mother has said, "The Matrimandir will be the soul of Auroville," and that it represents "the Divine's answer to man's aspiration for perfection." Many are convinced that everything will follow from its completion. There's even a rumor, provenance unknown, that it might snow over Auroville when the Matrimandir is built.

The Matrimandir's foundation stone is laid at dawn on February 21, 1971—Mother's ninety-third birthday. (She does not attend the ceremony; given her poor health, the Mother will not one time set foot in Auroville.) Satprem is there. He's dressed in white robes, sitting on the ground alongside other notables from the Ashram, a tight look on his face. Three flames are lit, devotional music is played, and a recording of the Mother's voice announces, "Let the Matrimandir be the living symbol of Auroville's aspiration for the Divine."

The ceremony has been held somewhat prematurely. The land for the Matrimandir is not yet fully purchased, and the very next day, even as Aurovilians start digging in the area, a group of twenty villagers descends upon them and chases them away. Work commences in earnest only a few weeks later, after considerable haggling with local landowners. Starting in mid-March, a dozen or so Aurovilians gather every morning, armed with shovels, pickaxes, and crowbars. They face a formidable task: the foundation pit to support this structure will occupy more than seven hundred thousand cubic feet and require the excavation of around forty thousand tons of red earth. No machinery is on-site, but sometimes the Aurovilians are supplemented by crews that come in a blue bus from the Ashram. There is no hired labor; the Mother has said that the Matrimandir should be built only by devotees.

From dawn to midmorning, and then again from midafternoon to evening, they chip away at the compacted soil. Hand to hand they pass earth in metal pans, balancing the weight on their heads, emptying the pans into rusty wheelbarrows whose contents are piled along the circumference of the site. The work is grueling, and there isn't a corner of shade. Sometimes morale fails or tempers rise. But for the most part, the excavation is conducted in high spirits and with a deep sense of purpose.

For many Aurovilians, these early days of digging will rank as among the most hallowed of their lives. Ruud Lohman, a former Franciscan monk from Holland who has left the order to join Auroville, writes in his diary:

> That crater is not just any crater. Right from the start it had something to do with the soul of Auroville. Nobody is digging anymore to dig a hole, but rather to absorb the spiritual force at the excavation site and by digging the red earth to the rhythm of nature to dig into one's own subconscient. . . . The crater has a force, one discovers things which might otherwise take a lifetime to discover.

John is among the first workers at the site. He comes out in the blue bus from Pondicherry or, if he's spent the night in Auroville, as he increasingly does, cycles up the road from a friend's house. He isn't typically one for manual labor, but he seems captivated by the sanctity of this effort, and he works determinedly, usually shirtless and in a straw hat.

He likes to work alone; it's a form of meditation. While others take late-morning breaks, sipping chicory tea or lemon juice under a thatch stall, John keeps digging in the high sun. One day around lunchtime, an American man shows up and points to John's tall silhouette, blurry behind the heat waves. The man asks who the shirtless thin guy out there is, and someone says he's a recent arrival, a rich Harvard graduate named John Walker. The American man is known to be irascible. He looks at John, shakes his head, and sneers, "If he keeps going like that, he'll never make it out of here alive."

A LIVING LABORATORY

JOHN IS HAVING LUNCH at Goyle's Guest House. He's sitting in the dining room, in a wooden chair, at a square table with a cotton cloth cover. Portraits of the Mother and Sri Aurobindo look down from the walls. Waiters in white uniforms carry Goyle's refined dishes on silver trays: freshly caught fish in a lemon-butter sauce, rice pilaf with cashews and raisins, roast chicken with potatoes, maybe a lemon meringue pie.

Goyle stands in the corner, a short man with thinning hair surveying all of this through thick spectacles, chatting occasionally with his guests. John uses silverware he's brought from America, and it's monogrammed with his initials. He praises Goyle's cooking, comparing it to meals he's had at the Four Seasons in New York. Sometimes he reads old copies of international newspapers or magazines, perusing the stock market pages or checking the price of gold. Goyle has seen a lot of people come through town, but he's never seen anyone quite like John. Goyle often says, "John's problem is that he was born a swan but wants to be a crow."

An Aurovilian woman joins John at his table. She lives in Kottakarai, the community set up by those organicist refugees from Silence. They start talking, and John is all over the place. He says he's thinking of buying a house in Pondicherry; or maybe he'll move out to Auroville. Then again, he kind of wants to be closer to his parents. They're getting older and he misses them; he wonders if he should return to America. The woman lets him wander, then asks, "But haven't you seen the Mother?" John says he has. "So, where are you going?" John smiles; he resolves to spend more time in Auroville.

Most of his friends are now living in Kottakarai. He starts going out there on a newly purchased white Raleigh bicycle, and sometimes he takes the one-rupee bus from Pondicherry, jammed in with farmers and their crops, their chickens and goats. Initially he spends a night or two in the community, sleeping at a friend's house or in the open, on a cane mat under the stars. Nights turn into weeks, and soon John is spending months at a stretch in Auroville. But he always keeps his room at Goyle's, in the back of the guesthouse. It's his foothold in civilization, a more refined outpost to which he periodically retreats.

Auroville is a little over three years old, but life remains rudimentary. Kottakarai doesn't have a well yet, and its residents bathe, only occasionally, by immersing themselves in rusty metal barrels carried by bullock carts from other communities. They crouch under trees and behind bushes when they need to go to the bathroom, carrying mugs of water to clean themselves. Sometimes after a big rain the paths that lead to the community are flooded and they must wade through knee-high water to get in and out of their homes. They buy a wooden cart, pulled by a bullock named Morris, to help navigate the inundated fields.

John starts sleeping in the loft of a tile-roofed building located near the center of the community. The tiles are cracked and the roof leaks into a metal bucket that pings through the night. The building also contains a silk-screen workshop on the ground floor. It prints brochures and pamphlets and is part of an effort, repeated across other communities, to create small commercial units that could generate an income for Auroville. These include pottery studios, incense factories, and an incipient electronics unit (Auroelectronics) that will go on to make some of India's first computers. John helps fund many of these enterprises, and he works in Kottakarai's silk-screen unit, too, alongside a German man named Gerhardt. They smoke copious amounts of bidis and get ink all over their clothes and into their skin. They take a lot of breaks, walking over to the village tea shop, where they smoke more bidis and eat idli and dosa while farmers crowd around a shared newspaper.

Eventually, John moves into his own hut, a small raised capsule by a casuarina forest. He contracts hepatitis and is bedridden for a time with yellow eyes. One day a thief from the village forces open the flaps of his capsule and steals his alarm clock, pillow, and clothes. "Half of one's possessions [gone]," John writes to his father, adding, "Which further on, some days later, are found to have been unnecessary in the first place. One wakes up quite well without an alarm clock. The wind in the tree tops is far better than strident clicking and ticking."

To his family, John refers to Kottakarai as "my minor gulag." But he's always loved a fresh start, and he pours himself into the work of building this new community: digging an open well, clearing the land of weeds, irrigating saplings with jugs of water that he balances on his head as he walks across the fields. At night, John and his friends gather around a bonfire and read aloud from *Savitri*, Sri Aurobindo's epic verse reworking of an ancient Indian legend. In the poem, a widow, Savitri, follows her dead husband, Satyavan, into the underworld and negotiates for his life with the god of death. Death ultimately relents and releases Satyavan. The Mother says that Sri Aurobindo has "crammed the whole universe" into *Savitri*, and many Aurovilians consider the poem an allegory of all that they are trying to accomplish. John and his friends shout it out exuberantly over the bonfire, as if to conjure up the new world.

From a letter home to his parents, which John sends during this time: "So for the moment I don't stand so much as squat, poised to take off, so full of the joy of soft breezes and soft sounds, bird calls and leaf rustles, and in the distance the workers starting to work—making a dream come true. For sure, I'm well and happy and wish for you that it is also so, so good it is to be here, and to be."

Kottakarai is one of approximately fourteen communities that emerge across Auroville in the early 1970s. Each is a world unto itself; they all have their own character, and they all coalesce around a particular purpose or set of activities. Some communities—Fertile, later Aurogreen—are focused on ecological work. Others on the borders of Auroville—Promesse, Hope—serve as outreach stations, their geographic locations providing an interface to life beyond the plateau. The notion grows that Auroville is a living laboratory— a testing ground for new ideas about economy, society, and consciousness. Really, though, Auroville consists of a number of dispersed laboratories; every community is experimenting in its own way, each searching for a distinctive model that could radiate outward and illuminate a new path for the planet.

It's a time of ferment, of great creativity. Aurovilians will look back on this period, the first decade or so of the project's existence, and say that they were the most imaginative years, when it felt like anything could happen. Intentional communities are like people; they have life cycles. These young years are a moment of great plasticity and innovation. They will be followed by a certain adult caution and then, as some will bemoan, a middle-aged stasis.

In Kottakarai, a Dutchman named Jaap, trained as an electrical engineer but now one of Auroville's self-taught ecologists, collaborates with village farmers to refine methods of agriculture. The farmers share their knowledge, acquired over centuries, of when and how to plant. They show how stinking dead fish can be buried alongside saplings to keep away insects and animals; and they teach Aurovilians how to make small cracks in water-filled clay jars so that the water seeps out and irrigates over time. For their part, Aurovilians teach villagers how to use calendars rather than the moon and stars to time their harvests, and they install diesel pumps to improve on ancient rain-fed irrigation methods. Aurovilians also introduce an important transport innovation, swapping the old wood-and-metal wheels of bullock carts for rubber tires. Someone tells the Mother about this innovation and she's amused; even in the jet age, she remarks, the city of the future must be built by bullock cart.

The residents of Kottakarai also search for answers to some of the most difficult questions that confront Auroville, concerning economy and finance. In

"A Dream," the Mother's document that established the founding principles of Auroville, she wrote that "money would no longer be the sovereign lord." Aurovilians grapple with the practical implications of this precept. How can Auroville grow—how does it survive?—in a world where money is very much the sovereign lord? How will people feed themselves? How will they build homes and buy clothes?

The economic model (if that's what it can be called) that emerges is somewhat improvised, and not particularly original. Life is financed through a combination of donor funds, mostly raised by the CFY, the organization set up by the Mother to administer Auroville, and small-scale industries such as the commercial units in Kottakarai. A basic—very basic—level of sustenance is provided by the CFY, which offers residents free housing, some food, and a few essential living items (soap, toothpaste, combs, tongue cleaners) through a system known as Prosperity. The monthly cash value of Prosperity is around 125 rupees ($17) for adults, and 75 ($10) for children. Most Aurovilians struggle to eke out a bare subsistence, and wealthier members of the community, such as John, play a big role in keeping them afloat. He adds to the CFY's allotment with food and other goods he's purchased in Pondicherry, over time spending thousands of dollars on his friends and neighbors. He's also known to slip an occasional packet of marijuana into the allotment. This comes to be known as John's Prosperity.

Kottakarai's residents pursue their goal of fostering a closer relationship with their Tamil neighbors; this makes the community a good laboratory, too, for Auroville's prospects as a multicultural town. The Mother has called the Tamil farmers and fishermen of the area "the first citizens of Auroville," but early encounters have mostly been transactional, characterized by land purchases or employment, and often tense. Can these two populations coexist harmoniously, and maybe even productively? The residents of Kottakarai are determined to fulfill the Mother's vision of Auroville as a "Tower of Babel in reverse." They set up a library in the village, and a small health center that primarily treats parasitical and skin infections. They also build a volleyball court where the populations play together, and Kottakarai is one of the first communities to open its well to the villagers. Every morning, farmers and housewives line up with their clay jugs and fill them with water that is reputed to be cleaner and healthier than that from the old, contaminated wells that otherwise dot the area.

In the villages, sentiment toward these outsiders is ambivalent. Some people find the foreigners who cycle around, red-faced and sweaty under the sun, amusing; white people usually show up in chauffeured cars. Many are incredulous about the way these people dress—the men in their loincloths or lungis, like Indian farmers, the women in scandalous little shorts and sleeveless tops. Auroville comes to be known as *nanga nagar*, or naked town. But many villagers also appreciate the simplicity with which Aurovilians live, and they respect the community's spiritual foundations.

One Aurovilian man will remember negotiating for a plot of land with a Tamil owner near Kottakarai. Auroville pays a deposit for the land, but then has trouble coming up with the rest of the money. Legally, the owner is entitled to keep the deposit and the land. The Aurovilian visits the owner one night, talks to him about the Mother and Sri Aurobindo and what the community is trying to achieve. The owner ends up forgoing the remaining payment. "It's all right," he says. "It's for a good cause."

Other villagers, especially older ones, are more skeptical. They remember colonialism, and they warn about a repeat. Such fears are heightened by rumors that the government plans to forcibly acquire thousands of acres for the project (this never happens). One elder in Kottakarai, nicknamed Dadikar for his long white beard (*dadi* means "beard"), warns his people of "slavery." Dadikar is a fiery man and a member of the panchayat, a traditional village assembly. He tells kids to refuse the sweets handed out by Aurovilians, warning that they're poisoned and that they'll induce a trance that will make the kids do the white people's bidding.

At least one boy is dubious. His name is M. Sundarvinayagam, and he goes by Sundaram. He lives in the village with his father, a widowed roof-maker. Sundaram watches the white people come in, sees them clear the land, observes as they erect their huts and dig wells. He plays on the volleyball court they build and, despite Dadikar's warnings, eats the ladoos, jalebis, rasgullas, and other sweets they offer him. He doesn't often get treats like these in the village.

Sundaram notices one white man in particular. He doesn't know the man's name, but he knows that he's an Aurovilian, and he sees that the man is tall and skinny, with a long face. The Aurovilian gets around on a white bicycle, a cloth bag slung over his shoulder, and he hands out biscuits and chickpeas, and sometimes pens, to Sundaram and his friends. The man seems calm, he smiles a lot, and Sundaram thinks he's friendly. One day the man waves Sundaram over. *"Tambi, inge va,"* he calls, in broken Tamil (Young brother, come here). Sundaram walks over and asks. *"Ina aya?"* (What, sir?) The man shakes Sundaram's hand and says his name is John. He asks Sundaram if he'd like to start spending more time in Kottakarai community, with Aurovilians.

So Sundaram starts hanging around with the white people. He visits their homes and sees how they live—modestly, in huts, like villagers—and he starts doing odd jobs for them: buying cigarettes or bidis at the village provisions store, driving a bullock cart with loads of compost and feed. When Aurovilians plant a field of millet, Sundaram is given the job of protecting the crops. He walks the land, beating an empty metal tin with a stick to keep parrots away.

After a while, Sundaram drops out of school and starts spending his entire days in the community. His father isn't pleased. He had hopes for his only son; he wanted him to get a solid government job, maybe as a teacher. But now Sundaram works with the white people from early in the morning until late at night, and he eats most of his meals with them, too, in Kottakarai's collective kitchen. Sundaram tries to reassure his father. He says the Aurovilians treat him well, as an equal, and he's working because his father is old and he wants to earn enough to support him. And, also, Sundaram says, "Being with them is the same as being in school. Every day, I learn so much. It's God's grace to be able to live with a different culture."

The truth, though, is that living side by side isn't always straightforward. Interactions between Auroville and the villages can often seem like a procession of misunderstandings and disagreements. Geography—the land—emerges as one of the biggest flash points. While wealthier villagers are largely pleased with the prospect of this new township, thinking it will boost the value of their properties, smaller farmers are often less thrilled. They complain when Aurovilians fence off their communities and prevent livestock from grazing freely; they are also unhappy with the profusion of trees, which they say shade their fields and stunt their crops.

One day there's a confrontation outside Kottakarai, where Aurovilians have been building a mud dam in a canyon. They build it with good intentions, to halt erosion, but now the six-foot-high wall is complete and it's blocking water for downstream villagers. Early one morning a group of about one hundred shirtless farmers descends upon the canyon, armed with shovels and *kattis*, or sickles, intent on breaking the dam. Aurovilians race over, there's a lot of shouting and shoving, and one Aurovilian is slapped a couple of times. The situation is finally settled when a Tamil man who is close to Auroville and speaks a little English mediates between the groups, and the Aurovilians agree to bring down the dam.

Such heated encounters play out across the plateau. They are often defused, as in that canyon, by local Tamil people who have ties with Auroville. Some of these people end up leaving the villages to join Auroville. Sundaram is one of them; he hesitates initially when he's offered a hut in the community, worried about leaving his father, but then he starts spending nights in Auroville, and he transfers his clothes and possessions and begins English lessons. Henceforth, he, like all other Tamil Aurovilians, will have to negotiate a complex web of loyalties and affiliations; his life will be a balancing act between cultures.

One afternoon Sundaram invites John to the home where he grew up in the village. John walks over, bends down as he enters the low hut, its walls made of thatch and its floor a mix of cow dung and earth, and then he sits outside on a bamboo-framed bed strung with coconut rope. Sundaram tells his father that John and his friends are taking care of him now; they're his new family. He shows his father an egg with his name written on it in black felt pen. Every day, he says, the community distributes eggs like these, hatched from its collection of chickens. Sundaram is included in the distribution; he's one of them.

Sundaram's father offers John some water in a clay bowl. He notices that John drinks the water without touching the bowl to his lips, and he's impressed that John is familiar with this custom. Later, his father tells Sundaram, "I'm sorry, I misunderstood these people." He says that he now sees that they're nothing like the colonialists. Sundaram is relieved when he hears this; his two worlds feel a little less irreconcilable.

Diane is among the first to live in Kottakarai. She moves in along with two-year-old Aurolouis and Larry. Guido has left Auroville for Rameswaram, where he now lives with Guruji, and Larry is like a father to Aurolouis. Also, Diane is pregnant with Larry's child, a daughter whom the Mother will name Auralice. Larry builds the family a hut by a casuarina grove. The wind whispers through the trees at night and it's soothing, but the grove also attracts drunkards and gamblers; sometimes their arguments awaken the family.

Couplings are easy and transitory in this new society. Auroville's hippies have predictably open-minded views about sex and marriage. Parenting is fluid and, like everything else, unconventional. To the many aspects of life Auroville is trying to reinvent in its laboratory, we must add the family unit. Aurolouis has two fathers and so will Auralice: Larry and, later, John. Really, the idea is that everyone is a child of the Mother's; the whole community is one big family. Larry will explain it to me like this: "We didn't want to repeat any of that nuclear-family stuff that we'd grown up with. We weren't into jealousy, possessiveness, none of that. Marriage felt like ownership, and that's not what we were doing—not for things, not for people. We were all in this together; it felt like we'd all take care of each other."

Not everyone in the Mother's world shares quite the same views. Tales of promiscuity in Auroville filter back to Pondicherry, dismaying the administrators and planners. The Mother herself complains that Aurovilians are "living like rabbits and animals." She says children born out of casual affairs are "ill-conceived, ill-formed, underdeveloped." In March of 1972, the topic of Diane's relationship with Larry comes up in a conversation between the Mother and a member of the Ashram.

"What is this? Going after one man and another!" the Mother reportedly says. "We are trying to be above humanity, but these things are animal things, below humanity." She adds, "Tell her [Diane] that they can be good friends, but for good friendship kissing is not necessary, nor sexual activity."

Mother's admonitions come too late: apparently no one has told her that Diane is already six months pregnant. Still, word filters back to Kottakarai, and Diane and Larry do try for a time to sleep on separate mattresses. But the mosquitoes are annoying at night, they have only one big net, and ultimately the mattresses are pushed back together and the errant couple are once again in the same bed.

Auralice is born on the morning of June 21, 1972. She comes out with a distressed face, a look that her parents feel indicates a premature awareness of life's hardships. But Diane's labor has been easy and relatively painless. A woman assisting in the delivery is struck by Diane's calm, and what she will later call her capacity for surrender. This is Diane's talent, will always be her gift, and it teaches the woman something about how to relate to the divine: if you really let go, she feels, if you give yourself to faith, then you will be guided.

Around this time, too, a young American woman moves into Kottakarai with her Indian husband and their infant son: my parents, and me. I have only the dimmest memories of this period, and much of what I remember is probably filled in by subsequent recounting. I recall a sense of openness. I'm sitting on the front tank of my father's Jawa motorcycle, the breeze sticky and warm as I sing. I seem to recall playing with other kids by the Matrimandir's foundation pit, the enormity of that cavity—and its aura of holiness, which we absorb from the adults around us—awe-inspiring.

We live in a single-room hut with bamboo walls and a thatch roof, and outside the hut, connected by footpath, there's an open-to-air bathroom with a hand pump, and a metal bucket and mug for bathing. Our house has no electricity and we use kerosene lamps at night. Next door, in a pit filled with muddy water, a black buffalo heaves and grunts; a man has bought it to make cheese.

Here's another memory (or at least a story I've been told). My family is visiting with Diane and Larry in their hut, and Diane lifts me and tickles me under my chin. My father, who like most men is not immune to Diane's charms, gifts her a brass statue of Krishna, with ruby eyes. She cherishes this statue, and it kindles a deep affection for the god. On the last day of her life, she will clutch her brass Krishna, one of its eyes now fallen out, and hold it close to her heart.

My father is twenty-six years old when I'm born, my mother twenty-four. She's from Pipestone, Minnesota, a small farming town, the eldest in an Irish Catholic family of ten. My father's parents were Hindus who lived in Pakistan and were forced to flee to India during the partition that took place at independence, in 1947. They lost everything in the bloody conflict, struggled to rebuild in New Delhi and Agra, and then made their way south, attracted like so many to Sri Aurobindo and the Mother. My father grew up in the Mother's orbit. He attended her evening French classes in the Ashram sports ground, and after classes she would give him and his friends treats, cashew sweets or roasted peanuts. As a teenager, he often sought her permission, which she granted in writing, to cycle out and explore a wild land outside Pondicherry known as the Red Hill.

So my father knows this area well, has inhabited it since childhood. He was also among the first generation of Indians to go to America for an education, and many of them stayed and built new lives and brilliant careers. It wasn't at all foretold that he would leave those opportunities and return to India. Like many in the community, my parents' decision to live in Auroville has been guided by the idealism of the sixties. "We really thought we could change the world," my father will often tell me. "Maybe we were crazy, but we thought everything was going to be different, and that we could be part of a revolution."

My parents' lives converge in 1969, at an anti–Vietnam War gathering at the University of Denver. My mother is handing out flyers in a wood-paneled dining hall, and she gives one to a dark-skinned young man with long curly hair and a mustache. They get to know each other; he talks about the Ashram and the Mother, and then he goes to India for a holiday, and when he returns, he tells her about cycling out to a canyon where some hippies have built a hut and are planting a forest. Soon my parents embark on an overland trip through Italy, Greece, and Egypt, and then they board a ship in Port Sudan, destination Bombay.

This is my mother's first time outside the United States. It won't be long before she's living with that long-haired man in a hut by a field in South India, and I will always marvel at the audacity (or was it naïveté?) it takes to make that trip. Is she searching for adventure? Does she know what she is getting into? I ask my mother years later, and she says she never dreamed she would end up in a place like Auroville; girls from rural Minnesota didn't possess the vocabulary to have such dreams. "I didn't come with any big plans or ideals," my mother tells me, sitting in a cane chair on her porch in Auroville. She's a schoolteacher in the community, and she's worked in education for some thirty-five years, often fighting considerable headwinds and resistance from a town determined to reinvent, along with everything else, traditional learning. "I mean, I found Auroville very interesting, and it's been a wonderful place for me to live," she says. "I'm so happy I discovered it, but I never set out to come to a town like this. Sometimes I still can't quite believe I live here."

Dreamers come in many flavors. Some, such as John and Diane, are intentional; they're romantics and they're conscious of their search, even if they're unsure of what they're looking for. They're eloquent and often vociferous about their restlessness. Others, such as my mother, are quieter. They stumble into their dreams. I will talk to her over the years, and she always seems reticent, as if bashful of the idealism—or whatever it was—that brought her to Auroville. There will always be these two contingents: a loud and vocal cohort of dreamers, and then a more latent one. One of the challenges the community faces, will face increasingly as it matures, is reconciling these different kinds of idealism.

One day in Kottakarai an American man named Roy walks down to a palmyra grove and watches as a metal barrel is unloaded from a bullock cart. The barrel has been modified by the addition of a door and internal shelves, so that it can serve as an oven. A mason lays a brick base under the barrel, then erects an arch above it. The area is cleared of shrubs and saplings; a carpenter builds a wooden table.

Roy goes down to Pondicherry and buys a can of wheat berries. Back in Auroville, he crosses into the village and heads toward a large cast-iron mill, under a shed with sheet-metal roofing. The mill is an antique from colonial times. Roy pours his wheat berries into a funnel, a villager turns the wheel to ignite a kerosene engine, and then the funnel sputters and shakes until ground wheat, or flour, comes out.

Roy takes the flour back to the oven. The next day, he bakes a couple of loaves of whole-wheat bread. This is the start of the Kottakarai Bakery. It begins humbly but grows quickly, until it's producing some two hundred loaves a day, as well as buns and cakes, all of which are distributed across Auroville.

Roy is soon joined by Larry, John, and Sundaram; as usual, John provides much of the money. The four of them gather every morning and collect casuarina poles for firewood, chop the wood in a clearing, and kindle the fire with pages from newspapers and kerosene. It's fun, kind of exciting, to be doing this all together for Auroville. The bakery feels like one more step in the community's efforts to build a self-reliant economy.

They face a variety of impediments. Some days the area stinks terribly; the bakers hadn't realized that village farmers used these palmyra trees to hang the placentas of newborn calves. It's a local superstition, believed to enhance fertility. They must work without a thermometer or timer, pacing themselves instead by the village bus schedule; they put bread in the oven as the bus drives one way, pull it out when the bus returns. Bus schedules being what they are in this part of the world, the bread sometimes burns.

They work outdoors, exposed to the elements, and when the monsoon arrives, they are forced to hastily erect a thatch roof. They have to contend with mosquitoes, geckos, ants, and frogs that hop up to the table and get stuck in the dough. Once a thick rat snake slides onto the bakery's sandy floor, and Larry jumps up, shouting, "Sonofabitch! Sonofabitch!" Sundaram chuckles as Larry lands directly on the stunned rat snake—which, uncharacteristically for this aggressive species, slithers quickly away. The whole bakery effort is really a makeshift, shoestring affair. But this, it seems, is how Auroville will emerge: ad hoc, amateurishly, a miracle in the way it holds together. Even as the administrators in Pondicherry lament the hippies, it's the hippies who ingeniously, persistently—almost lunatic in their stubbornness—keep digging, building, planting, cutting, damming, watering, and baking. One man will later characterize Auroville's pioneers as "idiot savants of endurance."

The bakery starts with one fundamental principle: there should be no exchange of money in Auroville's economy, and hence, no one should have to pay for Kottakarai's bread. Like many of Auroville's ideals, this noble ambition is more easily articulated than effectuated. Wheat isn't free, after all, and neither is use of the village mill. The bakers come up with a workaround that sidesteps the problem without quite solving it. People who want bread will go down to Pondicherry to buy wheat berries for themselves (money isn't taboo over there), then come back and give it to the bakers. This type of sleight of hand is characteristic of the approach Auroville takes to building its alternative economy. Over the years, it will open the community to charges of hypocrisy and wishful thinking: pretending that money isn't involved doesn't actually make it so.

The cashless experiment at the Kottakarai Bakery doesn't last long. It starts to fall apart when one man who has bought a kilo of wheat berries puts his bread on a scale, finds it only weighs 750 grams, and gets suspicious. He throws his bread on the ground and accuses the bakers of cheating him. Another man, tired of cycling into Pondicherry, grows similarly irate. "I'm tired of this stupid story," he snaps at the bakers. "Here's some cash, you go get the fucking wheat. Just let me buy some bread!"

Finally, the bakers relent. They start charging three rupees for a loaf of bread, and twenty-five paisa for the jaggery muffins they've added to their inventory. "It was like the reinvention of money," Roy, the first baker, tells me later. "We soon figured out that this thing about no money was never going to work."

John has worked elsewhere in Auroville before the bakery, but this project represents his first substantial commitment of time to the community. Although he still keeps his room at Goyle's Guest House, he's spending fewer nights in Pondicherry now. He seems invigorated by the bakery, galvanized by the opportunity to set up something so elemental: feeding the new world.

He awakens every morning at dawn and sits in his capsule with the flaps open, his long legs over the side so that they hang just above the ground. He smokes a bidi and opens his leatherbound copy of *Savitri* and reads from it aloud, as if to the trees. Then he walks over to the bakery, greets his co-workers, and sometimes spends a few moments with Auralice and Aurolouis, who like to hang around under the tables or play with blocks of firewood. He stands over a pile of logs, using a metal ax to chop rhythmically, as if following the cadence of an inner mantra.

Later, after the bread is in the ovens, John is often seen meditating with eyes closed under a neem or peepul tree, enveloped in smoke from incense sticks fixed into the ground. He sits straight, aiming for a stillness that he knows rishis and yogis are able to achieve. Sometimes the squirrels and dogs come around. One time a dog, mistaking John for a plant or a stone, urinates on him to mark its territory.

At the end of the day, under an orange-and-purple sunset, John heads to the fields holding a bag of freshly baked muffins. He greets the farmers and laborers as they return to the villages, trudging exhaustedly back to their homes. "Take this," John says, a smile on his face, and he looks them in the eye. "Take this for your work."

He's eccentric, no doubt; some people think this white man in the fields is bizarre. Mostly, they think he's kind. Stories about John's generosity continue to spread, within Auroville but also now in the villages. People with debts know they can count on him, as do people who need a new bicycle, whose roofs are leaking, whose water pumps are broken, or parents who worry about getting their children married or educated. An old Tamil man who works in the bakery is always dressed in the same tattered loincloth. One day, unprompted, John buys him a new saffron dhoti and shirt. Stunned, the man runs his hands over the clothes, and after that he starts calling John "Swami," an honorific with spiritual connotations. This is the thing about John, they say: he just watches, notes the need, and then provides without being asked.

Another man will tell me about approaching John for help with a ticket to America. The ticket is already booked, but the man doesn't have sufficient funds to pay for it. Without hesitation or questions, John hands over twenty thousand rupees in cash (around $2,600). When the man thanks John profusely, John replies that it isn't his money anyway; it's the Mother's money.

Years later, I tell this story to Gillian, John's sister. She's still anguished by her brother's death, furious after all this time at Auroville and everyone around him. She blames them, thinks they were careless and that they took advantage of John. "It wasn't the Mother's money," she says. "It was *my* mother's money."

The checks arrive by airmail and are placed in wooden cubicles at the Ashram post office in Pondicherry. They are accompanied by letters from John's parents—tender, curious, clearly expressing longing for their son, bemused by his strange trip but trying not to prod. The checks are drawn on the Riggs Bank in Washington, DC, or on Coutts & Co., a bank in London where his mother maintains an account. John also has an investment account at Schroders, an asset management company, which contains a bequest left by his great-aunt Bee. He expresses a desire to sell all his holdings and donate the proceeds to Auroville, but Walker Sr. dissuades him, and they're instead sold in increments of between $2,000 and $4,000, which nonetheless translate into princely sums where John is living.

He takes the checks to a bank near Pondicherry's city park, walks over to the manager's table in the back, and produces them with an ironic flourish. The manager knows this man; not many people in the area show up with this kind of money. "What'll it fetch?" John asks with an exaggerated drawl, and the manager proceeds, unsmiling, to press buttons and pull a few levers on a machine, figuring the amount in rupees as the contraption jiggles and rings and thumps. Sometimes John takes the checks to an Indian friend who operates an illicit money-changing business. The friend deals mostly in cash, and he's initially reluctant to accept personal checks. But John assures him that his parents' financial instruments are as good as those issued by the Bank of England, and the friend soon learns that this is true.

He pleads with his father to give money directly to Auroville. John says— perhaps exaggerating a little—that a single check for $3,000 could keep all of Auroville's Tamil members fed for five months. He speaks of the environmental work being done in the community, of the Matrimandir, of all the money that's needed to build this ideal city. Walker Sr. is a practical man. He expresses trepidation and asks about Auroville's organization:

> How is it governed? Who decides how the money is spent? Do each
> of you contribute? Do you have a budget? I know you have a utopian
> society, but is there any chance it will ever be self-sustaining? Do you
> support many people who have nothing to contribute?

These questions are all far removed from the daily reality of Auroville, which is not only lacking in organization but adamantly against it and anything that smacks of structure. Aurovilians like to speak about operating by the rules of "divine anarchy." John replies to his father by quoting the *Rigveda*: "Who knoweth these things? Who can speak of them?" The problem, he adds, now quoting Lao-tzu, is that "the Tao which can be expressed [in words] is not the eternal Tao."

Walker Sr. no doubt finds all of this a bit impenetrable. He asks for more detail, and this time John replies by quoting Sri Aurobindo's maxim "All life is yoga." "So if I am to write to you of my life I can only write to you of the yoga," John says. "Are you interested? This life that I live is not understandable in terms of familiar analysis. You see it gets complicated, for the truth is simple—so simple as to surpass our comprehension. But I want you and [mother] to know that I am blessed by more than happiness, by the possibility of a progress that can be infinite. *That* is the infinite. As I said, it's not so easy to understand."

One afternoon, John is sitting with a friend by the Matrimandir. "You know," he says to his friend, "if my parents wanted, they could build this whole place in one go. Just like that." The sky is blue, a play of swirling cotton-candy clouds. The friend feels that John says this without glee, and certainly not as a boast. He can't quite place it, but in the way John describes his family's wealth there's something mournful, like a yearning.

John goes with this same man to an antique store in Pondicherry. The owner greets John effusively; he's a good customer. As they're looking around, a cassette deck plays Bob Dylan's "Just Like a Woman." The song is about Edie Sedgwick, John's friend from his Harvard days; Sedgwick was also close to Dylan. The man accompanying John is a huge Dylan fan, something of a groupie, and John turns to him and says nonchalantly, "Oh, I know that woman. She was a good friend." Moments like these remind John's fellow travelers in Auroville—and perhaps John, too—that for all their shared participation in this project, he comes from a very different world.

In the fall of 1972, John decides that he will, after all, visit his family in America. He catches a ship from Madras to Singapore, and from there flies via Tokyo and

Kyoto—where he checks into a "big jazzy hotel"—and then on to Honolulu and San Francisco. He arrives in New York bearing gifts: Japanese Zen sketches for his parents, tailored clothes for Gillian's new romantic partner, the documentary filmmaker Albert Maysles.

Gillian and Albert have recently purchased an apartment in the Dakota building, and John stays with them. The Dakota is a landmark overlooking Central Park. It's home to celebrities such as Lauren Bacall, Judy Garland, Boris Karloff, and, later, John Lennon and Yoko Ono. The Dakota is decorated with elaborate gargoyles outside, and opulent mahogany interiors.

John has come to America mostly because he misses his family; he wants to be with them for Christmas. But he has another reason, too. The American presidential campaign is underway, and John is a fervent opponent of Nixon, whom he accuses of purveying a "totalitarian tyranny." John is determined to support George McGovern, the liberal Democratic senator from South Dakota, and he's convinced that Indian spirituality has a role to play in the outcome of the election. He and a friend drive up and down the East Coast in an old station wagon, chanting, "Om McGovern, Om McGovern, Om McGovern!"

McGovern loses in a landslide and John remains in New York, with Albert and Gillian. Albert is something of a celebrity. In partnership with his brother, David, he's known as a pioneer of direct cinema, and their documentary on the Rolling Stones, *Gimme Shelter*, has gained them a cult following. A stream of luminaries—Vanessa Redgrave, Leonard Bernstein, the filmmaker D. A. Pennebaker—comes through the apartment. John mostly keeps to himself. He goes for walks in the park, he meets a few people in New York who have visited Auroville, or who are familiar with the teachings of the Mother and Sri Aurobindo.

Among those people are Robert and Deborah Lawlor, who have recently left Forecomers. They tell John that they're burned out by the land, and they're now living in the south of France, where Robert is writing a book on sacred geometry. John is distressed to hear that they're quitting. He corners them in a mutual friend's apartment on the Upper East Side and subjects them to a forty-five-minute rant about the decline of Western civilization and the end of what he calls "the era of the machine." He insists they've made a big mistake by moving away from Auroville. He seems worked up, and Robert feels that John is behaving erratically. Gillian notices this, too; she wonders what her brother is getting up to in India.

He likes to meditate on a coffee table in the living room of the Dakota apartment. He lights candles and incense, opens a window onto Central Park West. He sits on the table cross-legged in a lungi and closes his eyes. He stays like that for hours, sometimes with rose petals strewn around the table. Albert finds the whole thing ridiculous. He's the son of a postal clerk from Boston and grew up during the Depression. He's down-to-earth and doesn't have much patience for these kinds of fancies.

One day Albert walks into the apartment while John is meditating. Albert approaches the table, blows out the incense and candles, and shuts the window. He walks away without saying a word. Later, Albert asks someone, "When is that boy going to get out of his tree?"

ARCHITECTS OF
IMMORTALITY

EVERY UTOPIA IS AT ITS core an attempt to reinvent humanity. The Soviets anticipated a New Man and a New Woman who would embody communist values such as self-sacrifice and austerity. Thomas More, in *Utopia*, portrays an ideal society that molds human nature toward perfection. Transhumanism foresees a bionic species to improve on nature's version; it's possible to see our culture's boundless optimism about technology, and in particular the start-up ethos, as the twenty-first century's predominant strain of utopianism.

The Mother says that babies born in her cradle will be more conscious and have an enhanced sensitivity. She suggests that they may serve as "intermediary beings" to a more evolved form of life, and that they will "begin the new race." In this sense, children birthed on Aurovilian soil would be half an evolutionary step ahead; they will embody Sri Aurobindo's vision of a supramental human being.

By the end of 1972, sixty-six babies have been born in Auroville. Most of them carry the moniker *Auro*, as if branded by the new world: Auroson, Aurofilio, Auroanandan, Aurora, Junauro, Aura, Aurokumar, Aurokarl, Marcauro, and Diane's two children, Aurolouis and Auralice. These babies emerge in a steady patter from a small clinic in the community of Promesse, a former customs outpost between British and French India, on the tarred road that leads from Pondicherry to the Red Hill. They are carried to the Ashram by enthusiastic parents, who line up outside the Mother's room, waiting for an opportunity to place their newborns on her lap. The Mother caresses the babies, gazes on them with her soft eyes, then goes inward and searches for a name to match the identity of their souls.

People have high hopes for this first generation. That's how it always goes in new worlds: the youth are expected to purge the foibles of their ancestors. From book 3, canto 4, of Sri Aurobindo's *Savitri*:

> I saw them cross the twilight of an age
> The sun-eyed children of a marvellous dawn,
> The great creators with wide brows of calm,
> The massive barrier-breakers of the world
> . . . .
> The labourers in the quarries of the gods,
> The messengers of the Incommunicable,
> The architects of immortality.

Rumors of immortality have long wafted over the Ashram and Auroville. As we've seen, one of the central tenets of Sri Aurobindo's Integral Yoga is a determination to pass beyond human consciousness and form; this would seem to imply the possibility of surmounting mortal constraints. During Sri Aurobindo's lifetime, there were persistent whisperings that the master was working to conquer death. When those expectations were dashed, the whisperings attached themselves to the Mother. This transference was partly fueled by a pamphlet circulated within the Ashram, which explained Sri Aurobindo's passing as "a colossal strategic sacrifice . . . in order that the physical transformation of the Mother may be immeasurably hastened and rendered absolutely secure." Or, as Sri Aurobindo told the Mother one day about the possibility of his physical departure, "You will have to fulfill our Yoga of supramental descent and transformation."

Immortality is a godly aspiration—you could say it's utopian. Nonetheless, the anticipation that a successful yoga might succeed in banishing death captures the imagination of early Aurovilians and establishes a conceivable (if distant) goal, alongside more earthly ambitions such as reinventing the economy and society. This belief in spiritualism's ability to temper human matter—and biology—is central to the story we are unraveling here; it plays an important part in the deaths of John and Diane. We shall return to them shortly. But first, to understand Aurovilians' attitudes to mortality (and immortality), we must briefly step back in time.

The first Aurovilian baby is born on June 25, 1967, eight months before the community's inauguration in the amphitheater. The Mother names him Auroson. He is wide-eyed, chubby cheeked, and blond, the son of a German father, Frederick, and a Swedish mother, Charlotte. Frederick and Charlotte are the first people formally admitted into Auroville by the Mother—officially, the first Aurovilians, though Robert and Deborah Lawlor will be the first to actually live on the land.

When Auroson is born, Charlotte is twenty-eight, a mother of three from a previous marriage in Uganda. She comes from an artistic family in Sweden; while living in Kampala, she was part of a circle of writers and journalists at the vanguard of an African intellectual renaissance. Frederick is a child of the Second World War. He watched Allied bombers fly overhead as a boy, and he foraged for metal piping and begged for chocolate and oranges from American soldiers amid the ruins of Munich. Like so many of his generation, he's devastated and bewildered—how could the country of Goethe and Rilke descend to such barbarity?—and perhaps this sense of disorientation is what brings him to the Ashram.

They arrive in Pondicherry separately. They meet the Mother, soon they are devoted to her, and then they find each other and move, unmarried, into a whitewashed colonial house on Rue Dumas, one block from the ocean. They are a handsome couple, Charlotte blond and delicately featured, Frederick broad shouldered and square jawed, with an elegant, aristocratic manner. They are good archetypes for the Mother's new township. On weekends, they journey out to the Red Hill, where they are building a large concrete house that will be one of Auroville's first solid structures. The Mother calls the building Auroson's Home.

Before Frederick and Charlotte's baby is born, the Mother sends them a note. If it's a boy, she says, call him Auroson; if it's a girl, Aurosylle. Frederick is surprised because he assumes that the Mother would know the gender of their child. On the morning of June 25, as the pangs of labor announce themselves, Charlotte and Frederick rush to the community of Promesse. They make for a building under a leafy tamarind tree, with a room that has been hastily painted and equipped with running water for the occasion. The Mother has named this building the Maternity Clinic; she says it's intended for "children of the Divine."

The boy is born at two in the afternoon, and his arrival causes an immediate furor. People descend upon Promesse, eager to glimpse this progenitor of a new species. An Italian photographer captures the moment for posterity. The poor baby is like a celebrity. When the family visits the Ashram, they are surrounded by curious onlookers, many of whom reach out to touch the child's cheeks, as if seeking a piece of the divine. "It was a very special time," Frederick will say of these early months. "You really felt like a new chapter of Sri Aurobindo's and the Mother's manifestation had opened up. Auroson's birth was one of the events which was signaling a new world."

On February 28, 1968, the day of Auroville's inauguration, All India Radio carries a special broadcast about the town. Frederick is one of the speakers, and he's asked what kind of world he imagines his son inhabiting in a decade. His response captures all the optimism of a new parent—and so much more:

> Ten years from now Auroson will have a city-in-the-making as
> his playground. His games will take place on the scaffolding of

the future.... A city flowing with light and water will be at his disposal.... A planetary city [which] will always be changing and change itself....

Auroson ... will not experience the machine as other than himself, but as an extension of his body. Computers will answer his questions, televisions and radio telescopes will narrate cosmic stories.... Auroson-Auroville-Aurobindo—a mantra, a progression, and a promise. At ten, Auroson will be playing in twin cities: the city of joy in his heart and the city of hope, in South India.

From the beginning, the boy seems fragile, as if burdened by the weight of expectations. He has a way of staring astonished, and his mother feels he's "shocked by life and our ignorance and unconsciousness"; his father thinks the boy seems "defenseless." He's sick a lot, mostly with respiratory infections. At the Mother's suggestion, the family goes for a time to Bangalore, some two hundred miles away, hoping that the higher altitude and cooler climate might help.

In the spring of 1968, Auroson is almost a year old and it's hot, and Frederick builds a small pool for the family in the courtyard of their house on Rue Dumas. One day the baby is in a chair having a meal with his parents in the courtyard. He's struggling with a ripe mango, and it slips and slides delightfully, leaving orange stains across his face and torso. Frederick decides to go upstairs for a rest.

The next thing he hears is a scream from the courtyard—"one of those primal screams," he will recall—and he rushes out to a balcony and sees Charlotte standing over the pool, holding Auroson's wet, limp body upside down. Frederick runs to the courtyard and tries mouth-to-mouth resuscitation, the sweet taste of mango in his mouth. Auroson is unresponsive.

They flag a cycle rickshaw and rush to the Ashram, taking the body wrapped in a blanket. One of the Mother's attendants tries to stop them, but they refuse to say what has happened; they will only tell the Mother. The attendant finally allows them past, and they find the Mother recently emerged from her bathroom, dressed in a bathrobe. She sits in a chair and Frederick puts the baby, still wrapped in the blanket, on her lap. The Mother says, *No, no, no,* and then something like, *So he sneaked away.* Frederick and Charlotte sit silently, in shock, beyond tears, on the carpeted floor. Frederick feels like a stone. Charlotte searches for that place, deep in the pain, almost under the pain, where there is no more pain.

The Mother tells them to take the body to the hospital and show it to a doctor. For a moment Frederick has hope; he thinks maybe the Mother knows that the boy can be revived. Then he realizes that she's just being pragmatic: she wants a death certificate. The Mother has multiple roles. She is a spiritual guide, for many the divine incarnate. She is also an administrator, the woman running the show, who must attend to practicalities and legalities.

Later—maybe it's the same day as the drowning, maybe a few days on—the parents are back in the Mother's room, and she's consoling them. She tells them that what they consider to be a catastrophe is actually a grace. She's always known that Auroson wasn't happy to be the first child, that he suffered from the pressure. He has come to her in dreams and visions, expressing discomfort and a desire to leave the world. The Mother says that Auroson's body was too brittle for the task at hand; his soul needed a new container.

She tells the parents not to grieve, and that she will keep the soul safe. She asks them to bury Auroson in a temporary location, in a hermetically sealed coffin that can later be reopened. Make a new body, the Mother says, and I will reinsert the soul. When you are ready to bring him back, let me know; I'll do what's necessary. She taps her left shoulder when she says this, as if indicating the place where Auroson will stay, protected, until the parents are ready to reincarnate him.

Stories get around about the Mother's conversation with Charlotte and Frederick. Her words provide at least some kind of explanation; they soften the blow. Still, Auroson's death is a shock, and not only to the bereaved parents. He drowned on May 4, 1968, just a couple of months after Auroville's inauguration. The tragedy shakes some people's confidence. They wonder if Auroville is too early, if perhaps it is ahead of its time. At the very least, this is a bumpy start.

About a year and a half after the drowning, Frederick and Charlotte visit the Mother in her room and tell her that they are ready. The Mother suggests that December would be a suitable month, and the new child, the second Auroson, is conceived shortly afterward, at 10:00 p.m. on a terrace in Auroville. His father will describe a lovemaking that is "impersonal," as if "totally taken over by something else"; he feels he doesn't recognize Charlotte during the act.

The second Auroson will grow up to be a close friend of mine. Always, this legend hangs over him—his life a metaphor, a symbol of how death can be surmounted through faith and the permanence of the soul. His story inspires many Aurovilians, but it weighs on him. One day, we are teenagers hanging out in his room, listening to music and reading magazines. I remember it as being afternoon, the bright light filtering from outside through orange curtains, and he speaks to me of his burden hesitatingly, reluctantly. He tells me how his brother was exhumed from his hermetically sealed coffin and, on the Mother's instructions, buried in the garden of this house, Auroson's Home. He now lies outside, under a marble tombstone. Auroson tells me that one day when he was a toddler he walked out and urinated on his brother's grave. "I guess I'd had enough," he says. "I'd had enough of always having to be Auroson."

Late on the night of December 5, 1972, a massive cyclone crosses the coast of Tamil Nadu. The eye of the storm is some twenty miles north of Pondicherry (about five miles north of Auroville), and the rain and hurricane winds, which rise nearly to a hundred miles per hour, cause considerable damage. Eighty people are killed in the surrounding villages, and thousands left homeless. In the courtyard of the Ashram, the large copperpod tree that stands over Sri Aurobindo's Samadhi loses several branches.

The following morning, Satprem visits the Mother for their regular appointment. He comes with a woman named Sujata, a Bengali member of the Ashram who is now his spiritual companion. Sujata has been in the Ashram since the age of nine, and Satprem has entrusted her with typing his hand-written notes from these conversations. Satprem observes that the Mother seems downcast today. She's suffering from a cold, and she dwells on the havoc of the night before. Over the sound of axes chopping at the damaged tree below her room, the Mother surmises that something must be truly amiss for such a storm to strike at the heart of the Ashram. The cyclone, she suggests, "is a warning from Nature."

The Mother, ninety-three years old, tells Satprem that she is puzzled. Although in many ways her consciousness is stronger than ever, her memory seems to be fading; she forgets what she's done within half an hour. Satprem tries to cheer her up by handing her a white hibiscus flower that has survived the cyclone. The Mother has her own names for plants; she believes each one has a spiritual quality, and she has named the white hibiscus Grace. She hands the flower back to Satprem, who replies, "I would like the grace of belonging exclusively to you."

Over the following weeks and months, the Mother speaks of various physical infirmities, and of excruciating pain in her body. She tells Satprem that she has a constant sensation of being ill, although she knows very well that nothing is actually wrong. Over the years, the Mother has continued to work on her yoga of the cells, striving to arrive at a place where "death does not exist." Now she tells Satprem that she believes her ailments stem from a conflict between her human consciousness, which remains mired in the physical, and the supramental consciousness toward which she's aspiring. "The old things seem puerile, childish, unconscious," she says; at the same time, she feels that something "tremendous and wonderful" is taking place within herself.

Even as the Mother suffers, she continues attending to her responsibilities in the Ashram, although on a reduced schedule. She comments on Satprem's translations of Sri Aurobindo's writings, she steers her township, and she meets with visiting dignitaries. In early 1973, she receives a visit from the Dalai Lama, who asks whether his dream of a more perfect world—economically prosperous, yet based on Buddhist principles of love and compassion—can ever manifest in Tibet. The Mother assures him that this dream is possible, although it may take a long time.

Satprem grows increasingly agitated. Every time he visits the Mother, he departs convinced that she's in the midst of a competition between death and transformation, and that the fate of humanity hangs in the balance. No doubt he is also distraught at the prospect of losing the Mother, upon whom he has grown increasingly emotionally dependent. Sometimes, when Satprem asks eagerly about the progress the Mother is making, or when he beseeches her to persevere in her search for cellular immortality, he sounds like a man pleading for himself.

One day, toward the end of their meeting, Sujata tells the Mother that she has a wish. Satprem is too anguished, she says, and she asks the Mother to alleviate his suffering. The Mother asks why Satprem is so tormented, and Sujata, giggling, says it's simply his nature. Satprem grimaces and the Mother takes his hands in hers; she reminds him to always remain open to the divine.

Three months after that encounter, Satprem visits the Mother and finds her looking weak. Her voice wavering, she says she feels that she's coming up against all the obstacles of the old world. Sometimes she wonders if maybe the divine wants her to leave; she has no fear about that possibility. But she adds that she keeps asking if she should go, and she receives no answer. Then, when she asks if she should stay, she receives a single word in reply: *Transformation*. The Mother takes this to be an encouragement to keep going with her yoga until she has achieved a breakthrough.

Her face is pale and her breathing is halting. She takes time between words, long pauses that are filled with the bells of wandering peanut vendors in the street below, and the distant hum of the ocean. Then the Mother tells Satprem that she may, in fact, have found a solution. It's never been tried before, but she believes she can put her body to sleep while, inside, the work of cellular evolution continues. She has doubts that others will recognize what she's doing, and she expresses concern that the authorities and even some members of the Ashram will insist on pronouncing her dead and prematurely interring her.

She speaks about entering a state of "catalepsy"—a trancelike condition in which the body remains rigid and unmoving, as if mimicking death, and under which, she believes, the transformation could manifest. She cautions that the trance could last days or weeks, even longer, and she wonders if there is any way of preventing uncomprehending people from short-circuiting the process. Satprem assures her that he won't let that happen, and that he will make sure her project reaches completion. In truth, he has his own misgivings.

As the Mother has grown frail, tensions have built around her. There is jockeying for position, and new resentments and jealousies have begun to manifest. In particular, a strong mutual antipathy has grown between Satprem and a man named Pranab, a robustly built Bengali athlete who heads the Ashram's physical education program. Pranab is close to the Mother (he's often referred to as her "bodyguard"), and he's a rough, somewhat forceful man. Satprem characterizes him as a "brute," and accuses Pranab and his associates of trying to limit his access to the Mother and spying when he and the Mother are together. Satprem and Pranab are like two jealous children, rivalrous brothers vying for the love of their parent. Their tensions will have long-lasting repercussions.

On April 7, 1973, Satprem is with the Mother when Pranab enters her room. They have been discussing the transformation and the cataleptic trance, and now Satprem tries to tell Pranab about all of this, especially the Mother's request that her body should remain untouched. As the Mother sits in her chair, hands folded in her lap, a ferocious confrontation ensues. When Satprem tries to explain, Pranab is curt and dismissive. "I am not interested," he says. "Whatever happens, happens. I am there to stand up to the last. . . . I don't want to listen also, Mother."

The Mother asks Pranab if he is sure he doesn't want to know, and Pranab replies abruptly that he does not. Satprem tries again to explain about the Mother's yoga and the importance of leaving her body untouched. He adds that, should the unthinkable happen, it will be essential to leave the Mother's body undisturbed. At this, Pranab explodes. "*Who* is disturbing her?" he shouts. "If anybody is disturbing you, Mother, amongst us, he can be off!"

The Mother tries to say something, but Pranab interrupts. "Mother, don't tell anything," he says. "You go on: eat, sleep, and work, and don't try to make anybody explain me [*sic*]. I know what it is, what everything is. Better everybody keeps quiet!"

The conversation continues in this heated vein, with the Mother feebly trying to interject every now and then. Finally, Pranab shouts that he's had "enough of humbug!" and forces everyone out of the room. Satprem bids the Mother goodbye in a tender, choked voice. "*Douce Mère,*" he always calls her (Sweet Mother). He clutches a white lotus as he leaves. On his way out, he sees someone and predicts that one day, soon, he is going to be shut out of the Mother's room.

Years later, Pranab will remember this moment, acknowledging his anger, adding that he lost control over himself because he felt the conversation had turned unhealthily lugubrious, as it often did when talk turned to the transformation. He tells an associate that every time Satprem was finished with the Mother, he left her exhausted. Pranab was trying to divert the Mother's mind, he says, cheer her up and get her to stop focusing on death.

The summer of 1973 rolls in. Even by the standards of the region, it's harsh. In Auroville, the water table descends, and wells and fields go dry. Such hunger and starvation haven't been seen since colonial times. In the village of Kottaka-rai, a Tamil mother is found selling her breast milk to a tea shop, trying to pass it off as coming from a cow.

Outside Auroson's Home, in a bed of dung compost, a man plants ninety-five roses. He does this to mark the Mother's ninety-fifth year. They are red and pink, and he plants them with love and dedication; he even receives a card of encouragement from the Mother. But the roses soon shrivel up and die in the heat.

One day that summer an Aurovilian Frenchman named Alain is cycling down the beach promenade in Pondicherry. It's late afternoon and the road is filled with men and women on their walks, seeking relief in the cool seaside breeze. He cycles past the tennis courts where the Mother used to play, along the whitewashed lighthouse, and then he hears a voice calling his name. The voice belongs to Roger Anger, and he appears to be in some distress.

The chief architect tells Alain that Auroville's finances are in dire straits. Thus far, the CFY has raised and distributed much of Auroville's funding, but this has largely been done in the name and on the charisma of the Mother. Now that she's sequestered in her room, the funds have all but dried up. There's no money, Roger says, nothing to build the city, and hardly enough to feed its residents. "No Mother, no money," he keeps repeating, trying to impress upon Alain the gravity of the situation. Roger asks Alain to set up a meeting in the community; he says that Auroville needs to take charge of its affairs.

The meeting takes place shortly thereafter in the amphitheater. It will go down in history as Auroville's first general meeting. In preparation, a plan for a revamped economic structure is developed, and a few hundred cyclo-styled copies are distributed. The plan has a hand-drawn sketch showing how money should flow from a central Common Fund to various other communal facilities such as a Fund for Development, a community kitchen, and a central purchasing unit. The proposal also outlines a number of principles

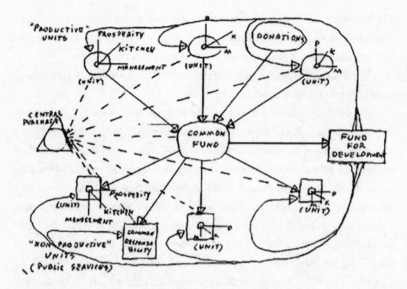

for Auroville's economy, including this cardinal one: "The same amount of money for the maintenance of each Aurovilian." The monthly maintenance is set at 150 rupees (about $20).

There's a flurry of subsequent activity, gestures toward systematizing the economy. A Central Food Distribution Unit is set up to collect produce from farmers and to purchase in bulk. A proposal is submitted to the Mother for a center where Aurovilians could receive essential supplies without having to pay. She is enthusiastic and writes, "*Pour Tous*" (For All), on the proposal. This becomes the name of a cashless cooperative that will be located in an asbestos-roofed shed near the community of Aspiration. The prospects for all these efforts are, however, profoundly uncertain; nothing can get around the reality of Auroville's increasingly precarious financial situation.

The sense of precariousness is heightened, too, by growing awareness of the Mother's condition. Whispers about her failing health reach the community, along with rumblings about some kind of monumental struggle she's in. When Aurovilians visit the Samadhi, they hear shouts from upstairs in the Mother's room, and they listen as her attendants exhort the Mother to walk, eat, and take her medications. The Mother's cries of anguish pierce their meditations. Across the plateau, there's an apprehension that hardly dares articulate itself: Could the Mother really leave us?

One day an American man from Kottakarai, a close friend of John's and Diane's, has a dream. He's at the Ashram with a crowd, and he sees the Mother lying in state on the Samadhi. He kisses her feet, and he feels a tremendous surge of energy emanate from her body. The man wakes up and recounts this dream to a neighbor, who says he's just had a similar one. They're astonished, and the American man cycles down to Pondicherry, where he asks an Ashram elder about the significance of the dream. The elder tells him to put such thoughts out of his mind. "You needn't be concerned," the elder says. "This is in the atmosphere. It's all just a formation."

For Satprem, the topic of the Mother's death is taboo—the notion a form of treachery, a breach of faith and a betrayal of her project. Hasn't she repeatedly told them that she's not going to die? Don't they understand about the transformation? Shortly after his confrontation with Pranab, Satprem reports indignantly to someone that Pranab has been overheard telling a man to prepare for the Mother's departure. Another senior member of the Ashram concurred with Pranab's assessment; Satprem concludes bitterly that they are all in a conspiracy against the yoga.

His last meeting with the Mother takes place on May 19, 1973. He and Sujata climb to the Mother's room, and they find her hunched over in her chair, turned in the direction of Sri Aurobindo's tomb, a beam of light illuminating her neck. Sujata hands the Mother a hibiscus flower with a red heart. The Mother has named this flower Power. She holds the flower and says that power is really necessary right now.

She inhales uneasily, and their conversation is punctuated by moments when she seems to withdraw into herself. She holds Satprem's hands and tells him that she no longer wants to eat, but that her doctors and attendants are insistent. This infuriates Satprem, who is convinced that the Mother's lack of appetite is a sign of progress, that the body and its physical needs are releasing their hold. He quotes to her from *Savitri*: "Almighty powers are shut in Nature's cells."

The Mother says that her condition is declining, and she asks Satprem if she shouldn't perhaps just slip out of her physical body. He strongly rejects the suggestion. Satprem insists that the work in the cells is advancing, and that the Mother is being led through the valley in order to reach the top of the mountain: only by approaching so close to death, he says, by almost touching it, will she be able to find a way to surmount mortality.

"Ah!" the Mother says. "That's it."

"It must be done now," Satprem says, and he adds again, forcefully, that she mustn't give up or lose hope. He will later write that he feels momentarily as if he's resisting the Mother—or, perhaps, he's just fighting the pull of death, the pernicious suggestion that he feels is so palpable in the air.

He's with her till shortly before 11:00 a.m. She closes her eyes, she moans, and then he leaves the room. The next day, the Mother suffers a decline in her condition. As followers wait outside her room, one of her attendants steps out with a grim look on his face and says, "I don't think Mother will ever see people again." Henceforth, access to her room will be restricted to two doctors and just four or five associates. Satprem is not included. He will never see the Mother again.

She stays under close medical supervision for the remaining months of her life. From outside, Satprem rages against the litany of medicines imposed upon her. He is particularly incensed when he learns that the doctors are giving the Mother Siquil, a sedative.

The doctors continue to insist that the Mother should eat. They say she needs twenty to twenty-five ounces of nourishment a day, and they give her vegetable soup, milk, almond paste, mushrooms, artichokes, and fruit juice.

Meal times are often a struggle. The Mother lies on her back in bed, her eyes closed, and the attendants have to force-feed her.

The most detailed account we have of the Mother's final days comes from Satprem's adversary Pranab, who continues to see her until the end. After her passing, he will give a talk in which he outlines her final weeks. The talk is remarkably matter-of-fact in its details of illnesses and ailments, its sheer physicality. Years later, these details will continue to cause discomfort among some of the Mother's followers. As one Aurovilian man will tell me, "I really don't think Pranab ever understood who the Mother was. I think he just thought she was some kind of ordinary guru or something—just another one."

Pranab's account details the Mother's hiccups, her bedsores, a paralysis in her legs, and the pills and syrups the doctors administered to her. "Every morning we gave Her [some medicine]. She took it without any objection that day," Pranab says, speaking of November 17, 1973. "Her breakfast She took very well, lunch also. . . . After Her lunch, I was with Her; I noticed that She was making some strange sounds, and sometimes lifting Her hands, but as She used to do this often in Her sleep, I did not pay much attention."

That night, the Mother's condition worsens. The sounds from her throat increase, and her head begins moving in an uncontrolled way. At 7:05 p.m., a doctor arrives; her heart is still beating, but slowly, with long intervals. The doctor compresses her chest, but his efforts are in vain. At 7:25 p.m., the Mother is declared dead. The official cause of death is heart failure. Witnesses report that the moment is peaceful, and that she leaves her body without great struggle. "She went out like a candle," says one person.

Mindful of the Mother's statement that she might be in a trance, her attendants leave the body undisturbed for three and a half hours. At 11:00 p.m., they clean her with eau de cologne and dress her in white satin. Key members of the Ashram are informed, but the public is kept in the dark. At 2:00 a.m., the Mother's body is carried downstairs and placed on a bed in a room near the Samadhi. She is covered with a gold-laced silk shawl. Flowers are strewn on the floor, incense is lit, and heavy fans are placed throughout the room, to alleviate the heat generated by a battery of neon lights.

Meanwhile, word spreads. Men and women are awakened from their sleep, and they head, bleary-eyed, toward the gates of the Ashram, which remain closed. Among the crowd: John Walker, recently returned from America, now walking with a group of seven or eight Aurovilians. They stand outside in the street, silent and stunned. At 4:15 a.m., the Ashram's gates are opened and a tide of devotees—"her children one and all," an observer notes—sweeps in. Many sob quietly; a few weep loudly.

Surrounded by that crowd, John notes a happy synchronicity. That very night, even as the Mother was fading, Aurovilians achieved a major milestone at the Matrimandir. Recent months have been devoted to finishing four ten-meter-high pillars to support the spherical structure. The triangular tops of the last two pillars were completed in an all-day concrete pour on November 17, leaving Aurovilians red-eyed, covered with cement powder, and ears buzzing from machinery. The final touches to the pillars were laid between 7:15 p.m. and 7:30 p.m., almost exactly the time the Mother left her body. "She knew her home was ready for her," John later tells a friend. "She timed it perfectly."

Satprem is not one of the insiders informed early of the Mother's death. He learns of it hours after the fact, through hearsay. At around 5:00 a.m., he enters the Ashram and sees her—she with whom he has spent countless hours, of whose deepest secrets he considers himself the guardian—as a member of the crowd, a common man. He's struck by the concentrated look on her face, and he's convinced that she's still very much waging war, working internally on the transformation.

He's horrified that her body has been brought down so early and subjected to this spectacle. The crowds, the flowers, all the incense: it's like some ancient religious ritual. And the neon lights, whose heat reflects off a zinc roof: they couldn't have picked a better way to decompose the flesh. But, really, why should he be surprised? The whole thing is playing out just as she feared. They didn't believe her, and they didn't heed her instructions. Satprem believes he's witnessing a huge mistake, an earth-shattering calamity. In the rush to declare the Mother dead, he sees an assertion of the old world—all its privilege, all its vanities—against the potential of a new evolutionary reality.

He sits by the Samadhi for ten minutes. An Ashram elder calls him into his chambers and asks for assistance in translating an announcement to explain the Mother's death into French. The elder shows Satprem a draft of his note, which begins, "The Mother's body belonged to the old creation." Satprem considers this a falsehood. He refuses to help, and he returns outside, where he sits once more amid the jasmine and incense.

He stays at the Samadhi all day, suffering a terrible headache, a feeling that his head will burst. In the evening, he gets up and leaves the Ashram, wanders toward the ocean. As he walks, his body starts shaking, the crushing disappointment all at once eases, and Satprem experiences a great wave of joy. He hears bells over the universe, and he has a soaring realization: nothing is actually interrupted, no force can block the Mother's project of transformation.

He believes he hears the Mother's voice, and it tells him that if he doesn't want the transformation to be a failure, then it is up to him: he must continue the fight against death. Now everything becomes clear. Henceforth, Satprem's mission—his crusade—must be directed against the all-pervasive odor of mortality that has hung over humankind since the beginning of time. For the rest of Satprem's life, until his own dying day, he will insist: the Mother never really died, death itself is an illusion, and the Mother's yoga is a weapon to pierce the illusion.

For two days, the crowds gather. They spill in from across the country and the world, line up outside the Ashram, while policemen in shorts and red kepis keep order. People sit for hours on the floor by the Samadhi. Indian women in chaste white saris juxtaposed alongside Western women in tight, revealing outfits. Farmers and fishermen in soiled lungis and turbans side by side with merchants and traders who have traveled from Bombay, Calcutta, and beyond. The Mother's world is capacious.

They are bereft, but there is a certain comfort, or at least a sense of validation, in the widespread recognition the Mother's passing receives. Pink telegrams pour in to Pondicherry. The president of India issues official condolences. The prime minister, Indira Gandhi, who has met the Mother three times, extols her as "a dynamic, radiant personality with tremendous force of character and extraordinary spiritual attainments." A public holiday is declared, and obituaries are carried in, among other publications, the *New York Times*, *Le Monde*, *Newsweek*, and all the leading Indian papers.

At 8:00 a.m. on November 20, three days after the Mother's death, she is lifted from her bed and placed in a rosewood coffin lined with layers of felt and white silk. Her hands are clasped together and rested on her folded knees. Six men in white shorts fix twenty-five screws into the coffin, and it is lowered with ropes and positioned above Sri Aurobindo in the gray-white marble of the Samadhi, which has been chipped open. Two Ashramites scatter rose petals over the coffin, another group lays a sheet of black Formica, and then four slabs of concrete are placed.

Satprem watches all of this. As the Mother is carried to her tomb, he notices that she still has that look of fierce concentration on her face. "A Lie. An enormous Lie," he rails. "That death was a dreadful lie."

Udar Pinto, a Goan member of the Ashram who had been close to the Mother, visits Auroville a couple of weeks after her passing. He is known to many Aurovilians as the master of ceremonies at the community's inauguration, and some people have asked him to help them understand recent events.

He meets with a group in a thatch-roofed meditation space near the Matrimandir. Like everyone else, he grasps for explanations. He talks about different forms of evolution, and varied passages to the supramental being. He suggests that the Mother's transformation was cut short due to the pettiness that surrounded her. "Our filth and dirt we threw upon Her, and as our Mother, She took everything upon Herself from Her children, blind and stupid though we were," he says. He encourages the crowd to aim at greater harmony, and to a stronger sense of purpose in building Auroville.

Someone asks Pinto if, in view of the Mother's passing, the project of physical transformation has been curtailed. Should we give up on our personal yoga? Pinto rejects the suggestion. "There is no reason why someone should not now succeed in transforming a human body to a Superhuman one," he says. "The Mother has opened a pathway for us to follow, by Her great work. The Divine may take someone to His end."

Is Diane in that crowd? Is John? I can't place them with certainty. But I know that this is the message that goes out across Auroville: nothing is over, the transformation can still happen, and it is up to each individual now to continue the yoga in his or her own body.

Satprem moves with Sujata to an estate in the countryside. Nandanam is a ten-hectare garden leased by the Ashram, located between Pondicherry and Auroville. It's a serene orchard, with bouncing white rabbits, peacocks, and doves that peck at an expansive lawn. There are mango and tamarind trees, large rosebushes, and plantations of pineapples, papaya, and banana. A canyon runs behind the estate, and at the end of the day Satprem walks alongside it. "Mother, do you hear me?" he cries into the canyon. "I am here. Do you hear me?"

Using his pension, he builds a house, with a room downstairs for Sujata and one upstairs for him, surrounded by an open-to-air terrace. He paces this terrace and, through his grief, holds on to the insight he was given as he left the Ashram and walked to the ocean: the Mother's work must continue, and his part is instrumental. He feels a tremendous sense of responsibility, and he decides that he will start by opening the world's eyes to the Mother's project of transformation. Satprem plans to write a book about her life and yoga, based on their conversations. Sitting cross-legged on the floor of his room over a desk, he plunges into the project, a torrent of writing that will last eight months and turn into a nearly fourteen-hundred-page trilogy.

But even as Satprem writes this trilogy, a bigger project grows in his mind. He wants to publish the full, unexpurgated transcripts of his conversations with the Mother. He's convinced that the world must see them in their entirety, and that their publication is part of righting the falsehood of her death. This project will culminate years later in a thirteen-volume set known as the *Mother's Agenda*, or simply the *Agenda*. Satprem compares publishing the *Agenda* to building a temple: it is a sacred mission, one that will open a channel to the divine and help bring about an evolutionary leap forward.

In December of 1973, Satprem watches as a large flock of black birds emerges in the sky over Nandanam. They rush toward a tree in the garden, swarm all over it, and voraciously eat its fruit. Satprem thinks the tree represents the *Agenda*. But what of the birds—what is symbolized by the black creatures that rush so menacingly at the fruit?

The following day, he asks Sujata to inform the Ashram of his plans to publish his conversations with the Mother. He has over three hundred hours of recordings, stored on tape spools, and thousands of pages of notes and transcripts. The Ashram is distinctly unenthused. Its elders, who now manage the institution, would rather publish an edited version. Satprem counters that no one has the authority or spiritual knowledge to edit what the Mother said. But the elders resist, arguing that Satprem has no legal rights over the contents of those conversations. Satprem recoils against what he takes to be an instinctive conservatism, a reactionary resistance that threatens the new order.

It is the beginning of a protracted battle. Many will be caught in this battle directly—and some, such as John and Diane, such as Auralice, will be swept up indirectly.

AUROLOUIS'S WELL

FREDERICK, THE FATHER OF AUROSON—of two Aurosons—
tells me about the day the Mother died. We're sitting outside his apartment in
2017, forty-four years later, on a balcony with views of the Matrimandir. The
Mother's Temple is now long completed, a massive sphere covered with 1,415
sparkling golden disks that rises like a sun from the flat earth. The building is a
cross between a town square and a holy temple, a social and spiritual glue that
binds this community together. It is surrounded by an oasis of green lawns and
gardens, and I can see families walking there now, and a few men and women
sitting under the Banyan Tree in meditation.

Frederick remembers the early morning of November 18, 1973. He and
Charlotte were sleeping on the terrace of Auroson's Home. Just before dawn,
someone shouted from below that the Mother was no more. No one ever said
the Mother was dead; people only said that she left her physical body. Frederick and Charlotte bathed hastily and drove their motorcycle into Pondicherry.
They stood in line outside the Ashram, tears in their eyes, then filed past her
body and sat in meditation at the Samadhi. They were both numb, and now
Frederick compares the experience to the death of his first son.

When Auroson died, he says, he had the Mother to console him. But when she was gone, he was alone. "She never prepared us for the possibility that she would leave her body," he says. "I was totally blown away. Actually, I'm still in shock. I didn't believe it then, and a part of me still doesn't believe she's gone."

I ask Frederick how he recovered—how he summoned the conviction to pick himself up and continue building Auroville. This is something I've always wondered about the adults of my world. They were utterly devoted to the Mother, and many of them were convinced that the transformation was imminent. How was it that her passing didn't puncture the dream? I ask Frederick how he held on to his faith.

"There you go again," he says, and he smiles indulgently. This isn't the first time we've had some version of this conversation. I've known Frederick since I was a boy, and I feel as if we've been dancing around the topic of faith for decades. "As usual, you're trying to grasp these things with your mind, Akash," he says. "But you can't. Faith doesn't work like that. Faith is an adventure into the unknown; it's either there, or it's not."

Still, I say, bear with me. Walk me through this experience. You and the mother of your child move to Auroville full of anticipation. Your vision of the future is radiant. Then your son—the first son of Auroville—dies; and then the Mother is gone. These certainly weren't part of the radiant vision. Help me understand how you keep going. How does all of this *not* break you?

"I don't know whether you've ever had extreme physical pain?" Frederick asks me. "You wonder, 'How can people bear pain like this?'" He talks about mountain climbers who get stuck under boulders, who must amputate their arms so they can free themselves. The body has a way of anesthetizing itself. You keep going by not stopping; faith has its own momentum.

"Eventually, you open up and you find within yourself a large hole," he says. "You have no idea what to do with this hole. It's so painful you can't come close; it's as though the nerve endings are exposed. And then slowly, slowly, I find I can touch the rim of this wound. The nerves are still exposed and it's still painful, but at least I can touch it. Honestly, I think that hole never completely filled. But it doesn't feel like a thing that stops me any longer. It's a benign absence, a vacuum. The loss isn't as painful anymore but it's still unknowable—and, yes, unknowable things often express themselves in scary ways."

Frederick stops talking and he has a distant expression on his face. I feel as if he's touching the wound now, testing it even as we speak. "Sometimes it seems to me that there's a divine in this universe gauging how much we can bear," he says. "I remember the first Auroson in all his luminosity. I'm taking him in a pram to the Ashram, and the sun is rising and its rays are in his fluffy blond hair—he was otherworldly. I'm thinking of him as the next stage of evolution, and the question I ask myself is this: How much light can be manifested amid the darkness? How much light is supportable on this planet? When Auroson dies, it's as if there's an overdose of light."

Frederick looks at me and returns to my original question: How did you—how did Auroville—keep going? "Of course there's always an invasion of despair or doubt," he says. "That happens all the time. It's part of the power of aspiration that it moves through this area of darkness."

A man once told me a story about how he came to Auroville. I was sixteen years old. His name was Patrick, and he was from Australia. Patrick had heard that I was applying to boarding schools in America, and he wanted to know why I was leaving Auroville. I told Patrick that I felt I needed some experience in the real world. I said I loved Auroville, but I worried that without an education and some recognized credentials, I would be defenseless.

Patrick scoffed. He told me about an exam he had taken many years ago, as a young man in his country. He said he was sitting in a room full of students; it was an important exam, and everyone was quiet and concentrated. Suddenly, he had a revelation. He realized that this whole situation—this game of academic degrees, elite networks, and careers—was a charade ("bullshit," he called it). He slammed his hand against the desk and walked out of the room. He abandoned his education and moved to Auroville. He said he never had any regrets; that decision saved his life.

"You know what your problem is, Akash?" Patrick asked me when I explained why I was going to America. "Your problem is that you're too mental. You don't have faith; you don't know how to let go."

I spent much of my childhood hearing stories like these—about the importance of moving beyond the intellect and the mind, about devotion's power to surmount human limitations. My friends and I were told about the new world and the transformation, about how we were models for a more perfect version of humanity. We didn't necessarily believe all these stories (and not *everyone* told them to us). But we didn't question too much either. It was all part of the matrix we inhabited, a world we knew was filled with unusual ideas and people, but that we also felt was very pure and honest. We had the implicit faith of children. We loved Auroville precisely for its unusualness—because our parents and teachers were trying to build something different.

I grew up, and in my teenage years my mind took a more analytical bent; I started questioning. Thomas Merton writes that "reason is in fact the path to faith, and faith takes over when reason can say no more." We all live somewhere on that continuum—that stretch of road between doubt and certitude, questioning and belief, resistance and surrender. Patrick, and Frederick, were right. I lived as a boy and still live now closer to the side of reason. My mind is filled with reservations and misgivings. I look for proof, and I go instinctively to the weak link or logical fallacy in a statement.

The truth is, I've always mistrusted faith a little. Maybe it's because I've grown up around its surfeit. And also, I've seen what faith can do.

Faith is like an open wound that has gradually lost its sting, Frederick says. Another man tells me that faith is an elastic band: it stretches to encompass the situation. A friend in Auroville, someone I grew up with who doesn't seem afflicted by the same problems of doubt as I have, compares his faith to a red-hot burning stove. "Either you touch it and you're zapped," he says, "or you're too scared to touch it and you'll never know the sensation."

The Mother is gone, but Auroville must continue. At the Matrimandir, work goes on, now with the help of hired labor, who have been employed, after much debate, due to frustration over the slow pace of progress. There are divisions and divergences, disputes over architecture and accounts. Aurovilians argue about the dimensions of the building, and they bicker over competing designs for the gardens and the amphitheater. But no one doubts that this "divine mystic ship" (as one man calls it) must manifest, and that its completion is vital to Auroville's spiritual purpose.

A series of four vertical concrete ribs start coming up on the structure. A thicket of scaffolding, some six miles of metal pipe, is laid from the bottom of the foundation pit to support a slab that will underlie the Inner Chamber, or meditation hall. This building is bold and structurally daring; an engineering firm forecasts that it will cost some $2.6 million, which seems utterly beyond the means of Auroville's struggling economy. But Aurovilians do what they do best: maintain their belief and persist. The community sets itself a goal of completing the Matrimandir by 1978, which would mark the centenary of the Mother's birth.

The forests of Auroville keep growing, too. Trees don't stop for death, and neither does wildlife. The once uninhabited—uninhabitable—plateau sees a growing amount of fauna. Jackals now prowl the canyons, and sometimes a shy fox. New species of birds are sighted and heard: red-vented bulbuls, purple sunbirds, and flocks of grey partridge that scurry noisily across the flat topography. There are reports of rabbits, porcupines, monkeys, even the occasional deer. As Auroville grows greener, so it grows more alive.

New people keep trickling in, too, applying for membership to the CFY, which conducts interviews with applicants and functions as a gatekeeper from its offices in Pondicherry. These people won't ever meet the Mother, but they read her and Sri Aurobindo's words, and they see their photos everywhere. The founders' framed portraits have grown ubiquitous, now adorning dining halls, libraries, shops, and many homes. People stand in front of the portraits and fold their hands in veneration, sometimes prostrating themselves. Shortly before the Mother's death, *Newsweek* ran an article titled "The Next Great Religion?" Many people frown on the increasing displays of religiosity, which the founders

always cautioned against. But religion, like faith, also has a momentum. Once the deification begins, it's hard to stop.

At midnight on January 1, 1974, Aurovilians gather in the amphitheater, in front of a mound of sticks and logs. A bonfire is lit, and the orange-and-yellow flame rises into the sky, illuminating the emerging Matrimandir while the assembled men and women concentrate in collective meditation. This bonfire meditation marks the start of a new ritual; the community will gather here and reaffirm its commitment throughout the decades.

"There is an awakening among the residents of Auroville to the necessity of making Auroville a 'self-supporting' community," proclaims an internal bulletin from this period. "Obviously, this will not be an easy task and will require a determined effort over a considerable period of time. We will also have to remember that the basis of this endeavour must always be an inner progress and transformation."

Life must go on in Kottakarai, too, where the community spreads into the surrounding fields. More houses come up, and the bakery expands, sending its bread and muffins—and now also cookies and jams, tofu, and peanut butter—across town. Sundaram works twelve-hour days; he and Larry are pretty much running the bakery. John still works there, too, although his attendance is more sporadic; once again, he's lost focus. Sometimes Diane comes over to see Larry or check on Auralice or Aurolouis. The kids play on the ground, often by the ovens, and this upsets Diane, who thinks Larry is insufficiently attentive. Larry and Diane get into screaming matches that embarrass the others.

Like everyone, Diane struggles to reconcile herself to life without the Mother. She complains of feeling heavy and lethargic, of an uneasiness she's never before known in Auroville. Of course she's convinced that the Mother's project must continue, and she wishes very much to be part of the transformation. What she really wants is to be at the Matrimandir, participating in the construction of the Mother's Temple. But she's weighed down by two young children, stuck all day in the community, and this adds to her feelings of heaviness, and also mounting resentment toward Larry.

She keeps herself busy with classical Indian flute lessons, and by planting a vegetable garden outside their hut. Watching her children interact provides her with a measure of solace. Auralice doesn't speak much, and Aurolouis is her medium; he translates his sister's wishes and thoughts for adults. "My sister wants a glass of milk," he says, or "My sister doesn't want to go outside right now." Diane tells someone that watching Auralice and Aurolouis together is "like a fairy tale."

Eventually, Larry moves out of the hut he built for them. He and Diane have bickered almost from the day they got together, and it's only gotten worse since Auralice's birth. Now there's another shift in Diane's romantic life. She starts spending more time with John. They talk at the bakery or in the community kitchen, or sit together in the fields as they explore a shared affinity for *Savitri*. They've both memorized long passages, and they stare into each other's eyes and engage in recitation contests, seeing who can go on longer; Diane inevitably wins. She steals across the community at night, visiting John in his capsule and often spending the night there. She leaves her kids alone at home. That's how it is all over Auroville: there's little crime, and everyone knows that the Mother is watching over things. Children roam freely, with minimal adult supervision.

There are some precarious moments. One night Diane goes to Pondicherry, and Auralice and Aurolouis are sleeping alone in the hut, under the ostensible watch of a neighbor. Auralice has a bad case of conjunctivitis; her eyes are painfully crusted, and she tosses and turns in her sleep. A kerosene lamp is suspended from the roof, hanging by a strand of coconut rope. Suddenly the flame from the lamp starts climbing the rope, rising toward the thatch ceiling. Fortunately, the rope snaps before the fires reach the thatch, but then the lamp crashes to the ground, the kerosene spills, and the floor is engulfed in a blue flame. The neighbor who has been watching the kids rushes in and extricates them, then goes back in and tosses the cracked lamp through the window, putting out the fire. While Auralice sits outside, rubbing her eyes, John comes over and asks the neighbor, "Is there some kind of strange native custom around here that involves tossing flames out of windows?" He is oblivious to the tragedy that almost took place; the neighbor never mentions it to Diane.

Another time Aurolouis is in a palmyra grove, talking to plants. This is one of his favorite games. He leans over flowers and bushes and says, "Hello, my name is Aurolouis." He speaks deliberately, enunciating "Au-ro-Lou-is," as if articulating the syllables for someone who is hard of hearing. He sees a snake on the ground and he picks it up. Maybe he does this because he's recently been around an adult who similarly toyed with a harmless green tree snake; Auralice heard about the snake and was sad she didn't get to see it, and now Aurolouis wants to show this one to his sister.

But this snake isn't harmless; it's a highly venomous viper, and it bites Aurolouis on the hand. No one notices until about half an hour later, when his arm swells up and he starts having trouble breathing. He tells people what happened, and they load him onto a motorcycle and race him to JIPMER, a man holding the boy in the back and slapping his face to keep him conscious. It's touch-and-go at the hospital, but the doctors administer antivenom in time.

Aurolouis returns to Kottakarai, to a big hug from Diane, and relief all around. They're thankful that he's all right, and comforted, too, that the Mother's protection remains strong. There can be no doubt, especially in Diane's mind, that the Mother saved this child.

As Kottakarai grows, so do its farms. The area occupied by the community expands from an original half acre to around sixty acres, and a team of some dozen people—Aurovilians and village laborers—now work in the fields. What began as a small exercise in self-sufficiency for a handful of residents has developed into one of the largest farms in Auroville. Every day, the agriculturalists of Kottakarai fill bullock carts with rice, millet, eggplant, tomatoes, and chilies, and send these loads to other communities. As Auroville's economy stutters, such endeavors play an increasingly vital role in feeding its residents.

Gradually, water becomes a problem. Kottakarai's single well is no longer sufficient to irrigate its growing farms, and the community's residents decide to dig another well, closer to the crops. John takes the lead on this effort, displaying his customary vigor at the inception of a project. He bankrolls the well, and he also designs it. He conceives of an open square hole in the ground, twenty-three feet long on each side. He adds a series of steps leading into the pit, and a small sandy deck, like a beach, at the bottom.

He hires eighteen workers from the village. They're managed by a supervisor nicknamed Houndi, or donation box, for the large lump that protrudes from his stomach. Houndi and his team gather every morning and dig with crowbars and shovels, and they carry the earth away in woven cane baskets. There are hiccups along the way. Some days the workers don't show up, and sometimes money gets stolen or equipment goes missing. Once, John loses a leather wallet containing fifty thousand rupees (more than $6,000) intended for salaries. Sundaram finds the wallet on the ground in a palmyra grove and takes it to John, who is pacing anxiously near the well. John counts the money and he's ecstatic. He hugs Sundaram and chants, "Sri Ram, Sri Ram," invoking a Hindu god over and over.

Around six months into the project, John's energy flags, and the workers are sent home. The partially completed well sits there, a twelve-foot pit with six feet of water at the bottom. Still, the project hasn't been entirely in vain. People from the village come by to fill their jars and buckets, and Kottakarai's farmers manage to extract a little water with a swape, a long pole with a bucket at one end and a counterweight at the other. And the well finds another use, too: on hot days, the kids of Kottakarai and their friends from other communities use it as a swimming pool. They jump in and splash around, and they hang around the sandy deck that extends above the water.

On the afternoon of June 15, 1974, Diane visits a couple of friends in the community. She's accompanied by four-year-old Aurolouis and Auralice, who is almost two, as well as a few other kids. Diane is cheerful and chirpy, dressed in a knee-length floral dress, looking characteristically radiant and very hippie. She and her friends sit together and drink coffee out of pottery mugs, and they talk and talk and talk, and the kids get bored and want to go swimming. Diane keeps Auralice with her, but she sends the others ahead, saying she'll join them shortly.

Ajit, one of the friends Diane is visiting, has to go on a milk run for the community. He walks down to the well, checks on the kids, and sees that they're happy in the water—all except for Aurolouis, who is sitting on the deck looking forlorn. Aurolouis has never been enthusiastic about the well; he doesn't know how to swim. Ajit goes back to his house and tells Diane that Aurolouis looks lonely, and he suggests she go down to keep him company. "Ya, ya," she says in her Flemish accent. "We'll go down in five minutes." She and her friend, Ajit's companion, are still deep in conversation, punctuated by Diane's giggles.

Ajit gets on his bicycle and rides around the community, with an aluminum pail tied to his back carrier. He finishes distributing the milk at around four in the afternoon, and he stops by the village tea shop for a smoke. As he heads back to the community, he sees a group of adults hovering near the well, their movements frenzied. He gets closer and hears screaming, and his heart sinks.

Aurolouis waited for the other kids to leave, then got into the well. Now his body is on the ground, and everyone's around it, shrieking and yelling. Diane is howling, and Auralice is on the ground, in the mud, crying. A man runs over and tries mouth-to-mouth resuscitation; he's a former member of the Dutch navy and he pumps Aurolouis's chest, as he's been trained to do. He pumps and pumps but Aurolouis doesn't move. How could this have happened? Another Aurovilian child, another exemplar of the new species—once again, drowned.

He is buried the next day in a morning ceremony held behind the family's house. His body is placed in a small wood coffin, and a red rosebush is planted above the pit. People gather from all over the plateau. There are tears and, as always, much conjecture about messages and meaning. One woman reports having seen Aurolouis's coffin as it was being built before the funeral. As she watched, she had a feeling that the special souls who had been placed in Auroville for a special purpose seemed disappointed. For her, these drownings are a symptom, indications of a collective failure.

"What kind of sign is this, what kind of warning?" asks one Aurovilian man in his diary, shortly after the drowning. "Are we even ready to build Auroville? What are we doing to force you, poor little man, poor Louis, to take such a huge step? Louis, come back in a new body!"

Word gets around that Aurolouis was seen speaking to the second Auroson recently. Maybe, people speculate, Auroson told him something about coming back in a better body. Auroson's mother, Charlotte, is in the crowd at the funeral, and she's dismayed at what she takes to be the community's lingering "unconsciousness." She feels a force—a "tremendous grace, like rain"—descending on the assembled mourners, and she laments that they're unable to absorb it. "What a sorry state we remain in," she reflects.

"Aurolouis, my little lion," Diane moans. She's devastated. But she displays, at this impossible moment, a fortitude and iron will, a capacity to quickly right herself that she will evidence again and again. Even by the standards of Auroville, Diane's faith is resolute. Soon she starts telling people that she's convinced Aurolouis died for a reason. It was the Mother's will, she knows it, and to question the drowning would be to question the Mother. Diane refuses to go down that path; she won't allow anyone in her presence to ask why.

There are layers of psychology here, shades of cognitive complexity. "You know some people ask me if I feel guilty that he died," Diane says one day to a man. "But if I felt guilty, then it would mean I was doubting the Mother. No, that would be impossible."

If Diane has one regret (at least one that she articulates), it's that the Mother is gone, which means she can't reincarnate Aurolouis, as she did for Auroson. Seeking another way, Diane comes up with a plan. She will go down to Rameswaram and find Guido, Aurolouis's father, who is still living with Guruji. Diane knows that the Mother has praised Guruji's powers; she wants to make another baby with Guido, and she intends to ask Guruji if he can insert Aurolouis's soul into the new child.

She takes an overnight train with a friend. They go by third-class, non-air-conditioned carriage, crowded with pilgrims and farmers, through the flat land of Tamil Nadu, and then onto a shaky bridge above aquamarine waters. Rameswaram is on an island in the Gulf of Mannar, near the southern tip of India. They alight from the train and climb into a horse cart that carries them through the quiet town: the single market street lined with a couple of provisions stores and a gold seller, and the soaring temple, one of the holiest in India. Soon they are outside town, in an undulating topography of low yellow dunes, and then arrive at a tile-roofed house. This is Guruji's home, where he lives with his wife and children; it has been built with financial assistance from the Mother.

Guruji is a round man with a shaved head, and big horn-rimmed glasses. He comes from a long line of holy men, and he's always dressed in the fashion of a high priest: shirtless, a white dhoti, beads around his neck and arms, a string pulled diagonally across his torso. He receives Diane and her friend on his veranda. He sits on a wooden bench, and they sit on the red cement floor. He seems to know already about the drowning.

It isn't clear what Guruji tells Diane—what assurances (or otherwise) he gives her about the possibility of reincarnating Aurolouis. What is clear is that Guido will have nothing to do with the plan. He's taken a vow of celibacy; and besides, he's furious with Diane, enraged with what he considers Auroville's irresponsibility. His son is dead, and he blames the adults who should have been watching over him. Diane and her friend spend the night in a guesthouse in town, then they take the train back to Auroville the next morning, where Diane must pick up the pieces without Aurolouis.

A young girl sees John around Kottakarai shortly after the drowning. He's gardening, and the girl, who was a friend of Aurolouis's, asks why the boy died. "The Mother said that everyone is born with a fixed amount of karma," John answers. "Aurolouis died because he used up his karma."

John writes to his family about the drowning. He tells them about how Aurolouis was seen speaking to Auroson, and he says there's no doubt that Aurolouis will soon return in another body. John remembers the night before Aurolouis died. Diane was putting the boy to sleep, and Aurolouis begged his mother to pull the white bedsheet all the way up to his chin; he looked like a mummy. Perhaps, John speculates, the boy had some kind of premonition. John remembers, also, a hug that Aurolouis gave him about a week before he died. It was deep and joyful, seemingly out of nowhere, and John has read that shortly before Sri Aurobindo left his body, he gave a similarly spontaneous hug to one of his disciples. John thinks Aurolouis was saying goodbye; the child knew he was going to die, and maybe he chose to die.

Not everyone subscribes to such narratives. My mother is sitting with Diane and some friends around this time in Diane's hut. They're having a cup of coffee or tea, and people are talking about Aurolouis's soul, how he chose to go and will return at an appropriate time. My mother has been away from America for around five years. She's excited by Auroville and the new world it's trying to manifest, an eager participant in this brave journey. But there are various pathways within the journey, and not all Aurovilians subscribe to the same version of reality. My mother doubts some of these theories about Aurolouis, although she tries to be respectful and doesn't say anything.

Racing around on the cement floor of the hut, as the adults talk about death and reincarnation, are two shirtless young kids on wooden scooters. The scooters are a gift from John, and the kids are Auralice and Akash—dipping in and out of corners, squealing with delight as they narrowly avoid furniture and other obstacles, forming an early friendship whose inception they will not remember, but that will last a lifetime.

"How we wish you were here with us," John's father writes to him, in a card sent along with a check. "If you want to give me a longed-for present, please write me a description of a typical day. What does it consist of? Shopping, cooking, swimming, meditation (how long?). Do you have a garden? I desperately want to feel some empathy with you, but I need more data. Please let me have it. Please continue to write often and send us photographs, anything that will help us feel close to you."

John's family reads his letters from Auroville, and their reaction is similar to my mother's. What kinds of stories is John telling us? What strange beliefs has he adopted? Gillian is horrified; her parents are more confused. They simply don't know what to make of the life John has chosen, and Walker Sr. in particular struggles with the distance that separates him from this son with whom he otherwise shares so much: a first-rate intellect, a Harvard education, a love of Renaissance art and classical literature.

Gillian is sitting with her father on the beach at Fishers Island. It's late summer, midday, and the sun is fitful, in and out of clouds. They're alone; everyone else is walking, or swimming in the gray Atlantic. Walker Sr. is in pants and a shirt, with elastic suspenders. He's wearing a canary-yellow jacket and a white straw panama hat. He's always formal; his children know little about his interior life. But now he starts talking about his faith, and about his conversion to Catholicism as a young man in Italy.

He was raised a Presbyterian, although he never had much belief. He has come to Catholicism circuitously, as part of his passion for art; he believes that art and religion are timeless, the only possible defenses against the tragedy of what he calls "human transience." Sitting on that beach, he indicates to Gillian that his relationship with religion remains uneasy. Speaking about a Benedictine monk with whom the family is close, Walker Sr. says, "You know, Father Hilary always said faith comes easily to your mother, like daffodils in spring. It's so much harder for me. I have such terrible periods."

He stands up and limps off the beach on his polio-afflicted leg, supporting himself with a cane. Gillian has a sense at this moment of a vacancy in her father; she knows that he's a searcher, and that he still hasn't found what he's looking for. This father and son are more alike than they may seem.

To honor Aurolouis's memory, John decides to complete the well. The diggers are reengaged, and a team of four Aurovilians and some twenty village laborers are assembled. They begin every morning at seven, when John carries them hot tea and ragi (millet) porridge from the community kitchen. They climb into the well and dig with crowbars, and they load the wet earth in metal pans and hand them along a human chain, to be dumped outside. They work in this way until water starts spurting from the walls of the well, and then they fill bullock carts with hundreds of cubic feet of lime, which they dig from the ground outside a nearby Kali temple. They mix the lime with stones and cement to create a waterproof layer that covers the walls. The water turns green from the lime.

They inaugurate the well one evening, under a golden light. A small group of Aurovilians assembles, and they burn incense and play spiritual music on a cassette player. Everyone who can swim jumps in, and after some time, a young girl who doesn't know how to swim, who has been afraid of water until now, also gets in. Miraculously, she stays afloat. "I can swim! I can swim!" she calls out to her mother. John, smiling, tells them that this is a gift from Aurolouis. She will not drown; she cannot drown. An Englishman dives into the green water, and when he surfaces, he says, "Thank you, Aurolouis. Thank you."

PART II

It is more pleasant and useful to go through
the experience of the revolution than
to write about it.

—Lenin

There is a tyranny in the womb
of every utopia.

—Bertrand de Jouvenel

A FAMILY AFFAIR

"THERE ARE DESERTS THAT HAVE to be crossed in this yoga and I seem to be in the midst of one," John writes to his parents. "But the monsoon is on its way physically, and perhaps spiritually as well. It is a matter of perseverance or merely stubbornness and then after a time the skies open and the path becomes clear. I have faith and hope still intact, and the belief that the pursuit is worthwhile."

Something breaks in John after Aurolouis dies. The Mother is gone, her children are drowning: Was it all an illusion? Diane tries to prop him up. Faith is often contagious, but the well was John's project, he financed and designed it, and he's filled with guilt. He's afflicted by doubts, and questions about what he's doing in Auroville. He suffers a familiar loss of purpose.

In early 1975, John books a one-way ticket to New York. He doesn't say much to anyone about why he's leaving, and he doesn't talk about returning. He just packs a cloth duffel bag, takes a taxi on the bumpy four-hour drive to the airport in Madras, and from there flies to Bombay, where he passes through immigration and leaves the country.

He makes a stopover in London. His father has recently retired from the National Gallery, and his parents now spend most of the year in England.

They divide their time between a country home in the village of Amberley, West Sussex, and a book-lined flat, sublet from their friend the philosopher Isaiah Berlin, in the Albany, an apartment building near Piccadilly Circus. They continue to spend time in the United States, on Fishers Island and in a rented home in Hobe Sound, Florida.

He spends nearly a week with his parents, in their stone cottage in Amberley. They walk the Downs together, and John plays croquet with his father in the back garden. In the evenings, they sit by a fireplace in the drawing room, and the three of them sip olive martinis under crystal chandeliers, the walls adorned with paintings Walker Sr. has acquired over his career. Mrs. Locke, the house-keeper, cooks dinner: shepherd's pie, steak and kidney pie, or perhaps Yorkshire pudding, which they take in a dining room at a table with Hepplewhite chairs. It's quite a change of scenery.

More change awaits in New York, where John stays again in the Dakota, this time in a ninth-floor studio Gillian and Albert have added to their ground-floor apartment. John has a key and comes and goes as he pleases, and before long he's looking up old acquaintances and exploring former haunts. He wanders the downtown arts scene and shops for meats at an Italian market on Columbus Avenue. He frequents expensive restaurants on the East Side, where he treats friends to meals of escargots and champagne. He's slipping into an old skin.

People notice something different about John on this trip. There's less fervor, and none of that proselytizing about Auroville to which he subjected Robert and Deborah Lawlor on his last visit to New York. He displays a new ambivalence about his life in India. Weeks pass, months, and he's still in the city. He starts talking about applying to a religious studies program at Princeton, maybe working toward a PhD. His family holds their breaths. Is this India whimsy finally over? Will we get him back?

He likes to wander Central Park at night. He goes alone and stays out late. Gillian wonders what he does, but she doesn't ask. One time he comes back carrying two wooden sailboats. They're toys, or models, and they're painted red, and he tells Gillian he bought them from a man he met near the Pond, an expanse of water at the southern end of the park. He asked the man how much he wanted for the boats, and the man said, "As much as a woman costs." John tells Gillian he paid the man enough to buy a woman.

He places the boats in a window in Gillian's apartment, overlooking the park. Later, Albert will share a dream he has about them, and he and John come to believe that the boats are a symbol and carry a message. Everyone faces a choice in life—stay put where you are, or chart your own course.

He's reserved, like his father, he's secretive and deeply private. He's always been like that, and the people around him know not to pry. Prying makes John run away. His family is aware that he's having doubts about Auroville, and they feel it has something to do with the death of Aurolouis, and perhaps others. They don't know much more, and they don't ask; they're trying to keep John around.

But there is, in fact, more—other reasons John is considering staying in America. At the Spring Street Bar, in SoHo, he confides to friends that the Mother's Ideal City is turning out harder to achieve than he had imagined.

Human nature is so damn persistent. He alludes to arguments and disagreements, some kind of conflict back in Auroville. He lets drop that his Indian visa may be at risk; it's possible he would be denied reentry. Again, he doesn't give out too many details. But he leaves a definite impression that there's trouble in utopia.

The Mother has been gone for more than a year now and she's left a vacuum in her wake. For nearly half a century, she held her world together. Her authority was unquestioned, her leadership always provided answers and direction. No detail was too small, no decision too trifling. But now the Mother is entombed in the Samadhi, under layers of concrete and marble, and the long-submerged rivalries of those around her, already evident in the clashes between Satprem and Pranab, have started rising to the surface.

Some of the disagreements John has left behind are high-minded and ideological. Many are petty, products of the usual all-too-human ambitions and bruised egos. There are murmurings about money and who gets to handle it, jostling for power, and maneuvers to inherit the Mother's mantle. The sharpest divisions have emerged between the residents of Auroville and the administrators of the CFY, the body tasked by the Mother with running her project. Aurovilians have always chafed a little at this arrangement, and at the sense of remote control from offices in Pondicherry. Now, like an orphaned child coming into its own, the community starts challenging the CFY. Aurovilians raise questions about the way donations are collected and assets used, and they demand more input into how the project is governed. There is growing talk about the need for "independence" and a "revolution."

The residents of Auroville are confronting a quandary that has faced intentional communities throughout the ages. What happens when the founder dies? What structure, what kind of governance, can replace the charismatic authority that has initiated and held these places together? Such questions will multiply over time, building ultimately into a vicious and at times violent battle that pits neighbor against neighbor, friend against friend, and divides families. The 1970s, Auroville's first full decade of existence, are a tumultuous, fraught time. The community is engulfed by its revolution, an insurrection that tears at the seams of the Mother's dream, revealing the dark and often extremist underbelly of utopia.

"You may not be interested in war, but war is interested in you," according to Leon Trotsky. No one will escape the flames of Auroville's revolution—not Diane, not John, not Auralice, nor the scores of combatants and innocent bystanders whose lives (and hopes for a more perfect world) will forever be singed by this disheartening period in the community's history.

The buildup to revolution is incremental, a gradual ratcheting up of tensions that begins shortly after the Mother's death and mounts steadily in the subsequent months. But if there's a precipitating event, a moment that could be said to ignite all-out conflict, it takes place one morning in December of 1975, a few months after John has already left India, in an airy room in a colonial house in Pondicherry. It's around 10:00 a.m., overcast outside, and the air is thick with monsoon humidity. Inside the house, an Aurovilian man named Amrit, a Japanese American from California, is sitting at a long wooden table. A fan turns slowly overhead, hanging from wooden rafters. Facing Amrit, on the other side of the table, are three Indian men and a woman, all dressed in white robes.

Amrit is thirty-two years old. His original name is Howard Shoji Iriyama, and he was born, in 1943, in the Gila Relocation Center in the desert of Arizona, a Second World War internment camp to which his parents were consigned. He spent his childhood behind barbed wire and gun towers and then, when the war was over, amid the poverty and discrimination suffered by the Japanese American community. After graduating from Stanford, he worked as a volunteer with the Student Nonviolent Coordinating Committee (SNCC) in Mississippi, registering black voters and facing down angry white mobs. These experiences imprinted in Amrit an acute distaste for prejudice and oppression. They led him to Auroville, to its promise of a better world, and they will prove central—albeit in an unpredictable manner—to his role in the unfolding battle.

139

The people facing Amrit are members of the CFY's Executive Committee, which manages the organization's day-to-day affairs. They are here to discuss Amrit's visa renewal. To live in India, every foreign Aurovilian must have his or her visa recommended to the government by the CFY. Until recently, that's been a formality; the Mother made the decision, and all it took was a willingness to commit to the project. But the Mother is gone now. What unfolds this morning in Pondicherry is akin to a tense legal hearing, or perhaps an inquisition.

"You know that in Auroville we must collaborate," one member of the Executive Committee says to Amrit. "Do you understand? Are you willing to collaborate?"

Amrit replies that his only allegiance is to the truth.

"But are you willing to collaborate?" the first member insists.

Amrit: "Much depends on the outcome of the situation in Auroville. I am willing to abide by what Aurovilians decide."

First member: "All you have to do is say, 'I will collaborate,' and you will have your visa."

Amrit reiterates that he is willing to do whatever Auroville decides. "I don't clearly understand what you are saying," the first member of the committee says. "Let us not beat around the bush. I don't want to speak nicely, then stab you in the back. I say clearly that if you are not willing to collaborate, we cannot extend the guarantee for your visa."

The conversation continues in this manner for some time, until the Executive Committee comes around to the real issue at hand. A few weeks earlier, Amrit was one of a group of individuals who signed a document establishing a new trust, the Auroville Society. This trust would allow the community to manage its own affairs and represents a de facto declaration of independence. The CFY, incensed, is determined to get Amrit to remove his signature, and in this way for the trust to be dissolved.

Another member of the committee now confronts Amrit: "If you support the new society, then we can have nothing to do with you. Do you support the new society?"

Amrit: "Yes, I support the new society."

"Then we can have nothing to do with you," the second member says.

There's a silence in the room. A crow caws outside; devotional music plays from the temple next door. The first member tells Amrit, "We can forget the past and start anew." Amrit feels a tightness in his body, but he's unwilling to submit. Later, he attributes this refusal to his experiences combating injustice as a young man, and to what he calls a "Japanese stubbornness." He feels the Executive Committee is trying to bully him, blackmail him into acting against his convictions.

First member: "Then it is clear."

Amrit: "You will return my application papers for the visa?"

First member: "The decision is to be finalized by the Executive Committee."

Amrit: "Then you will inform me of your decision?"

"Yes, of course," replies the first member, and the hearing is over.

Amrit rises to his feet. He nods at his interrogators, and they nod back. The mood is more awkward than tense; there's even a vague exchange of goodbyes. Still, as Amrit cycles back to Auroville—through the quiet streets of White Town, past the Ashram, up the Red Hill under a midday sun, the sea sparkling, green—he has a definite sense that some kind of Rubicon has just been crossed.

He returns to the community and tells people what happened. Word spreads quickly, facts transmogrified in the small-town rumor mill. Reactions vary: shock, outrage, sadness, more than a little fear. Aurovilians are reminded that their situation is tenuous; they are foreigners in India, a country that has only recently emerged from colonialism and that remains deeply suspicious of Westerners. They have dedicated their lives to this project, staked everything on it, but they receive no equivalent commitment in return. The future, until recently so promising, now seems more menacing.

The weeks and months following that December morning are marked by a series of ill-tempered encounters and clashes, acrimonious accusations on both sides of bad faith, venality, and disloyalty to the Mother's legacy. If the CFY's intent was to tamp down Auroville's budding mutiny, then its confrontation with Amrit, followed subsequently by threats to several more visas, has the opposite effect. The CFY's paternalistic attitude only stiffens the determination of Auroville's young rebels. Meanwhile, the CFY grows ever-more exasperated with what it considers the insolence of these dissolute hippies, who appear to be reliving their days on the barricades. There are some half-hearted attempts at reconciliation, efforts to foster a dialogue. Increasingly, though, the Mother's world feels sundered; a line is being drawn between Pondicherry and Auroville.

A number of parallel skirmishes emerge. In a Pondicherry court, the CFY files an injunction suit to dissolve the new trust and argues that it is the rightful proprietor of Auroville and all its assets. Aurovilians counter that the community's Charter—the *Mother's* Charter—clearly states that Auroville "belongs to nobody in particular" but instead "to humanity as a whole." The Charter, submits the CFY, is a spiritual document, not a legal one. Strictly speaking, it has a point. But this legalistic interpretation feels for many Aurovilians like a betrayal of the community's ideals, a repudiation of its effort to break through old forms of ownership and property. This is precisely why they're fighting.

Writing of conflict and dissension within Brook Farm, a nineteenth-century intentional community in Massachusetts, Ralph Waldo Emerson described "a French Revolution in small, an Age of Reason in a patty-pan." So it now feels in Auroville, where the evolving battle represents a curious amalgamation of the trivial and the epic, its stakes both trifling and monumental. The arguments, after all, are among a mere handful of people who occupy a tiny corner of South India (Auroville's population now numbers around three hundred). They have known one another for years, and they are like squabbling cousins.

But for those caught up in the battle, it feels like anything but a squabble. The very future of humanity—and of human society—seems to be in play. Where is the line between respect for authority, on the one hand, and the principles of self-determination and individual liberty on the other? Can the world's perennial divisions and corruptions be replaced by a new model that embodies unity and harmony? Aurovilians are convinced that they are fighting for freedom, equality, and the virtues of idealism. The CFY believes it is upholding order, hierarchy, property rights, and pragmatism. Both sides sincerely believe in the integrity of their position; these oppositions have played out across history.

Soon the legal and cosmological jousting starts having a tangible effect on the ground. The CFY cuts much of Auroville's funding, further squeezing the community's faltering economy. Prosperity, that regular allocation of food and other essentials, is all but terminated, as is a meager but essential five thousand rupees (about $600) that the CFY has been distributing every month for green work. Across the plateau, fields and farms grow fallow, and buildings sit incomplete, their protruding metal rods rusting in the coastal humidity.

Hunger and malnutrition stalk the community. Aurovilians are reduced to eating mostly what they can grow (and make), a diet that consists of millet, spinach, rice, bread, tofu, and the ubiquitous cluster beans—hearty but tough and chewy—that sprout up in seemingly every backyard. Under this pressure, the town's communal economy starts to buckle. One man will later recall walking into Pour Tous, Auroville's cash-free food distribution center. He sees an apple on the shelves and, as he has many times before, starts biting into it. Someone stops him and says he'll have to pay; there's no more money in the collective account. Years later, the man tries to convey the sense of dislocation and despair this episode gave rise to. "I could never imagine that I would have to pay for an apple in Auroville," he says. "The thought had just never entered my mind." At this moment, he tells me, he found himself reckoning with the full, terrible implications of the Mother's departure.

Inevitably, children suffer along with adults. I'm too young to experience these hardships directly, but Auralice, who is two years older, will remember the deprivation and hunger, a general sense of scarcity. Meals in Kottakarai's community kitchen are reduced to spartan portions; days are often spent in a series of amusing (to children, at least) games that involve foraging and hunting down sustenance. Auralice and her friends hang around the bakery and snatch hot loaves of bread as they're loaded into bullock carts. They steal money from adults and sneak away to the village tea shop, where they buy curd rice, a single serving for four or five children.

Perhaps fittingly, they find some of their most prized meals at the Matrimandir. Diane has started working part-time in the gardens surrounding the structure, fulfilling her long-cherished desire to be part of the Mother's Temple. She rides there nearly every morning on her white bicycle, and sometimes Auralice goes with her, sitting on the back carrier. Then, as Diane mixes compost or digs holes for saplings, Auralice gets together with friends and they clamber down into the Matrimandir's foundation pit, some thirty feet below, where they hunt for crabs. These small brown-shelled creatures dart nervously in and out of a muddy, sedimented pool.

Auralice and her friends catch the crabs and hit them with sticks, to knock them out, then throw them in an empty tin and carry them to a Tamil woman who works in the vicinity. She fries them on a wood fire with spices and salt. The children relish these meals of what they call "crab curry," one of their few sources of protein during these lean times. "We were like hunter-gatherers," a friend of Auralice's and mine will say years later. "We were always scavenging for our next meal." He says it cheerfully, nostalgically, and Auralice, who is sitting with us, joins in the laughter. We were just kids. What did we understand

about the mayhem, the disorder and disharmony, into which the adults of our world had so blithely plunged us?

There is disharmony in the world beyond Auroville, too, and this further contributes to the unease. Beginning in late 1973, India undergoes its most severe period of upheaval since independence. Protests against Indira Gandhi's Congress government spread across the country. Students shut down colleges, railway workers paralyze the nation's train network, and leaders of the opposition speak of "total revolution." In response, Gandhi takes a drastic step. On June 25, 1975, she declares a state of emergency. The government cuts electricity to newspaper offices and jails opposition leaders. This is uncharted territory; the very foundations of democratic India are being shaken.

Much of this drama plays out in the north, far from the relative quiet of Auroville. Aurovilians do feel ripples—one man complains that his copies of *Time* and *Newsweek* no longer arrive due to the media blackout—but the real impact is psychological. Gandhi and the Congress are generally seen as more friendly to foreigners (the prime minister's son Rajiv Gandhi is married to an Italian, Sonia Gandhi); the opposition is more nationalistic and is reputed to have ties with the leadership of the CFY. The prospect that Gandhi's position could be threatened comes at a bad time for the community.

The whole situation adds up to a general mood of drift and insecurity, a sense that things are coming unmoored. One Aurovilian who seems to acutely feel the peril of the moment is John. In a letter to his mother, mailed before his departure, he writes of "repressions" in the north, and of all the government's promises of aid to Auroville that have failed to materialize. "Not possible to go on like this," he writes more dramatically, in a staccato note to himself. "Eventually the shoals and capsizing. The last hope of humanity. We must get the motor started."

It's a difficult time, a frightening time. The members of the CFY are Indian, and largely wealthy; most Aurovilians are poor, and foreigners. For all their bravado, the community's revolutionaries are at an undeniable disadvantage. Desperate for help, for some form of patronage, Aurovilians turn to the Ashram. They send a note asking for guidance from a respected Ashram elder, a former confidant of the Mother's and Sri Aurobindo's. The elder's reply is delivered via bicycle messenger one afternoon, and it is not encouraging: "You are not yet ready for your freedom. Go back to the status quo and surrender all to The Mother. If you can do this, you do not know what Grace will come your way."

Some Aurovilians want to heed this counsel. They advocate dissolving the new trust and coming to a settlement with the CFY. But in a sign of things to come, a louder, more confrontational contingent carries the day. They declare that Auroville should turn instead to a person they believe will be more sympathetic to the community's cause: Satprem.

Satprem is still living with his companion Sujata in Nandanam, the estate outside Pondicherry. He wanders the grounds feeding the doves and rabbits, avoiding the large team of hired laborers that tend to the gardens. In the evenings, he exits a metal door in the back and takes his daily walk along the canyon. Mostly, he remains upstairs in his room, sitting on the floor and hunched over his desk, facing a meshed window with a view onto a mango tree that he believes harbors an ancient—though benevolent—spirit. He works tirelessly on the *Agenda*, the unabbreviated recording of his conversations with the Mother.

He has more than six thousand typed pages of transcripts tucked into a trunk. The trunk is hidden in his room, kept away from inquisitive, jealous eyes. Satprem is worried that the Ashram, which still vigorously resists publication, might try to steal his papers. He is particularly worried about his old nemesis Pranab, who remains the head of the Ashram's physical education program, and fears an imminent storming of Nandanam by a squad of gymnasts and athletes. In one particularly agitated moment, Satprem sets fire to fourteen personal diaries; he tells someone it feels as though he is burning his own existence.

He has largely withdrawn from public life. But when he receives Auroville's message asking for guidance, he replies quickly. Satprem's letter is read out one evening at a meeting held in the community of Fraternity, attended by some sixty Aurovilians. The letter begins by reminding Aurovilians that he has spent his whole life resisting institutions, in all forms. Even though he has been a member of the Ashram, he joined only so he could be by the Mother's side; he has never cared for rules or hierarchies. Turning to the community's predicament, Satprem writes, "The situation of Auroville, *whatever it may be*, is a last resort until everyone has lost their ego enough to see things clearly and to spontaneously obey the Rhythm of the perpetually changing Truth."

It's a cryptic, Delphic proclamation. Satprem may be waiting things out, watching to see how they develop. But it won't be long before his sympathies become clearer. In the CFY's proprietorial attitude toward Auroville, Satprem seems to hear echoes of the Ashram's claims of copyright over his conversations with the Mother. He comes to believe that he and Auroville are up against a common enemy, conservative old-world specimens who would block the transformation. He says several times that the Mother has left only two pure things, Auroville and the *Agenda*. In this way, and fatefully for Auroville, two struggles are fused.

Soon Satprem is corresponding several times a week with the community. His letters are carried from Nandanam by close Aurovilian associates, who drive their motorcycles through the back roads of Pondicherry and the canyons of Auroville. Often they arrive at Aspiration, that sprawling congregation of huts by the ocean, one of the first communities. Aspiration emerges as ground zero of Auroville's revolution.

Aspiration's residents assemble eagerly in the collective kitchen, under a gabled thatch roof and portraits of the Mother and Sri Aurobindo. They pass Satprem's letters around in silence, sometimes interjecting with whispered observations or exclamations. The whole process is a grave ritual, all solemn and serious; everything around Satprem always is. Eventually these messages filter out, emanating like gospel to the wider community. Satprem develops an ardent following in Auroville during this time. Many (but by no means all) of his followers are French; some go so far as to argue that he is the natural heir to the Mother and Sri Aurobindo.

Over time, the contents of Satprem's letters grow more overtly supportive of the rebellion, and even downright exhortatory. He inveighs against dark forces and practitioners of black magic. He tells Aurovilians that the planet is facing an existential moment, and that it is up to them to combat the powers impeding the next stage of evolution. He cautions against accommodation or compromise. "If you persist in believing . . . that one can come to terms with potassium cyanide, then there is no other solution but for you to become poisoned," he warns.

What emerges from these interventions is a maximalist, militant world-view—"an ugly black and white," as one person will later put it. Opponents are labeled Asuras (demons) and interpersonal disagreements are elevated to titanic occult struggles between the forces of darkness and light. "Truth is schismatic," Satprem says once to an associate. This deeply held belief in an absolute truth—an either/or reality—will over time impart a distinctly uncompromising flavor to Auroville's conflict.

Later, there will be controversy over Satprem's role in the revolution. His admirers will say that he saved Auroville, offered a moral beacon and a clarion call to action at a confusing time. Others will lament what they see as his divisiveness, an implacability that plunged Auroville into a depressing period of fanaticism. Father of Auroville's independence, or fount of its excesses? Architect of the community's freedom, or engineer of one of the darkest periods in its history? Either way, as the situation in Auroville heats up, Satprem comes to play a powerful, perhaps determinative, role in its insurrection. All that intensity, all that obduracy; the pain, the ferocity, the relentlessness, forged in the bowels of Gestapo torture chambers and two Nazi concentration camps—now they're guiding the birth of the new world.

The fields and forests around Kottakarai grow hazardous. Auroville and the CFY are fighting over territory. Aurovilians live on the land and cultivate it, but the CFY legally owns most of it, and its leadership wants these agitators gone.

Someone (it'll never quite be clear who) hires a group to patrol and protect the land. They're a rough crew, hardscrabble farmers and laborers, and sometimes they go overboard and resort to violence. They number about forty and come to be known as the watchmen. Aurovilians will always suspect that the violence is instigated; the CFY will deny it played any role.

One morning Sundaram is cycling from the Kottakarai bakery to visit his father in the village, when he sees a group of about ten Tamil men near the hut where Diane and Auralice live. These men—the watchmen—are shirtless, their mouths stained red from betel nut, and they carry long sticks fitted with hooked knives. They're pushing an Aurovilian man and woman, Diane's neighbors, and they're warning them to vacate the area. The Aurovilian man sits on the ground, indicating his refusal to move, and the watchmen pick him and the woman up by their hands and legs, swing them around while they taunt and curse. The man's glasses fall to the ground and the watchmen stamp on them, bending them out of shape.

Sundaram recognizes some of the aggressors; they're from neighboring villages. He asks why they're attacking Aurovilians, and they reply, "This isn't your business. You're one of us, why are you siding with the white people?" Sundaram runs back to the bakery, stands outside and whistles loudly, summoning a brown horse named Laxmi. He rides her bareback across the fields to Auroson's Home, where he finds a group of Aurovilians gathered in a meeting, at that very moment discussing the violence in the area. He tells them what's happened and they race toward Kottakarai, approaching from different directions to corner the watchmen. They catch three or four and interrogate them. Who are you? Who's paying you to do this? The watchmen smell of alcohol and refuse to answer questions. "Go back to your country," they say, and they call Aurovilian women whores. "Go back and fuck each other in your own land."

That night, the residents of Kottakarai gather as usual in the community kitchen. The servings are skimpy, and the mood is somber. This whole thing feels as if it's spinning out of control. Diane writes to a friend from Belgium of a "heavy dark period" and "a long journey far from peace." She doesn't specify what it is that weighs on her, but even Diane's faith must wobble on days like these.

Does she miss John? Does she long for his companionship in these troubled times? They are all free souls, so intent on shedding attachments; John and Diane seem to have no contact while he's in America. "There is so much love that sometimes it can create a bond that's too strong between people," Diane writes to her Belgian friend, explaining why she's living alone with Auralice. "All the love gets squeezed in a tight corridor. I have gypsy blood in me, probably from other lives."

Amid the deteriorating atmosphere, Auroville witnesses a number of exits. Some are involuntary: following the initial threat to Amrit, who manages to remain in India, a few residents are forced out of the country. Others leave the community more voluntarily. These include people such as John, who want to get away from the conflict; and my own family, who decide to leave Auroville for a time and move to Pondicherry.

My parents make this decision for many reasons. Mostly, they're tired of the disharmony and weary of the food shortages and near-monastic hardship of life. Also, as things fall apart in the community, they are increasingly worried about the prospects for my education; this worry will prove prescient. So we pack up our belongings one day, and we rent a rambling and somewhat decrepit house in Pondicherry's White Town. My parents enroll me in a school run by the Ashram.

We keep a small capsule hut in Auroville, which we visit on weekends. We see our friends, including some from Kottakarai, and sometimes we bring them food from town (cheese, vegetables, chapatis). My parents insist that this move is temporary. They are young, in their twenties, and I think they're trying to figure things out; we are in-between. But utopia is an all-or-nothing proposition. As Auroville radicalizes, so its geography is more tightly bound. You either live on the land or you don't; you're either in, or you're out. It's getting hard to be in-between. And it will get even harder.

Amrit attends a meeting at Auroson's Home one morning. About twenty Auro-vilians are assembled under a covered veranda, sitting around or leaning against walls, sipping tea and smoking bidis. The talk, as usual, is of the ongoing battle, the struggle for subsistence, and all the violence. Amrit has attended so many of these meetings since that December-morning tribunal with the CFY. Auroville has entered, as he will later put it, "the era of meetings"—an endless series of convocations and huddles, marked by long, meandering conversations and often-heated debate. The atmosphere of these meetings can be fiery. People who find themselves on the wrong side of the Collective, as the group leading the revolu-tion has come to be known, are denounced and browbeaten. Some laud the sense of solidarity and common purpose; others compare these meetings to show trials.

The crowd gathered at Auroson's Home turns to the topic of a man called Hendryk, who is a German neighbor of Amrit's. Hendryk is reported to main-tain links with the CFY. In particular, people say that he continues to receive Prosperity. Although most Aurovilians are now denied the CFY's material assis-tance, Hendryk still gets an occasional bar of soap or tube of toothpaste. "Why shouldn't I receive soap from them?" he asks when he's challenged. "What have they done to me?" Amrit has told Hendryk that he considers his continued acceptance of Prosperity unwise, a needless provocation of the Collective.

But at the meeting now, Amrit finds himself growing uneasy as some par-ticipants advocate a hard line with Hendryk. People are enraged by what they say are Hendryk's dual allegiances. They want to cut off the food and other support he receives from Auroville, and there's talk about evicting him from his house. Amrit has recently become aware of a changing tenor in Auroville's revolution; such talk triggers an old trauma, his long-standing aversion to in-justice and bullying. Amrit is slight and bespectacled; he's introverted and rarely speaks at these meetings. But now he stands up and, quietly, almost timidly, declares that he could never countenance such action against his neighbor. He says that if Auroville cuts Hendryk off, then the community is stooping to the same level as the CFY. He talks about freedom of expression, and about each Aurovilian's right to choose his or her own course of action.

There's a pause, then the meeting moves on. After it's over, a man pulls Amrit aside and pleads with him to reconsider his position. He tells Amrit that it was his situation, and his principled stand against the CFY, that inspired so many to fight in the first place. How can Amrit now support Hendryk's defiance of the Collective? Amrit holds his ground. "When the CFY is criticized for behaving like Nazis, then if we act the same way, what makes us different?" he asks. Later, the man is overheard telling others that Amrit is a "leak in the boat that has to be plugged."

The battle lines are shifting. New divisions are emerging, new allegiances and loyalty tests that will thrust Auroville's revolution onto terrain that is far more uncertain and morally ambiguous. Amrit, Hendryk, and several others will form a group of Aurovilians known as the Neutrals. In their own eyes, the Neutrals stand for compromise and conciliation; they advocate dialogue with the CFY. In the eyes of the Collective, especially those gathered around Satprem, the Neutrals will be seen as turncoats and fifth columnists who are too morally squishy to take the battle to the enemy. These are the opening salvos of an ugly civil war.

Early one morning in Aspiration, a group of about fifteen Aurovilians files toward a large hut that stands on high ground near the eastern boundary of the community. The hut is nominally occupied by the chairman of the CFY, but in truth he spends very little time in it, and a feeling of resentment has been building in the densely packed community, which suffers from a housing shortage. The Aurovilians force a padlock and remove a few items: a toothbrush, a razor, some clothing. They take possession of the hut and feel a sense of jubilation. They know this is only a token gesture, a symbolic show of resistance. Nonetheless, the community has felt so impotent in recent months; with this action, Aurovilians believe they demonstrate that they can stand up for themselves.

The next day a police inspector drives his Royal Enfield motorcycle into Aspiration, followed by two officers sweating on bicycles. Charges of burglary, breaking in, and unlawful assembly (a serious offense under India's state of emergency) have been filed against the intruders, and the police carry a list of names. It's a mark of the naïveté of Auroville's young rebels that they are astonished by the repercussions of their intrusion. "But what are you doing here?" one of the people involved asks the inspector. "This is just a family affair!"

The policemen ask a few questions and examine the hut. They hang around over the following days, so that Aspiration starts to feel like occupied territory. The Mother always said that there should be no police in Auroville, and their presence now feels sacrilegious. One man will compare it to the forced entry of the police during the riots of May 1968 into the Sorbonne, in Paris; he will evoke the sanctuary offered to dissenters during medieval times by monasteries and cathedrals. For Aurovilians, these uniformed officials in the heart of a residential settlement are further evidence of the CFY's disregard for the community's ideals.

Along with outrage, though, there is also some second-guessing. Children are scared, and a few adults are worried. Have we taken it too far? Are we all going to be expelled from the country, and Auroville simply shut down? Some people suggest returning the chairman's possessions and apologizing; they feel that de-escalation would be the wiser course. Faced with this vacillation, a Frenchman named Luc, who is close to Satprem, makes an offer, but with a condition. He will go ask Satprem what they should do; whatever Satprem advises, they must agree to follow.

That evening, Luc drives his red Rajdoot motorcycle to Nandanam. He parks in a clearing, then hunches over and squeezes through a path overgrown with spiky bougainvillea creepers, as though passing through a tunnel of thorns. When he emerges on the other side, he's astonished to find Satprem already waiting. No one has told Satprem that Luc would be coming. But now Satprem is there, as if expecting him, and he extends his hand and stares at Luc with his intense blue eyes. Without prompt Satprem says, *"Mon petit, il ne faut jamais avoir peur"* (Little one, you should never be afraid).

Satprem takes Luc up to the terrace of his house. They sit on the floor under a starry sky, and Luc explains the situation in Aspiration. What should we do? he asks. Should we apologize? Satprem closes his eyes and meditates. When he opens them, he replies with just two words: *"Mère sourit"* (Mother is smiling). Luc takes the message back to Aspiration, and it is sufficient: the action will stand.

Shortly thereafter, two police vans pull up in Aspiration, one empty and the other containing a contingent of helmeted troops. The police round up eight Aurovilians (seven French residents and an American man) and load them into the empty van. There's a moment of unintended levity when the van fails to start, and the police are forced to ask for assistance from the prisoners' compatriots. The residents of Aspiration oblige by pushing from outside, shouting, *"Oh hisse! Oh hisse!"* (Heave-ho! Heave-ho!), in unison while their arrested friends sit inside.

The Aurovilians are taken to a prison complex in Tindivanam, some twenty miles north of Auroville. Their cell is small and has a hole in the ground for a toilet, the air is filled with a stench, and piles of dead insects are all over. The floor is splattered with red pools that the prisoners initially think are blood, but later realize are accumulations of betel nut juice spat out by previous inmates. The food is atrocious, an inedible glop of red chilies.

That first night is a little rough, but the mood substantially improves by the next morning. The prisoners' better spirits are fueled by a sense of camaraderie, and also by a conviction that the CFY has overplayed its hand. The truth is out now; they believe that everyone will recognize the ruthlessness of their adversaries, and hence the righteousness of Auroville's revolution. When an inspector comes by after a few days and offers them bail on condition that they remain in Tindivanam, the prisoners reject what they call a "rotten bail." They say they will leave only when they can return to Auroville as free men. The inspector pleads with them: "Why are you doing this?" he asks. "Why don't you accept my offer? I'm trying to be nice to you."

Meanwhile, phone calls are made to foreign embassies in New Delhi, and strings are being pulled behind the scenes. Satprem plays a central role in these efforts. From his position as one of the Mother's closest aides, he has over the years cultivated a number of influential people, primarily government officials and industrialists, and now he uses his connections to help Auroville.

On a Saturday morning a week after the arrests, the prisoners are sitting around their cell, when Satprem makes an unannounced visit. He's dressed in shorts and a white shirt, and as he strides past a couple of astonished constables, one of the prisoners sees him and exclaims, "Oh, Satprem!" They all rush to the front of the cell. Satprem stands there and slowly, emphatically, runs his fingers along the metal bars. "It is in order to get rid of these that we are fighting," he says, looking intently at each of them, one by one. The prisoners freeze; their eyes well with tears. Satprem has come and crystallized their struggle. This isn't just a fight over a hut or visas in a single community. This battle is for the liberty of all humankind.

They are released later that morning, and they ride back to Aspiration in two taxis. Their comrades greet them jubilantly. It's clear to everyone that, with these jailings, the conflict has risen to a new level. This definitely isn't just a family affair anymore. The takeover of the chairman's hut marks a new, more confrontational phase in the revolution. It also cements Satprem's influence over the trajectory Auroville takes following the Mother's death.

That afternoon, the prisoners assemble with a group of about forty people in a large hut in Aspiration. They have named the hut Victory. They sit in a circle in Victory and meditate. Many will later say it is the deepest meditation they have ever experienced.

THE SACRIFICE

MANY YEARS AFTER THE REVOLUTION, an Aurovilian man will say of John, "He was very angular physically, but there were no angles in his attitude or way of being. He was like honey." From New York, John has been receiving sporadic reports of the unrest in Auroville. But he's left early in the course of the action, and he seems happy to keep his distance. He's a gentle, contemplative soul, utterly lacking the conviction and judgmentalism that have seized so many of his compatriots. That's not what John came to India for; that's not his idea of the yoga.

As the months have passed, he's become more deeply ensconced in his New York existence. His life is busy, a flurry of social activities and engagements. He meets old classmates, and he visits and stays with his cousin Theodore Friend, the president of Swarthmore College. He attends Gillian and Albert's wedding, held at a friend's Victorian mansion on Long Island, where he wears a pink silk Nehru jacket and mingles easily with the eminent, cultured crowd. Henri Cartier-Bresson sends a wedding present, a signed photograph he's taken of Henri Matisse; the installation artist Christo gifts the couple a charcoal drawing of a wrapped woman. Later, at a reception in the Dakota, John Lennon and

Yoko Ono occupy a couch while Gillian serves finger foods and John (Walker) slips in and out of the room, smoking cigarettes—and probably more—in a stairwell outside.

The author and editor Jean Stein, a doyenne of New York literary life, is writing a book about Edie Sedgwick. Sedgwick died of an overdose in 1971; her glamorous life and tragic burnout have come to emblematize the frustrated possibility of the sixties. John walks over to Stein's apartment on Central Park West several times, and he sits in her living room sharing memories. He talks about studying in Widener Library at Harvard while Edie sat by his side drawing, and of drinking with Edie and her gay crowd at the Casablanca. Once, John tells Stein, he hosted Edie at Fishers Island, where he took her to a party thrown by an heir to the IBM fortune. Edie was stunning in tight leotards, all eyes on her as she danced and cartwheeled under the moon, alone on a lawn sloping into the ocean, enveloped as always in an air of mystery and enchantment.

"When I first saw her in Cambridge, she looked like a Tamil child growing up in South India—huge eyed, those children are, with faces just like Edie's,"

John says to Stein. "There's that old Yogi axiom: the higher you go, the further you fall. She liked walking very close to extinction, always."

He spends most weekends at the family's home on Fishers Island. He drives there with Gillian and Albert in a green station wagon piled with groceries, and they take a car ferry from New London, Connecticut. Sometimes his parents visit from England. They fly the Concorde to America, then they take a small propeller plane from Groton to a landing strip on the island. They come with help—two or three women to clean the house, and Mrs. Locke to do the cooking. The help fly from England, too, but they take regular flights.

He meets a woman on Fishers Island. Her name is Prudence. She's a recent history and literature graduate from Harvard, and a new friend of Gillian and Albert's. Prudence is tall and earnest, curious and well-read. She's taken by the scene around the family—the artists, the filmmakers, the writers—and John appears taken by her sensitivity and intelligence. They strike up a few conversations, and soon they're spending more time together: hours in the garden, long walks in the pine forests and along the curved beaches. They listen to Joan Baez and Gabriel Fauré's Requiem; they discuss art and philosophy.

John tells Prudence about his time in India. He talks to her about Auroville and Sri Aurobindo, and about meeting with the Mother and how much that encounter affected him. He doesn't speak about the troubles or his disillusionment with them, but he does mention the PhD program at Princeton, and that he's thinking of remaining in America. Still, as summer extends into fall and winter, the trees on Fishers Island first red and yellow, and then bare, Prudence starts sensing a shift in John's mood. She isn't quite convinced that he'll stay.

In part, what Prudence feels is John's habitual inability to commit; he's always got an eye to the exits. Also, she thinks that John seems a little lost in America, struggling to find his place in a country that has changed so much since he left in the late sixties. Vietnam, the hippies, civil rights—all of that's increasingly in the rearview mirror. John has missed the trauma of Watergate. He still detests Nixon, and he refers to President Ford as a "puppet figurehead." But he doesn't quite get what the country has been through, and maybe he knows it. Prudence wonders if John sometimes feels like an anachronism.

Back in the city, he starts taking Prudence to Auroville-connected places—a hidden network of the Mother's believers and followers, like an underground in America working toward her dream. At 1050 Park Avenue, on the corner of Eighty-Seventh Street, they visit a spacious apartment owned by Marjorie Spalding, the heiress to a sporting goods fortune. Spalding has been to Auroville and is inspired by the project. She donates generously to Auroville-related causes, and supporters gather in her apartment for dinners, readings, and lectures by traveling gurus and philosophers.

Sometimes Prudence and John take a taxi to Brooklyn, where he visits an old friend from Auroville, a redheaded Irish American named John Kelly. Kelly is one of those who have left Auroville. He lives alone on the second floor of a wooden house, his apartment a mess of empty beer cans, discarded cigarettes, and dishes piled in the sink. John and Kelly drink and smoke weed together, and they read aloud from *Savitri*. Kelly is a performer; his voice is strong and melodic, like a bard's, and as he reads, John closes his eyes and bobs his head. Prudence looks at John and knows that, for all his talk of staying in America, he is very much at home here, steeped in this world of Eastern mysticism.

One day John and Prudence are in the garden on Fishers Island, and he pulls an orange Chinese-lantern seed pod off a stem. He holds it in his hand and embarks on a story about a homunculus man who lives inside the pod. It's a fabulous yarn, a dithyramb he composes on the spot. It goes like this: The pod is so bright, so luminous and beautiful, that everyone wants it, except for the poor homunculus who's trapped inside. The homunculus lives in a gilded cage. No matter what he does, how hard he pushes, he can't break free of his shiny orange prison.

John's imagination is a thing to behold. He's creative and brilliant, and so much fun to be with, especially when he's in a good mood. They laugh at this fable. But it's clear to Prudence that the story is also sad, and that John identifies with the trapped homunculus. He has a way of laughing into the distance, as if he's disassociated from his own mirth. Prudence wonders if the gilded cage is the life John has inherited from his father, or the one he adopted in India—or, perhaps, both.

They are in the Dakota one winter afternoon in early 1976. The mahogany paneling is heavy, a little oppressive. It's dark inside but bright outside, where the trees are leafless in the park and New York shuffles along, muffled and hatted. John tells Prudence he's been thinking a lot about India lately. He's been in New York for nearly nine months, and maybe the time away has been soothing, allowed for some perspective and eased some of the rawness of Auroville's disharmony. He's been wondering if he should return; and he wonders, too, if Prudence should come with him. He's not sure, and neither is she. So John lights some incense from Auroville, purifies three I Ching coins, and casts them. The resulting trigram is Tui, "lake over lake." John interprets this as propitious; they should go.

They don't talk about what this decision means. Why are they going? How long will they stay? Will they return? And what's going on between them, anyway? Prudence has a vague sense of another woman, maybe a whole family, in Auroville. John has bought clay-sculpting tools as a gift, and she gathers that the intended recipient is more than a friend. But Prudence wants to respect John's privacy, so they don't talk about anything. They just book their tickets and leave on a cold evening from JFK, flying to Madras via Rome and Bombay. On the tarmac in Bombay, John dives to the ground, kisses the earth, and proclaims, "O Mother India!" Prudence rolls her eyes; John can be so melodramatic.

In Pondicherry, they take a room at the back of Goyle's Guest House. John shows Prudence around town: the Ashram, the French villas, the beach promenade. He introduces her to Indian food and takes her to the Samadhi, where they meditate. Prudence sits on the roof of the guest house reading E.M. Forster's *A Passage to India*, and they spend hours together over Goyle's meals, the conversation always high concept and intellectual. John holds forth, and he's erudite and insightful, but sometimes Prudence feels he loses the thread, goes too far out on a tangent. She looks at him and wonders, Where are you, John?

Shortly after arriving in Pondicherry, John disappears. He's gone for a couple of days, he comes back, and then after a while he disappears again. This keeps happening. Every time he returns, he retreats to his bed and lies there, rising only for meals, as if stunned or overwhelmed. Prudence figures he's got another life in Auroville; she doesn't probe. One day John takes her on a walk, and near the Ashram they come across an attractive woman in a sari: Diane. The meeting appears to take place by chance. In fact, John has arranged it. The encounter is tense, a little awkward, and mercifully short. Prudence knows right away that this is where John disappears. In Diane, Prudence feels something intense, almost desperate. Diane is a strong, powerful woman. Depths and currents lie beneath her slight exterior, and Prudence has a sense that Diane will fight for what she wants.

Eventually, Prudence goes with John to Auroville, where they visit Kottakarai. The troubles rage on, as do their financial repercussions. A recently constituted Central Fund now disburses a mere 26,375 rupees ($3,500) every month for food, personal maintenances, and electricity, a 65 percent reduction from the community's budget before the revolution. More than ever, Auroville depends on contributions from its wealthier members; John's return to the scene is welcome.

The center of revolutionary action remains in Aspiration. Kottakarai is located on the other side of the plateau, its population consists mostly of Dutch and American hippies who smoke pot, and perhaps this explains why things are less heated. Years later, a resident of Kottakarai will tell me, "We didn't really have a dog in a lot of those battles. We saw the problems, we didn't want the CFY telling us what do to. But we thought those Frenchies down in Aspiration took things too far. They thought we were hippies, and we thought they were fanatics."

In Kottakarai, Prudence meets Auralice—a withdrawn three-year-old who alternates between Tamil and English. Her skin is nut-brown and she has round eyes, a wide mouth, and her mother's cherry lips. Prudence notes John's affection for Auralice. He carries her around on his shoulders, tells her stories and brings her treats—jam, dates, chocolate—from Pondicherry. He tickles her and places her on a blanket, then pulls the blanket along the floor as Auralice laughs. John keeps telling Prudence that he's moving back to America. But when she sees him with Auralice, sees him with Diane and all his other Auro-vilian friends, it's clear to her that he has attachments here.

One day John takes Prudence to Rameswaram, to visit Guruji. John has grown close to the priest, and, especially since the Mother's absence, reliant on him for spiritual guidance. They take a train through emerald-green rice fields and sugarcane plantations; they make a stopover in the town of Kumbakonam, where the platform is crowded with lepers who stick their gnawed-off arms through the carriage's metal grilles and beg for alms. In Rameswaram, they visit Guruji at his home, and later they walk with him to his temple at the top of a sandy hill. The views are spectacular, the ocean a shiny sliver on the horizon. John walks to the edge of a promontory and tells Prudence about an earlier visit to this place, when he threw an expensive silver watch into the plains below. The watch had been in his family for generations. "I was throwing away time," John says. "I was getting rid of the temporal."

They spend three or four days at Guruji's. John and the priest meditate together in the mornings, and Guruji offers John a private mantra, or sacred utterance, which he rarely does even with longtime disciples. John likes to sit with Guruji on his veranda and ask questions—about how to lead an ethical existence, about spiritual practice, and the order of the universe and John's place in it. Should he leave his American family and move to Auroville? Is he capable of committing himself to Sri Aurobindo and the Mother? John tells the priest he wants to surpass his bodily desires and that he's thinking of taking a vow of brahmacharya (celibacy). Prudence listens; she admires the integrity and sacredness with which John approaches his life.

This is a hinge moment in John's existence, although he doesn't know it. He is thirty-three years old and leading two lives, inhabiting two worlds. He is with two women who couldn't be more different. In Pondicherry, he leads a life of the mind with Prudence, and they share a common context in American East Coast society. In Auroville, John follows another type of existence: less mental, more elemental. There's potential for a spiritual partnership with Diane. What should he do? Who should he be? From a letter to his sister: "I am waging war—against what, I don't know." Sometimes you choose your battles; sometimes, life chooses them for you.

Prudence stays in India until the spring of 1976. John gives her his blue vest as she's leaving. Its lining is frayed, and he asks her to carry it to America so it can be fixed. Prudence takes a train to Bombay, and John calls her when she's at her guesthouse, about to depart for the airport. They talk for a while, and then he says, "So I'll see you soon, back in New York."

In fact, he starts spending more time in Kottakarai. He moves in pretty much full-time now with Diane and Auralice; they are living under one roof, for the first time as a family. They eat meals together, and John and Diane garden in the vegetable patch outside the hut. After dinner, they sit side by side and read the Mother and Sri Aurobindo, and they resume their old *Savitri*-recitation contests. They fight occasionally, too, bickering like an old couple. Diane can be headstrong, and the neighbors hear her screaming. Sometimes she throws a plate. Later, the neighbors find John and Diane sweeping their house, beginning at opposite sides of the room and working toward each other to the center, a ritual of reconciliation.

For Diane, these are settled times. Although she has long resisted domestic attachments, she seems content now to be with John. She's recovering from the trauma of Aurolouis's drowning, and she no longer speaks about reincarnating him. Auralice has started attending a preschool; it's a rudimentary setup, in an area known as Center Field, a thatch hut where eight or nine kids sit in circles and sing songs, but it means that Diane has more time to herself in the mornings. She's still working in the Matrimandir's gardens, but now that she no longer needs to keep an eye on her daughter, she's keen to move on to bigger tasks.

Diane knows that the most important labor is taking place on the construction site itself; that's where she wants to be. This work is more arduous and requires greater physical strength and concentration. Crews of six or seven perch themselves high up on the building and hoist metal pipes up from the ground, which they bind with clamps to create new sections of scaffolding.

They walk out on the two-inch hollow pipes without helmets or suspension, maintaining their balance by holding on to the scaffolding above their heads. They are barefoot and the pipes are painted black, to keep from rusting, and the metal absorbs the sun and burns their feet. When they reach the end of a section, they pull themselves up to the next level, rising vertically along the pipes, always without any protective gear.

There are a few close calls. A man falls from the building and dislocates his shoulder. Someone drops a wooden board embedded with nails, narrowly missing a person below. But no one is seriously injured, and these events reinforce a sense of invulnerability. This is, after all, the Mother's Temple.

Diane is accepted into the construction crew in May of 1976. It's a special time at the Matrimandir. After more than five years of labor—and hundreds of tons of steel and cement, and scores of concrete pours—the workers are at last reaching the summit. The vertical ribs that run alongside the structure are now bending inward, converging upon each other at a height of ninety-five feet. For Aurovilians, the imminent meeting of these ribs is highly significant: it represents a milestone in the Matrimandir's construction, and a landmark in the town's ambition to materialize its spiritual beliefs.

Diane awakens early every day, quickly bathes and feeds Auralice before taking her on her bicycle to school. Then she races to the Matrimandir, where she often arrives late, to the annoyance of her coworkers. She parks under a neem tree, removes her rubber sandals, and climbs a series of steel ladders to join her crew. She wears tight denim shorts and a cotton bandanna over her head, with a wrench in her belt loop. She's flirtatious and playful, poking people in the ribs and giggling. Men get excited, and they linger around her. A few people frown on that energy; they feel it's inappropriate for the solemnity of the task.

Sometimes Diane works the night shift. People are needed to guard the Matrimandir after hours, or to pour water over freshly concreted slabs. These are magical times. A deep black sky, and an endless sheet of stars. Dogs bark in the distance. A spotlight illuminates the structure's gray ribs, and bugs—thousands, maybe millions—are drawn to the light. They jump and swarm around,

swirling in fast-moving clouds. Diane is so happy to be here, she feels so complete. Amid all the strife, the obfuscating conflict, the Matrimandir's silence is a refuge. Nothing can shake this monolith.

On the night of July 12, 1976, Diane, John, and Auralice attend a party at a home on the outskirts of Auroville. About twenty people gather around a bonfire. There's a bucket with ice and cold beer, and they barbecue some chicken and potatoes. A man plays Bob Dylan songs on a guitar. The next morning, Diane is running late for work, as usual. Auralice feels lonesome, which is not usual. She begs her mother not to go to the Matrimandir and says she doesn't want to go to school.

Diane grabs Auralice anyway, and they rush out of their home. They stop by the neighbors', where Diane asks if she can borrow some bandages to cover a few sores on her foot. The neighbors are eating breakfast, and one of them notices that Diane has wrapped an improvised dressing around her injuries, a yellow scarf imprinted with images of a Hindu deity. She wonders if Diane will take it off before working at the Matrimandir.

There was a downpour overnight, and it was cool in the morning when Diane awoke; she's dressed in an orange-and-red turtleneck with long sleeves. But now the clouds have dispersed, the sun is out, and she sweats as she pedals fast to the Matrimandir. When she gets there, her crew is already at work. She pulls the stand on her bicycle and waves up at them. One woman lights a bidi, and a man rolls his eyes because Diane is late again. It's 8:15 a.m.

Diane is in a rush, so she decides not to take the ladder. She clambers up the scaffolding instead, moving quickly from level to level, hauling herself up with her arms and swinging her hips over the pipes. She's just below her crew when she loses her grip. She falls backward and the construction site is suddenly still, immobilized, total silence except for the sound of Diane's body as it ricochets off the scaffolding, layer after layer, her arms and legs thrown around as they hit the pipes, splayed out like a rag doll's, as she falls fifty feet onto the hard concrete, to the bottom of the foundation pit.

Thock, thock, thock. Everyone on the site will remember that sound. And some will remember a metallic sound, too, a clanking as Diane's wrench bangs against the steel scaffolding.

She hits the ground and they all jump into action. They slide down the pipes, crowd around her. It's apparent that she's hurt her back and they try not to move her. She's moaning, and her face is covered in blood. But she's alive! Her eyes are open, and they think it's a miracle, that Diane has survived due to the Mother's protection. The truth is that the scaffolding has broken her descent. One man who has been standing near the top of the structure looks down after her fall and sees how the pipes of the scaffolding are bent, dented where Diane's body has hit them.

Someone calls for a van to take her to the hospital. A man sticks a hand in her mouth to pull her tongue to safety. His fingers come out bloody, holding teeth; he wraps the teeth in a piece of cloth in case they're needed later. The van pulls up to the construction site, and they slide Diane onto a plank of plywood, a crude stretcher. They carry her up the foundation pit and place her—slowly, carefully—onto the floor of the van.

JIPMER, the government hospital in Pondicherry, is set in a sprawling, leafy campus. It's a chaotic, gruesome place, the crowded receptacle of so much trauma and drama. Patients and their families throng the campus—hoping, worrying, celebrating, badgering doctors, and setting up picnics on lawns.

The van pulls up outside the emergency room and Diane's friends go looking for a doctor. There's no one around—only a few patients, lying on the floor and huddled in corners, but not a single medical person. Finally they find a couple of orderlies, and together they carry Diane, who is now unconscious, into a low-ceilinged, tube-lit room. They lay her on a bed, its sheets stained and wrinkled, and the orderlies pull a curtain. They start moving her, trying to get her onto an X-ray table. Diane's friends feel the orderlies are being too rough, and they stop everything until a doctor can be found.

The doctor finally arrives, at the head of a retinue of ten medical students. He's a rotund man with a mustache, dressed in a white coat. He runs a metal scalpel against Diane's foot, nods meaningfully at her lack of reaction, then turns to the students, each of whom he instructs to do the same. Some fifteen minutes pass in this way. The doctor concludes that Diane's whole body is paralyzed.

The orderlies and her friends carry her into a room with a wooden X-ray machine. Her friends refuse to leave; they insist they will be the ones to turn her on the table. The results of the X-ray are apparent, even to a medical layman. A vertebra near the top of Diane's neck is dislodged by some two inches. She's also broken her jaw, a few lower vertebrae, her left arm, and a couple of ribs. As Diane is moved from the X-ray room to the ICU, the doctor opens a book for her friends and points to a paragraph on broken necks. "She will never walk again," he says. "Most likely, she will die."

John is in Pondicherry shopping for vegetables. He's weighed down by a heavy bag, navigating the crowded bazaar, when he sees another Aurovilian man. He heads toward the man and greets him with a smile. "Did you hear what happened?" the man asks. He doesn't know about John's relationship with Diane. John's face goes white. He leaves the bazaar and cycles straight to the hospital, joining Diane's coworkers outside the emergency room.

Auralice is at school. She's on a wooden swing attached by coir ropes to a large neem tree. All the other kids have gone home, and she's starting to get a little anxious, but only a little, because this is how it often is in Auroville. Adults get caught up in whatever they're doing.

After a couple of hours, an American woman comes over. She lives near the school, and she was working on the Matrimandir that morning. She witnessed Diane's fall and heard the sound of her body as it bounced off the scaffolding. Like everyone else, she's in shock. She sees Diane's daughter and realizes that no one has said anything to her. The woman tells Auralice that her mother has gone away, to Belgium, and Auralice won't see her again for a long time.

"I always wondered why she'd say that," Auralice tells me years later. "I mean, why tell a little girl her mother's abandoned her? I suppose she was lost for words. I guess none of them could figure out how to process the accident. It was just too big."

Auralice makes her way back to Kottakarai alone. She will not remember how she gets there; probably she walks across the fields, a journey of about a mile. She returns to an empty house, and a mostly empty community: Diane's friends are at the hospital. Auralice heads to the neighbors' hut, where she will spend the first few nights. The task of informing her falls to Larry, her biological father, who will return from JIPMER that night.

Work ceases at the Matrimandir for the day. The construction workers hang around a thatch stall sipping tea and deliberating the morning's events, then they head in a daze to their respective communities. Amrit, who was on the site when Diane fell, stands over the foundation pit and stares down to where she landed. He's always been afraid of heights, and this seals it for him. Amrit will never work on the Matrimandir again.

Another man on the structure that morning will later say, "When Diane fell, it was like the bubble went out of utopia. We just couldn't believe it. I mean, never in our wildest dreams could something like this happen at the Matrimandir."

Ruud Lohman, the former Dutch Franciscan monk, also on the scaffolding when Diane fell, writes about the event in his diary: "That morning, 13th July, Matrimandir was touched by Death or Something Dark. One could not touch it. Matrimandir was cold and distant; nobody could go up, most people left. I went to Pondicherry, it was too hard to even be around."

The Mother always said there are no accidents. Everything that happens has a reason. Aurovilians live in this mesh of significance, this universe where each event is freighted with symbolism. The Matrimandir is the Mother's Temple; it is the spiritual core of Auroville. Right away, it's clear to everyone that Diane's fall means something. It must carry a message, especially coming against the backdrop of all the recent disharmony. One Aurovilian man will later sum up the mood around town like this:

It was clear from the start that this fall was extremely symbolic. It was all tied in with questions. Is Auroville going to exist? Is Auroville going to be free? These were huge questions. The battle with the CFY was so intense; it felt like a battle to death, and the death could have been the death of Auroville.

Of course a materialist would say, "She just missed the bar, she fell." But we were all people who tried to look for the deeper meaning in things. We knew there was more going on. There was so much happening at the time in terms of forces and occult attacks on Auroville. Somehow, Diane became the sacrifice. The sacrifice of what? We were convinced that there were efforts to harm the soul of Auroville—to shoot arrows into its core, to lance its heart. Diane was a soft spot where all of that could play out.

As news of Diane's fall spreads across Pondicherry and Auroville, everyone has the same question. In community kitchens and homes, on sports grounds and in meditation centers, they ask, *How could this happen?* Shock gradually gives way to introspection, and the community turns to a search for explanations. People talk about the party Diane attended the night before; they wonder if she drank beer and was hungover (in fact, Diane is a teetotaler). Some mention the scarf on her leg—perhaps she slipped—and others to the flirtations on the site, which maybe distracted her. But the cause must be tantamount to the event. A fall from the Matrimandir cannot come down to something as base as a hangover or sexual flirtation. There must be more. The community thirsts for meaning.

Once again, Satprem steps into the breach. He and Diane have no prior association. But he's been following events in Auroville closely, watching its revolution, and he's distressed by what he considers the community's inability (or is it unwillingness?) to stand united against the CFY. He's particularly dismayed about the emerging group known as the Neutrals ("poison in the fruit" of Auroville, as he characterizes them to one man) and he knows that people from the Ashram and the CFY are still invited to work at the Matrimandir. This feels like a betrayal, a form of contamination. In Diane's accident, Satprem seems to see an opportunity—a teachable moment, perhaps a chance to cleanse the community's soul.

The evening of Diane's fall, a group of her friends is sitting on benches outside the ICU in JIPMER. The group includes John, Larry, and three or four others. Her inert body is visible from behind yellow glass, lying in a bed with protruding tubes and wires. Suddenly Satprem walks in, wearing tight shorts and a button-down white shirt. Everyone knows it's him right away, even those who have never before seen him. There's something about his cold-as-steel eyes and confident manner, an air of self-containment. Satprem is a man who knows his place in the world. He strikes one person in that waiting room as resembling a "bar of steel"—for which Diane's friends, bereft and disoriented, are profoundly grateful.

People stand and Satprem comes up to them, holds their hands, and looks them deeply in the eyes. He speaks soothingly. He assures them that the Mother is present and that she's watching over them. He goes up to a man who is sitting in the corner. Today is the man's birthday and he's holding his head in his hands, rocking it back and forth, singing despondently, "Happy birthday to you, happy birthday to you." Satprem puts his hand on the man's head and runs it through his long, flowing curls, as if caressing an animal. The man looks up, bewildered. Satprem stares at him, taps him on the chest, and says, "It's so easy. All you need to do is open up."

Someone has a word with the ICU attendant, impresses upon him the significance of this visitor. He says Satprem needs to be with Diane. Against hospital rules, the attendant allows Satprem into the ICU. Satprem walks to the back of the room and stands over Diane's bed, where he meditates. Then he sits by her side, and after a while he walks back out and consoles Diane's friends again. The Mother is with us, Satprem says, and he adds something else. He tells the friends that he was surprised during his meditation. He didn't just see the Mother in the room; Sri Aurobindo was there, too. Presumably, this suggests the significance of the event.

One afternoon a few days later, a man drives his motorcycle from Nandanam to Aspiration. He carries an envelope and, as always, a crowd gathers in the community kitchen. The envelope is opened and passed around, its contents read carefully in silence. Satprem's message is longer than usual, more letter than note, extending over several pages. This is his follow-up to the visit at the hospital. "To my brothers and sisters of the Matrimandir," the letter begins. "To Auroville."

What follows is a remarkable interpretation of Diane's fall—full of fire and brimstone, Satprem's words like the admonishing sermon of an old-school preacher. He insists that the accident was, in fact, not an accident at all. Following a "spiritual law," Satprem writes, Diane's fall is actually the "sign of a Falsehood." Those who insist otherwise are turning their heads away from the truth (the "Truth"). Since Auroville is meant to be a place exclusively for seekers of the Truth, and since Satprem is fortunate to see things a little more deeply, so it falls to him to share the reality of Diane's fall with the community.

That reality is difficult—"but people, alas, do not understand until they start receiving blows."

According to Satprem, an event such as this one occurring at the Matrimandir is a sign of the times—an indication of the divisions within Auroville and of the corruption of the Mother's dream. In the second part of the letter, Satprem returns to the core grievance that has eaten at him since the Mother's departure: the lie of her death, and the interrupted cellular transformation. He argues that the difficulties faced by Auroville in recent times—the violence, the financial hardships, the confusion of the revolution—have seeped in through the cracks formed by this original lie. Diane's accident should be understood as part of a dismal continuum; what took place on the Matrimandir is an act of collective karma.

Satprem's message reverberates across the plateau. Its effect is electric, transforming Diane's fall from an individual tragedy, a terrible personal accident, to a communal misfortune for which every Aurovilian bears a shared responsibility. His interpretation comes to define Aurovilians' understanding of what took place on that July 13 morning. More important, it shapes Diane's own understanding, her self-perception. It sets her—and John—on a radical, severe course that will culminate catastrophically. We begin to understand the snaking paths that will lead, more than a decade later, to their deaths in a hut by a canyon.

Many years later, after Auralice and I have returned to Auroville, she is sitting one morning in a café by the Matrimandir. A Tamil waiter approaches her. He comes over gingerly, hesitantly, and asks, "Sorry, but are you Diane's daughter?" Auralice tells him she is. "Oh, your mother sacrificed so much for Auroville!" the man says. He talks about how his family owned land behind the Matrimandir. He was born three years after Diane's accident; he grew up with stories about how much she had given for Auroville.

Auralice returns home more puzzled than upset. We have grown used to these incursions from the past. People approach us to share unsolicited theories about John and Diane, or observations about how much Auralice looks like her mother. Even after so many years, speculation abounds about the cause and meaning of Diane's fall. Mostly, we know how to handle these moments; we don't get surprised anymore, and we keep them in the past. But this idea of sacrifice: that's something new. "What do you suppose he meant?" Auralice asks me after coming back from the café, and I don't have an answer.

I'm just starting to research this book. I don't know about Satprem's letter yet, and I don't understand how his intervention changed the trajectory of Diane's and John's lives. Only as Auralice and I go deeper into this project—jointly, very much a shared endeavor—will we come to understand what the waiter was referring to: how John's and Diane's misfortunes intersected with a wider social discord, and how Diane's fall, and then their deaths, were the tragic resonances of another, more general fall in the community.

After several weeks in the ICU, Diane is moved to a private room, a narrow rectangle with a hospital bed in the corner and a small window looking into a patch of greenery. Disinfectant is in the air and the corridors outside are crowded with moaning patients on the floor. The doctors open Diane's trachea and insert a catheter so she can breathe. They shave her head, drill into her skull, and fit in metal plates that connect to chains, to put her in traction; her head is pulled back with hanging weights so that it is lower than her body, in an effort to reset the spine. The chains of the traction rattle when she moves.

A team of five attendants work in six-hour shifts to care for her. They feed and clean Diane, and keep her company. She can't eat solid food so she's put on a diet of soup and juice. John, who assumes the role of primary caretaker, buys a juicer and shops in the stalls opposite the hospital for mangoes, bananas, and apples. He also purchases a water mattress, which sags over the edges of the bed. Every couple of days, the attendants remove Diane's clothes and sponge her down. She will only let men clean her; she doesn't want women to see her damaged body. Her chin is flattened, as though eroded, and when she talks, she cups a hand over her face, to hide her shattered beauty.

Satprem comes several times to the hospital. Whenever he walks into Diane's room, everyone else clears out. He sits by her side, leans over, and speaks in a slow rhythmic cadence, accelerating and raising his voice when he wants to emphasize a point. Satprem assures Diane that the Mother is with her, and he casts her misfortune upon the wider canvas of Auroville's strife. Something is broken in Auroville, he explains, has been broken since the Mother's death, and that's why Diane's spine is now broken. In this way, Satprem concocts a reassuring—or is it devastating?—synecdoche, a transposition of a larger battle onto this one woman's individual struggle. He declares that a victory with two V's is at hand: her victory, he says, will also mark a Victory for humanity. Her suffering is part of divine suffering; her healing will be the healing of the world.

He asks Diane to write down her dreams and share them with him; this will allow him to understand the full dimensions of her situation. The assignment poses a challenge for Diane, since her head is held back by the chains of traction, below the level of her torso. Still, she makes valiant efforts, placing sheets of paper on her pelvis or thighs, and scrawling without being able to see what she's writing. One of her attendants, a man called Peter, guides her hand and tries to keep the lines straight. Peter is close to Satprem; he takes the dreams to Nandanam, and he and Satprem sit on a lawn and Satprem contemplates their meaning. He gives Peter messages to take back to the hospital. Diane awaits these messages avidly; she lives for Satprem's replies.

What is Satprem doing with Diane? Why is he spending so much time in JIPMER? Satprem's admirers will always insist that he is full of compassion; the Mother has after all renamed him—he who was formerly Bernard—"the one who loves truly." I do not doubt Satprem's compassion for Diane. But something else is going on, too. For two and a half years, Satprem has had one overriding concern, one preoccupation that has eaten at him and subsumed everything else: the death and premature entombment, as he considers it, of the Mother. It is this original sin, this root cause of Auroville's troubles, that he now sees a chance to remedy.

This, for Satprem, is the real significance of Diane's fall—and the meaning of her sacrifice. In Diane's splintered spine, Satprem believes he may have found a way to pick up the pieces of the interrupted cellular transformation. Henceforth, her body will be a vehicle, a laboratory for Sri Aurobindo's yoga of evolution. In this way, Diane's condition is intimately tied to Auroville's, and her fate to the community's revolution. It's a lot of weight to put on one woman's shoulders.

Years later, Peter will summarize Satprem's view of the situation like this: "He believed that she must work toward the transformation. She must embody as much of what the Mother was trying to achieve in her own body. She must become very aware of that and try to do that in her small body. The Mother's was the big body; she was an extension of that, and if she could do that, she could help cure Auroville of its problems."

There is one important consequence. Given the sacredness of Diane's mission, Satprem insists that Diane's recovery must be pure, relying solely on the yoga and without medical intervention. *"Pas de médecins!"* (No doctors!), he repeatedly tells her, even as he visits her in JIPMER, and he adds that she must at all costs resist hospitals and their paraphernalia. He says that the medical establishment can do nothing for her. When the healing happens, it will happen naturally—through sincerity and meditation, and most of all through her willpower and integrity, an undiluted aspiration toward the divine.

Peter continues: "It was a battle of light and dark for Satprem. He saw Diane's story as part of the total battle. There was Diane as representative of a personal trauma, but there was Diane as part of the big picture, the transformation, the forces of light overtaking the forces of dark. The fall was an indication of the play of darkness. It was all part of the same weave. It was an apocalyptic kind of battle."

He shakes his head when he tells me this. We're having lunch together in Auroville some twenty-five years after the accident, on an ordinary, sunny day. I feel that Peter himself can't quite believe the words he's saying. "It might sound crazy, I know it sounds crazy," he says. "But when we walked into that hospital room to be with Diane, it was like we saw the face of the Mother."

Diane looks at her face in a mirror in the hospital and complains to an attendant that she's ugly now. "No, you're not, you're beautiful," the attendant says. "Beautiful like this?" Diane asks, and she crunches up her features, accentuating the deformity of her broken jaw. Her voice comes out high-pitched and squeaky, as if her vocal cords are being squeezed.

She won't allow Auralice to visit her for more than a month after the fall. She doesn't want her daughter to see her in this condition. So Auralice remains in Kottakarai, sometimes staying with the neighbors, and sometimes with Larry, who now moves into Diane and John's hut. Auralice is scared and lonely, and she feels abandoned. She craves information and news about her mother, but no one will ever talk about Diane in front of her. One time a man shows Auralice a photograph from the hospital, and Auralice says, "My mama doesn't look beautiful anymore."

When she's finally allowed to visit, she and Larry make a chocolate cake for Diane in the bakery. Diane won't be able to eat it, but Auralice doesn't know that. She takes a bus with Larry and another girl from the community; Diane has suggested it might be easier if Auralice comes with a friend. Diane puts on a brave face. She smiles, playfully pulls at Auralice's pigtails, and asks about the preschool, which Auralice hardly attends any longer. There's no mention of the fall, no talk of why Diane is in the hospital or why Auralice hasn't seen her in so long. It's as if those chains of traction don't exist. Auralice knows, somehow she knows, that she's not supposed to ask.

Back in Kottakarai, Auralice plays a game with the friend who accompanied her to the hospital. They're in a hut, and one of them assumes the role of Diane, naked and wrapped under a sheet on a bed. The other plays a nurse who carries trays of food and drink to sick Diane, and sometimes gives her medicine. Auralice and her friend play this game over and over. She's a four-year-old girl trying to process it all. One day an adult sees them playing and reprimands them, tells them to stop their game right away.

Always, there will be this silence, this enveloping secrecy. Diane's fall is the result of evil forces; to name her condition would be to yield to the forces. Her situation is temporary anyway, Satprem has promised, and the healing is imminent. The two victories—victory and Victory—are around the corner. Diane is strong and unwavering, and she follows uncomplainingly the path Satprem has laid out, never voicing doubts or hesitations.

But silence corrodes; it never heals. Eight years after the fall and Diane will remain paralyzed, unable to walk, with no feeling below her waist; and still, no one talks about anything. Auralice is twelve years old now, on the cusp of being a teenager. She's stormy and one day she gets into an argument with her mother. Diane is sitting on the ground, supported by bolster pillows, her legs folded awkwardly under her. "Come here!" Diane orders her defiant daughter.

Auralice makes a face, not quite mocking, but challenging. "No, why should I?" she asks. "*You* get up and come to me!"

Diane is incensed; she orders Auralice to her side again. Finally, Auralice comes over and Diane slaps her. It's the first time (the only time) she's raised her hand against her daughter, and she's as horrified as Auralice. What have we become? For a moment, the mask slips. They clutch each other, they hold tight, and they both cry—cry and cry and cry.

A GOLDEN ROPE

SATPREM IS WALKING ALONG THE canyon behind Nandanam one evening. It's late August of 1976 and the summer is finally easing. The sun is a butter ball, soft, melting its glow over the compacted red earth and dusty scrub. The canyon is majestic; it imposes on the land, furrowing all the way to Auroville, where it joins Forecomers.

This walk is Satprem's daily respite, an escape from the rigors of the multiple battles he's waging. He follows the line of a ridge. He sits on the ground and watches the seagulls as they soar in and out of the canyon. Sometimes he feels as if he's drinking the quiet, or taking it in through the pores of his skin.

Three men emerge from a dip in the earth. They start walking in Satprem's direction, come right at him, and he knows at once that they are here to kill him. They move their arms, enacting what he takes to be a throwing gesture, as if signaling their intent to toss him into the canyon. Two of the men approach him and grab his hands; one unstraps his watch. The other man, apparently their leader, steps up to Satprem and looks directly at him. Satprem sees that the man has large golden eyes.

The assailant raises his hands to push Satprem into the canyon, but Satprem remains still. He's unafraid and his heart maintains a steady beat. There's no panic in him, no anxiety—nothing at all. He is utterly transparent, and this, he later explains, means that their hatred and murderous intent have nothing to latch on to. Satprem stares the man in the eyes, those golden eyes, and suddenly the man's arms drop, he turns and flees, and the others follow, all running away across the canyon. Satprem knows—he is sure—that they are fleeing his certainty.

He makes his way back to Nandanam and calls the police to report an assassination attempt. A man from Auroville arrives soon after; the police are already there, milling around, and Satprem takes the man aside in the garden and tells him what just happened. "I foolishly went and almost got myself killed," he says. It's only now, with hindsight, that he's a little shaken. But he's elated, too, because he has no doubt about what took place in that canyon: he found another way of being. Satprem later tells someone that in his stillness, his emptiness and transparency, he touched "unadulterated cellular matter," free of the mind and its fears and attachments. This transparency saved him. "One can't assassinate a current of air!" he exclaims.

Just under two months have passed since Diane's fall from the Matrimandir—two months since the open letter Satprem wrote about her to the community, and two months since she entered JIPMER, where she's now out of traction and with some mobility returned to her upper body, but with paralysis remaining below the waist. The letters still flow between her and Satprem; they contextualize her condition. A battle for truth. A divine sacrifice. The Mother's will. These are the high-minded phrases that describe Diane's everyday human exertions: the difficulties she has eating, bathing, urinating, satisfying an itch.

Satprem is in a heightened state. He's combative and suspicious, and even some of his closest associates wonder if he's a little paranoid. After the events of the canyon, he starts taking his daily walks with a bodyguard, a Nepali Gurkha who trails a few feet behind. A couple of Aurovilians start spending nights at Nandanam to protect him. All around, Satprem sees ill will, impostors and charlatans out to turn the Mother's and Sri Aurobindo's teachings into a new religion.

The Ashram continues to resist his efforts to publish the *Agenda*. Its elders hold to their original position that it is solely their prerogative to release the Mother's conversations with Satprem. Lawyers' notices abound, along with arguments over copyright, ownership, and financial restitution—all these base notions from the old world. Satprem writes to someone that he is surrounded by a medieval darkness. He has visions of death, of a vulture with golden eyes (just like the assailant's), of invaders rushing in from the distance under a column of black smoke.

He tells an associate he's prepared for any eventuality. He's read about a Czech student who burned himself to protest the Soviet invasion. If they try to steal his transcripts, he's ready to make the same sacrifice. He'll douse himself with gasoline and burn at the gates of the Ashram.

Satprem is a man of extremes. To his detractors, he can seem overwrought. But for him—and his followers—the stakes couldn't be higher. The struggle to publish the *Agenda* isn't simply a difference of opinion or a conflict between two factions. "One time there was a small mental vibration that touched an anthropoid, and that led to Einstein and all our knowledge," Satprem tells a man. He adds that just as reptiles grew wings and escaped their swamps, so the world now faces "the end of a geological or paleontological cycle, and the beginning of a new species." For Satprem, manifesting the *Agenda* is a matter of evolutionary destiny.

The man who visited Satprem in Nandanam after the assault in the canyon still lives in Auroville some forty years later. We get together one afternoon and he tells me the story of that day: how he jumped on his motorcycle to go see Satprem, how Satprem sat with him in the garden, police everywhere, and told him about his narrow escape.

I ask the man, "With all due respect, what did you think? Did you believe everything?"

"I have no reason to doubt Satprem," the man says. "For me he was a great rishi. They have different experiences, different truths. I saw him that day, and I am certain that something happened. I would never doubt what he told me."

There are things that happened in those years that defy explanation. I have trouble understanding them. I struggle to reconcile them with my conception of reality, and I'm sure some of you do, too. Maybe this is a failure of imagination. *Too mental.* Who am I to doubt that there are more things in this world than fit within my limited philosophy? I'm going to try to take these stories at face value. I will tell them to you, because this is how people experienced them, and you can decide what to make of them.

"It seems we pass through one of the darker nights of Auroville's soul," writes an American diarist a few months after Diane's fall. "One feels the intensity mount and mount until one almost becomes accustomed to it, and yet everything seems shrouded as if in a cloud, concealed, eclipsed. You try to see where it goes but you cannot, you only feel the intensity mount. We think it cannot go much further but it does; we think the curve cannot continue its descent but it does."

That moment in Auroville's history. Everything in turmoil, so much disaccord, Mother's absence insistently, awfully, palpable. Throughout the community, there are exhortations for renewed faith and unity. Auroville must stand together. But as always, the very concept of unity is contested. Unity for what? Whose version of togetherness? Even as the exhortations escalate, the community's internal schisms widen, and in particular those divisions between the self-anointed Collective and the Neutrals.

The composition and size of these respective groups will never quite be clear. The Neutrals themselves claim that up to a third of Aurovilians are sympathetic to their position; the revolutionaries who dominate the Collective insist that the Neutrals represent a much smaller minority. Most people do what they can to remain unaffiliated. While many Aurovilians support the battle against the

CFY, they are also dismayed by the growing extremism of the radicals. Associating with a known Neutral can invite ostracism, public censure, and even, in certain cases, being cut off from community food supplies. An ill wind is blowing through the plateau; the majority of Aurovilians try to stay clear of the storm.

"The enemy with whom we struggled so long outside ourselves now stands within, as intangible and deceptive as our own selves," continues the American diarist, presumably referring to the Neutrals. "The force of disruption and disharmony, before so easily identifiable, now enters among us and turns us against one another. Its face is our own."

Even as these internal tensions exacerbate, the conflict between the CFY and Auroville continues. Frederick, Auroson's father, is part of a group trying to assert the community's rights over public buildings. They are focused on a complex known as the Bharat Nivas (Pavilion of India), in whose basement the CFY has set up offices. Frederick spends a night in the complex with Auroson; this is intended as a demonstration of Aurovilian control. They are awoken early in the morning by a band of around six men—the watchmen—who arrive shirtless and inebriated, armed with iron rods. While Auroson runs to get help, Frederick, still in his underwear, ties himself with ropes to a concrete column. The watchmen cut the ropes and start hitting him with their metal bars. When other Aurovilians arrive, they, too, are attacked; one man suffers serious head injuries. The watchmen slip away after a time, but someone takes dramatic photos of an injured Frederick, splayed Christlike and dabbed in blood on a stretcher. The photos go around town; people are outraged.

Of course the Matrimandir can't remain immune. It's the heart of Auroville, and soon it's at the vortex of the disharmony. The community's disagreements seep into the construction site. There are heated, ideologically tinted arguments, bitter allegations concerning fundraising and how money is being spent. Work slows to a crawl. Some people decide that the CFY should be barred from the site, and one day a bus carrying visitors from Pondicherry is blocked by a group of boisterous Aurovilians sitting on the road ("half-naked apes, jeering and shouting," as a man on the bus will later describe them). The police are summoned, and when they arrive, a woman will recall, a person from the bus asks them to fire on the Aurovilians. "I thought I was having a nightmare," the woman says. "I thought I was going mad. This literally couldn't be happening in Auroville." The police do not fire.

One evening a group of about sixty Aurovilians is gathered in a collective meditation under the Banyan Tree. They are there to peacefully protest all the disharmony. They are interrupted by three vans of armed, helmeted police, who dismount from their vehicles and jackboot in sinister formation toward the assembled group. The police swing indiscriminately with their sticks at the protesters, who huddle together tightly, emanating spiritual chants. The police pack some forty Aurovilians, including three minors, into the vans and take them to jail. Several children are left behind without their parents. An observer will later compare the scene to a "battlefield," strewn with "sandals, bags and other personal articles." Once again, as after Diane's fall, there is horror that such an event could happen at the Matrimandir.

A few days later, even as the community is still reeling, my father receives some visitors at our home in Pondicherry. A group of Aurovilians has come to tell him about those arrests under the Banyan Tree. They say that Auroville needs help, especially from sympathetic Indians, and they ask if he'll bail out the jailed people. My father has started a leather-garments business; he has a little money. So he takes a car to the town of Tindivanam, and he hires a lawyer and visits the courthouse, where he puts up bail and signs a bond of surety in front of a black-robed judge. In so doing, he makes his loyalties clear. Our family is still living in Pondicherry, and I'm still attending school there. But my parents' hearts (and, I think, their imaginations) continue to reside on the plateau.

We have kept our hut in Auroville, and we come out on weekends. My parents see their friends, and I see some of mine, including Auralice. But it's getting harder for me to relate to these kids. I guess I've become a city boy. My clothes are washed and ironed, and I always wear sandals. My friends in Auroville go around barefoot, their ankles caked in red earth and scratched by thorns. They ride ponies bareback and run shirtless through fields, and they're very independent. Mostly, they seem to have so much free time. That's because they don't go to classes anymore. Auroville's schools are yet another casualty of the revolution.

In November of 1976, Last School, that center set up near Aspiration, is shut down. The revolutionaries have decided that Auroville no longer needs education—at least formal, classroom-based education. A slogan rings out: "If you want to learn about engineering, build a road; if you want to learn astronomy, observe the stars." A few brave individuals defy the Collective and continue to offer instruction in their homes, but it's all shaky. Education in Auroville, such as it is, disperses across the plateau to a multitude of informal home schools and tutoring sessions, where attendance by students (and teachers, too) is often sporadic. This is how Auralice continues to get a semblance of schooling. She attends classes in a house near Auroson's Home, and sometimes in a hut outside Aspiration, where a Frenchman and his wife offer lessons.

Auroville's freedom is enticing, and tantalizing. But it also has its perils, and my parents, who cherish the dream but want something more solid for their son, are struggling with this dilemma. Later, many children of Auroville will have a complicated relationship to this period in the community's history. Auralice, for instance, will remember a sense of autonomy and independence, the liberating feeling of roaming the land unsupervised with her friends, and just having the space to be kids. The adults of her world care deeply for her; they adore and even venerate the children of Auroville. She will also recall a feeling of abandonment and drift and resent missing out on critical, foundational years. "No one watched over us, no one made sure we were on track," she says. "We just did what we wanted and everyone told us that's how kids should be. It was fun I guess, and I always felt like we were surrounded by a lot of love. But it was also scary. I don't think we ever fully recovered from that time."

Symbolically, Diane is very much at the heart of all this tumult. The memory of her fall is still raw, its significance increasingly evident every day the unrest continues. Physically, she's now far removed. After about three and half months in JIPMER, Diane has been shifted to the Lady Willingdon Nursing Home in Madras, in an art-deco building some one hundred miles north of Auroville, where she's under the supervision of a clean-shaven Brahmin neurologist reputed to be one of the best in India.

The neurologist is an expert on cervical fractures. He notes that Diane's paralysis has lifted from her upper body, and he hypothesizes that the continued immobility below her waist might be due to a blood clot, which could dissolve on its own. Expressing guarded optimism about the prospects for a full recovery, he prescribes vigorous massage to restore circulation, especially of her legs. He counsels a stay in the nursing home of at least two months.

John accompanies Diane to Madras. He sets himself up in a garden suite at the Queens Hotel ($5 a night, no air-conditioning), a quiet establishment within walking distance of the nursing home. He doesn't relish his time with the doctors, but as always, he's happy to be away from the strife, and city life does have its advantages. John indulges in two hot baths a day and dips into a "steak fund" set up by his father at the hotel's restaurant, O Papa Ristorante, where a long-haired band plays American jazz songs. Once a week, he travels to Auroville to check on the mail and visit Auralice. She's still bouncing between staying with Larry and various neighbors.

At least at this point, John appears unconvinced by Satprem's instructions to Diane. He hasn't lost faith in doctors; he hasn't turned away from medicine. In letters to his parents from Madras, he's allusive as ever, but he refers to "a dear friend" who had an accident, and he asks them to look out for a good neurologist. He no longer says anything to his family—or to Prudence—about returning to America, but he writes that he might take his friend to England or Switzerland to see a surgeon. He tells an Aurovilian friend that he's making inquiries with a specialist at Stoke Mandeville Hospital, one of the world's leading centers for spinal injuries, located outside the English town of Aylesbury.

After a couple of months in Madras, with no signs of improvement, Diane decides she wants to return to Auroville. The hut she and John were occupying in Kottakarai is now too rudimentary for her needs, so John speaks to a mutual friend and arranges to borrow his place, a small concrete structure with running water and electricity in the community of Certitude, near Auroson's Home. They drive down early one morning in a blue van equipped with a bed in the back. We return, John writes to a friend, "with the faith that, in the words of *Savitri*, 'All here can change if the Magician choose.' May He so choose."

Word goes out that Diane is back in Auroville, but few people are allowed to see her. She moves between a mattress on the floor in the living room and one outside, on a veranda overlooking a walled garden. Her bathroom is equipped with a stool she uses while bathing, and a makeshift toilet, which consists of a hollowed-out chair connected via rubber pipe to a metal bucket. A handful of helpers—mostly friends and former neighbors from Kottakarai—attend to her, carrying her to and from the bathroom and emptying the bucket several times a day. The helpers never see Diane undressed. She is meticulous about her personal hygiene, and she only allows them into the bathroom when she is clothed.

Amrit is one of the helpers. He comes nearly every day and applies a newly acquired knowledge of acupressure to Diane's spine, arms, and legs. Diane lies on her stomach, and Amrit is struck by the difference in texture between her upper and lower body. The former is pliable and responds to touch; her legs feel like rubber, and she doesn't react—no pleasure, no pain—no matter how hard he presses.

Satprem also comes to see Diane, and his arrivals are always something of an event. The neighbors speak of his visits; they walk over, hoping to see or talk to him. Satprem sits with Diane and reminds her that the Mother has a purpose for her, and that her body is part of the battle against the ancient routine of decay and death. He says that she must work hard to touch the light of the sun at the center of her cells; just a single cell will do. Hearing of John's plans to take Diane to Europe, he counsels against the trip, warning that he's never believed in surgery, and cautioning that she's likely to find a heavy atmosphere if she visits a hospital. In a letter to a friend, Diane says that Satprem has assured her he's making progress: "He works day and night to make the Hour come— the world's and mine."

This is still early in Diane's struggle. The outlook remains hopeful, and her faith is buoyed by Satprem's assurances and the community's expectations of an imminent transformation. There are some beautiful days in that house, moments when the world seems bathed in the radiance of all that she is going to accomplish.

She sits on the mattress on the veranda one afternoon in January, the cool of Auroville's winter rising from the land. From the kitchen she hears an attendant singing "Twinkle, Twinkle, Little Star," and the garden in front of her is alive, blossoming in the postmonsoon freshness. Diane asks the flowers— and the birds and butterflies, too—to help her emerge from her morass. She remembers a friend who used to clap and sing for roses—because, the friend would say, aren't flowers living beings, too, just like us? Right now, in this garden, with all these flowers, Diane is possessed by a conviction that the dream is at hand.

A tape recorder plays Abdul Karim Khan, the Indian classical singer whom, Diane has heard, Sri Aurobindo admired. She listens to the singer's voice and it makes her think of a thirsty child in the desert. The child is parched, yet still he refuses to drink anything but clear rainwater. She is like that child: she refuses to take the easy way out.

Of course there are moments of weakness, of fatigue and despair. Another letter to a friend: "As soon as I forget that it's all for Him things become a hopeless mess with me, a miserable bundle of human substance right in the middle of it. I can't stand people. I'm sorry but sometimes it gets too much for me."

She never leaves the house, except for rare visits to the Matrimandir. She goes with a friend at night, when she knows no one will be around. The friend arrives in a white Citroën car, lifts Diane, and places her in the front, her legs dangling over the seat. (She never talks about that; it's as if she doesn't notice those traitor legs.) She balances herself with her arms against the dashboard, leaning in as they drive to the construction site. The friend carries her up a wooden ramp, and they sit on a concrete slab in the dark. She must think of what happened here, how could she not? She can't help wondering why. Has the Mother lifted her protection from Auroville? Is something irretrievably lost? Of course not. Satprem has explained; what's lost can be regained. They never stay too long. Diane's bladder is weakened by the paralysis, and she needs to get back home. They never discuss that either.

"Do you think Satprem gave her false hope?" I ask Peter, the attendant who carried the notes between Satprem and Diane while she was in JIPMER. Peter tells me about the terrors of the hospital: the metal plates drilled into Diane's skull, the catheter in her throat, the moaning patients in the hallways and the nauseating smell everywhere of disinfectant. "The link to Satprem was the one rope that she had," Peter says. "She was clinging to it, and she was clinging to it for life. It was like a golden rope. She was caught in this wild tempest and

that was her one chance at survival. I mean, without that, what was there? Just depression—nothingness."

It's true that in these early months Satprem's interpretation of Diane's accident ennobles and thus cushions her suffering. His attention burnishes her plight. I believe that Satprem's attention does carry her through. But already, early on, there are hints of how his project for Diane will turn. Even as John makes plans to pursue treatment in the West, Diane hardens her stance against medicine. She tells someone that Satprem has said hospitals are "worse than concentration camps," and she expresses a determination to never again enter a medical facility. She refuses to countenance visiting Stoke Mandeville, in England, even when a specialist agrees to see her and John offers to cover all expenses. She insists that the yoga offers a path so that "this endless stupid game of coming and going is no longer necessary."

Diane's neurologist in Madras is a spiritual man. He believes in the divine and admires the teachings of the Mother and Sri Aurobindo. But he's familiar with Diane's condition, he's seen her X-rays, and he knows the state of her spine. His initial optimism now faded, he tells Peter that no yoga has ever healed a severed nerve. He says that Diane must understand that she will never walk again. She must face reality and get a wheelchair, move ahead with life.

So Peter arranges a wheelchair from England. He writes to some friends, and they purchase one and send it to India by plane. Peter visits Diane in Certitude one day and they sit on the veranda and he tells her about his conversation with the neurologist; he talks about the wheelchair. Diane's face tightens. "You, Peter, you of all people, you should know that's not what Satprem wants me to do," she explodes. "You know that's not my yoga, and it's not what the Mother wants for me." She asks Peter to leave at once.

Later, Diane tells another man, "I don't want to be a happy cripple."

Now that Diane is back in Auroville, Auralice visits her and John almost every day. She hitches a ride with one of Diane's attendants or walks or bicycles from Kottakarai. Diane is an affectionate, doting mother. They sit facing each other on the floor, and Diane brushes Auralice's hair, clips her nails, spoon-feeds her even when Auralice is well past the age when she can feed herself (this will continue until Auralice is almost a teenager). She micromanages her daughter's diet, always asking what she's eating in Kottakarai and reiterating a long list of prohibitions: eggs, white rice, sugar, bread, and protein, which Diane seems to have turned against because the doctors foisted it on her in the hospital.

Diane herself rotates through a number of strict diets. She experiments with fruit-and-vegetable diets, raw diets, dairy-free diets, sugarless diets, and wheat-free diets. These regimes are all in service of her personal transformation, but often she seems to be imposing her compunctions on her daughter. Auralice obeys all the rules when she's with Diane and John in Certitude. Then she goes back to Kottakarai, or to friends' homes, and she indulges in jam and chicken (on the rare occasions it's available), and sometimes she chews pink NP bubble gum, which she buys at a shack in the village. She returns to Certitude and Diane praises her for being an obedient daughter. Auralice feels guilty; she's living two lives. One time she and a friend break into a wooden cupboard and steal some hash pancakes. They both get high, and the friend, who is seven years old, falls and cuts his eye. A few adults in the community find out and they tease Auralice: "Maybe we should tell your mother what you're getting up to so you can share your experiences with her."

Diane and Auralice are sitting together one day, and Diane is trimming the bangs on her daughter's forehead. "Little froufrous," she calls the bangs, borrowing from French slang. They're chatting easily and Diane seems relaxed, but then she sees that she's made Auralice's hairline crooked and gets upset. Diane tries to remedy things by trimming the bangs farther, but now they're too short. She gets agitated and erupts, "I'm so stupid! I'm so useless and I can never get it right! I always get everything wrong!"

"It's okay, Mama, it's not a big deal," Auralice says. But Diane is crying now, she's distraught and calls herself a poor mother, and all Auralice can do is put her arm on Diane's shoulder and try to console her. "They'll grow back," Auralice says repeatedly. "Don't worry, they'll grow back." Everyone who meets Diane remarks on her steadfastness, the equanimity and commitment with which she undertakes her assignment. Auralice will always have a sense of the volcanoes that lie beneath.

Larry, Auralice's biological father, decides to go for a time to America; the financial situation in Auroville remains dire, and he needs to earn money. So Auralice starts staying the occasional night in Certitude, remaining with her neighbors in Kottakarai the rest of the time. She grows closer to John during this period. They ride around Auroville on John's bicycle, Auralice standing on the back carrier and her arms on his shoulders, her head moving left to right, right to left, like a sentinel or navigator. They go shopping in Pondicherry for groceries, or fabric for Diane, who likes to stitch dresses for Auralice and vests for John. As Diane grows increasingly reclusive, Auralice and John come to share a private world: they are coconspirators, possessing a covert knowledge of life inside their house.

John sends poetic, adoring letters about Auralice to Gillian. "She comes into the play almost exactly like you," he writes to his sister, marveling at the proximity in their birthdays. "Having the same planets in the same positions, she is much like you, which makes her, at least for me, very loveable. Curious, the patterns that the infinitely varied infinite varies."

Auralice has a necklace that breaks and she's despondent. John asks Gillian if she could find a replacement, and Gillian sends a pearl necklace that belonged to their paternal grandmother. John marvels at how naturally this family heirloom fits. "There is something of the ocean in Auralice," he writes to Gillian. "To look at her sometimes when she is off drifting is to look at wave-flecked golden shorelines on distant palm fringed deserted beaches. Indonesia? But I've never been there. . . ."

John and Auralice embark one day on a joint mission to Rameswaram. They have decided to seek Guruji's counsel on Diane's paralysis. They take the night train, emerging early in the morning on the wooden bridge above Rameswaram's clear waters. They find Guruji in the garden outside his house, and John starts explaining Diane's condition. Guruji interrupts; he says he's well acquainted with it. He tells John that he's been studying the situation, he sees scope for improvement, but he needs a day to reflect further.

This gives John and Auralice the opportunity to wander the quiet town and swim under the sun in warm ocean waters that are reputed to be holy. They eat a lunch of idlis and chapatis at a canteen crowded with loud white spiritual seekers ("ugly ill-kempt rich hip bastards," in John's uncharacteristically severe judgment), and after lunch they visit Rameswaram's main temple, where they are swamped by beggars who recognize John and run up to him as he drops extravagant sums into their bowls and bags. Bhavani, the temple elephant, blesses Auralice on the forehead with her trunk, and Auralice shrieks with pleasure. They see the elephant again later, and when the animal trumpets a greeting, John tells Auralice that elephants have prodigious memories.

They return to Guruji's house the next morning. He's in a chair on his

porch; he says he focused on Diane during his daily puja, and he thinks he's found a way. Guruji tells them he's seen that Diane has a small broken bone in her back. He warns that an operation is probably necessary (there's a 60 percent likelihood, he says), but John says Diane won't allow that. So the priest advises massage three times a day with Lakshadi, an Ayurvedic oil, and regular hot baths to stimulate the muscles. He also shares a yantra (or sacred drawing) that he says Diane should trace thirty-two times before blowing on it and placing it in water. If she does this, he says, she may be better within a year.

John tells Guruji about Satprem's attentions and says that he and Diane are considering moving to Nandanam, to be closer with Satprem. At this, Guruji flinches; he advises John to stay in Auroville. In a low voice, almost a mutter, he says that Satprem is "sly," then quickly hastens to add, twice, that Satprem is "also good." The conversation ends soon after, and John and Auralice catch their return train. But the priest's aside is an indication of another rift in the Mother's world: Satprem has turned against Guruji, too.

The roots of this rift are obscure. The two men have been close, and Satprem has often expressed admiration for the priest. But now Satprem has grown distrustful of Guruji and quotes the Mother saying that Guruji came to her in a vision, attempting to impersonate Sri Aurobindo. The Mother seemed unperturbed by the episode, but Satprem takes it more seriously, and he turns the full force of his disdain onto the priest. Perhaps, too, Satprem is upset because Guruji continues to offer guidance to members of the CFY and the Ashram. Whatever the reason, Guruji, like so many others, now finds himself pulled into a conflict he never invited.

John and Auralice return to Auroville, and soon a conviction grows among the community's radicals that Guruji's followers must sever their ties with him. Satprem tells Diane that she must stop consulting the priest. This stricture weighs heavily; John and Diane have leaned on Guruji for years. But such is the fervor of Auroville's rebellion, and such is the reverence in which John and Diane now hold Satprem, that they have no choice but to comply. They will never see Guruji again.

In June of 1977, almost a year to the month since Diane's fall, Satprem is in Paris. One morning he and an associate catch a taxi to Avenue Marceau, which runs between the posh eighth and sixteenth arrondissements. They enter a large Haussmann building and mount a spiral staircase to the wood-paneled offices of Maître Mercier, a well-known lawyer who specializes in French copyright law. The meeting has been set up by Robert Laffont, Satprem's French publisher. This is an important occasion for Satprem: he has come to ascertain his legal rights over his conversations with the Mother, and thus his ability to bring out the *Agenda*.

Mercier is a chain-smoker. He coughs his way through the meeting, listening from behind a desk as Satprem tells him that he conducted interviews with the Mother for almost two decades, and about how the contents of these interviews contain the key to a new human order. The lawyer isn't too concerned about the particulars (he has no idea who the Mother is and doesn't seem very interested), but he has good news for Satprem. Under French law, the interviewer holds copyright over the contents of an interview. Satprem is legally permitted to use his conversations with the Mother. Satprem writes a check for the lawyer and they shake hands. After leaving the office, Satprem turns triumphantly to his associate and says, *"L'Agenda est libre!"* (The *Agenda* is free!)

A few weeks later and Satprem is back in India, determined to see this project through. He secures a meeting in New Delhi with Indira Gandhi, who has been voted out of office but remains a powerful political leader. She's accompanied by her two sons, Sanjay and Rajiv, and by Rajiv's Italian wife, Sonia, whose lipstick Satprem finds conspicuous. Satprem tries to impress upon them the importance of the *Agenda* and the significance of the Mother's yoga. He comes away feeling they were responsive. Things are looking up. He even expresses an unusual optimism about Auroville, telling someone that the community is finally getting closer to the Mother's truth.

Nineteen seventy-eight marks the centenary of the Mother's birth; it's a big occasion for everyone in her world. Satprem opens the year by traveling to the Himalaya with his companion Sujata. There, in a hotel in a small town, a man in black approaches Satprem and wishes him a happy new year. The man is a representative of the Ashram and hands Satprem a letter. The Ashram has gotten wind of Satprem's plans to push ahead with the *Agenda*. The letter contains a formal expulsion notice, accusing him of "anti-Ashram activities." The man also hands Satprem a printed calendar with a quote from the Mother: "All hearts are one."

How did the man know where to find Satprem? This encounter in the Himalaya reanimates Satprem's paranoia. He's convinced that he's being tailed, and that informants are tracking his every move. He races back to Pondicherry, arriving at Nandanam at two in the morning to find that the doors and windows of his house have been nailed shut. So this is what it's come to? Outraged, Satprem compares his feelings in front of the locked house to the sensation he had upon first entering Buchenwald.

Two loyal Aurovilians are called for. They arrive on a motorcycle armed with pliers and levers, dodge a posse of policemen sent to prevent forced entry, and fiddle around until they manage to open a window. At last able to access their home, Satprem and Sujata light incense and plunge into a ritualistic scrubbing and cleaning, a two-hour exorcism.

The police come and go over the following weeks, and Satprem's anxiety mounts. He complains about poison in the air and a feeling of psychological torture. It is becoming increasingly clear to him that he can no longer stay in Nandanam. In mid-February, he and Sujata pile into an Ambassador car with an American man, and they embark on a journey through the Western Ghats, a mountain range along the border between the states of Tamil Nadu and Kerala. Some of Satprem's influential backers have offered to help fund a new home for him; he is searching for a base from which he can complete the *Agenda*.

They travel for nine days, covering more than a thousand miles, passing through small hill stations and tea-plantation towns. Satprem is dismayed by the denuded forests, the timber logging and real estate speculation that he takes as evidence of man's rapaciousness. But the air is cool and the morning mist rejuvenating, and gradually he starts to feel a sense of possibility. After many dead ends—many scams, many dilapidated, ugly homes—they find what they are looking for outside a village called Kotagiri: two tile-roofed brick-and-mortar bungalows in proximity, surrounded by eucalyptus groves, original primal forest, all set in vistas of foggy rolling hills. The buildings are old and run-down, and will need a lot of work. But Satprem feels they have a definite power. Crucially, they are also isolated, far from any neighbors or prying, spying eyes.

They visit one of the bungalows on a cold winter morning. It's a windy day but calm inside, and the building has large glass windows that offer wide views onto the plains, sixty-five hundred feet below. It sits on a promontory, and Sujata christens the place Land's End—an echo of Finistère, France's westernmost district, a Bretton region that used to be known as the end of the earth.

They meet the owner. He pulls an envelope from his pocket, containing a document to establish his title. Their eyes are drawn immediately to the twenty-five-paise stamp on the envelope; it's a special issue for the Mother's centenary. The stamp contains a smiling image of the Mother, her head covered by a bejeweled crown, like a queen. The augury is undeniable. It is from here—not Pondicherry, not Auroville—that the *Agenda* will emanate across the world and usher in a new species.

The first of what will finally be thirteen volumes of the *Agenda* comes out on February 21, 1978, Mother's one-hundredth birthday. The book is in French and printed in Paris, its cover a bright red that Satprem says is the color of divine love. A copy is hand-carried from France to India for Satprem, and he asks a man to take it to Pondicherry and place it on the Samadhi. The man enters the Ashram at sunset, unsure of the reaction he will receive. He puts a copy of the book on Sri Aurobindo's and the Mother's marble tomb and stays there meditating deeply for about half an hour, amid a throng of devotees. No one seems to notice. He goes back to Satprem's mountain retreat and reports that his mission has been successful. The man has never before seen Satprem so happy.

The *Agenda*—this first volume, and then the twelve others—percolates across the Mother's world. For many of her disciples, at least those associated with Auroville, it is a gift, a dazzling insight into her divine yoga. The *Agenda* puts everything into context, and it offers a road map to Aurovilians for their spiritual endeavors. Now they see what she was trying to do, now they understand to what end Satprem has been exhorting them. So much hinges on the success of Auroville, and thus on their revolution.

A copy of the *Agenda* makes its way to John and Diane. They pore over it, John struggling with his limited French, acquired on summer visits to Switzerland, Diane translating for him. Like many others, they are in awe of the Mother's yoga. The book also has profound personal significance for them; although it doesn't reference Diane directly, the description of cellular transformation clarifies the task Satprem has set for her. John includes an excerpt from the *Agenda* with a letter to his father.

"I have hesitated to send this to you till now because it touches upon areas which are less susceptible to description than flowers on trees or crops in fields," John writes. "Maybe it conveys to you a sense of what Auroville represents. Not on the surface, but at a deeper level." In passing, as if to find common ground, he asks about Jimmy Carter (who has been elected president in 1976). John says he doesn't get much information about American politics anymore, but he's happy that Carter seems friendly to third world countries. He adds that Carter "has taken India by storm," and that people come up to him in the markets of Pondicherry and shake his hand and congratulate him for being American.

It's not clear if Walker Sr. ever reads the excerpt. He has recently written his own book, a collection of essays about the rich donors and collectors he cultivated during his time at the National Gallery, and he's been on a publicity tour of the United States. He's preoccupied with what he takes to be the insufficient marketing efforts of his publisher, and unhappy with the leathery chicken he's been forced to endure on the circuit. He writes a note to his son saying he's heard about the conflict in Auroville, perhaps through Prudence or Gillian, and he's concerned and offers to pay for a ticket out of India.

John writes with the tale of a holy man who could break his body apart and leave pieces in different parts of the room. "I am much like that but cover a bigger area," he says, explaining that their "untogether son" is with his parents in spirit but must remain in South India, with Diane, for what he increasingly believes is his calling in life. "The work that I do, the life that I lead, are deeply significant to me," he writes. "That I can be in India is for me a grace for which I am deeply grateful. I love this land, and I refuse to formulate or project any circumstances under which [leaving] would be necessary. The future, I repeat, I leave to the Lord. So, please, stop worrying. You have done well to have a child so well placed—believe me."

EMISSARIES

"FORGIVE ME FOR NOT WRITING in so long," begins another correspondence from John during this time, addressed to his parents at Fishers Island. "Letters have been started but abandoned as words failed and time has passed without my knowing. I would love to be with you at Fishers but at the present I must remain here with Diane. She shows slow signs of recovery but it is a very long process.

"Auroville is at the moment in a peculiar state of unrest," he continues. "We are trying to throw off the yoke of our overseers, weld some sort of harmony, but the divisions grow deeper, which is saddening. Emissaries have gone to Delhi hoping that the government would intercede on our behalf."

In the summer of 1978, an Aurovilian man named Michiel, one of John's aforementioned emissaries, is planning a visit to his parents in Austria. Michiel is in his midtwenties, and he's been living in Auroville for around five years. He hasn't seen his family in that time, and he's looking forward to visiting them and being back in his hometown. He stops by the office of a travel agent in Pondicherry and books an Air India flight out of Bombay.

A few weeks before Michiel is scheduled to leave, he receives a letter from the airline, saying there's going to be a VIP on the plane and they need more information about him for security purposes. When Michiel gets on the plane in Bombay, he sees that the VIP is Morarji Desai, India's recently elected prime minister. Desai, who defeated Indira Gandhi in 1977 to form India's first non–Congress Party government, likes to show that he's a man of the people. He flies commercial, albeit in business class.

Once in the air, Michiel corrals a member of Desai's retinue. He hands him a note for the prime minister, explaining the difficulties in Auroville and asking if Desai would be willing to discuss them. The plane makes an unscheduled stop in Tehran, where Desai disembarks into a helicopter and heads for meetings while the passengers wait. (In his efforts to prove he's a man of the people, Desai adds three unscheduled stops, and at least seven hours, to the original itinerary.) Shortly after the plane takes off from Tehran, the man from Desai's retinue steps back into economy class and signals to Michiel that the prime minister is ready to see him. Michiel makes his way to the front of the plane, where he finds the octogenarian Desai in a window seat in the first row. He's hunched over an article about himself in *Illustrated Weekly*, a newsmagazine. Atal Bihari Vajpayee, the minister of external affairs, who will later also be prime minister, is seated across the aisle.

Desai invites Michiel to take an empty seat by his side and launches into a series of disquisitions about spirituality, its various paths and manifestations. Eventually, the conversation turns to Auroville, and Michiel tells Desai about the ongoing conflict and asks if a group of Aurovilians could visit Delhi to present their case. "Yes, come," the prime minister answers in a gravelly voice.

A few months later, Michiel, along with four other emissaries from Auroville, alights from a taxi in front of the imposing Indo-Saracenic façade of Delhi's Secretariat Building, which houses the office of the prime minister. They have arrived without appointment; security is lax, and they make their way unhindered to the prime minister's outer office, where an aide is confounded by their unannounced arrival. "Do you think you can just show up and see the prime minister of India without an appointment?" he asks. Michiel tells the aide about his encounter with the prime minister on the plane, how Desai invited him, and finally, after a wait of about five hours, the Aurovilians are led into a massive wood-paneled office and seated at a desk. The prime minister, looking tired and all of his eighty-two years, is on the other side.

One of the Aurovilians, an American man, begins to describe Auroville and its goals and achievements. He tells Desai that hundreds of foreigners have left behind their lives and countries to "help India." At this, the prime minister shakes off his somnolence and rises from his chair. "India does not need any help!" he says loudly. Another emissary—one of two Indians among the delegation—will recall feeling a sense of relief at this sign of a pulse in his country's highest elected official.

Things settle down after this inauspicious start, and the prime minister gives his visitors a patient hearing. Along the way, he detours into one of his favorite themes, extolling the virtues of drinking one's own urine. This is a recurring preoccupation for Desai, who regularly praises the health benefits of this daily therapy to diplomats and audiences around the world (including, on a state visit to the United States, to a bemused Dan Rather on *60 Minutes*). The Aurovilians nod politely and steer the discussion back to their community. Desai promises that he will look into their concerns. He adds that he doesn't have much hope for their project, given that their "leader" is dead. But he concludes the meeting with this optimistic statement: "India is a vast country, and if four-hundred-odd people from many countries have assembled to pursue some spiritual goal, it can be accommodated. Such people should not be harassed."

The conflict is now multifronted. It continues in the courts and is ongoing in the trenches, the forests and canyons of Auroville. Increasingly, it is also being fought in the corridors of power—in New Delhi, Madras, Calcutta, Bombay, and other Indian cities. News of Auroville's upheavals has filtered into the national media. Bureaucrats and politicians are asking questions. This is no longer a matter for just provincial administrators and police officials.

The CFY would appear to have the decided advantage on this new front. But the raggedy and mostly impoverished Aurovilians will prove themselves surprisingly adept in the battle for political support. Sometimes, as in the meeting with Desai, their tactics are a little guerrilla. A more organized campaign is also underway, and Satprem is in the thick of it. From his redoubt in the hills, he sends letters and telegrams to his powerful friends, whom he's brought over to the twin causes of Auroville and the *Agenda*. These include JRD Tata, one of India's leading industrialists, and Sir CPN Singh, an influential diplomat and the governor of Uttar Pradesh, India's most populous state. A couple of years into the revolution, a sense builds that the tide could be turning; Aurovilians may not be quite so helpless after all.

But even as the battle marches on, appears to be heading toward some as-yet-indecipherable denouement, it suffers a crisis of identity. Revolutions always struggle to move beyond the nihilism of pure negation. Alexis de Tocqueville, the French writer and diplomat, compared them to novels: the hardest part is scripting an ending. So it is now in Auroville, where what began as a spontaneous, inchoate mutiny, an uprising *against* the CFY, must strive to articulate a positive vision *for* change. It turns out that rejection (saying what Auroville is not) was the easy part; the community must define what it wants to be.

Uncertainty breeds extremism. There is a default to purity. A purgatorial movement gathers steam. During the late 1970s and early 1980s, that incipient streak of radicalism in the community—Satprem's belief in a "schismatic" truth—hardens. Auroville's extremist faction gains new ascendancy, and it wields a determination to break through what it takes to be a crust of conventionality and complacency that has accumulated since the Mother's death. Education, medicine, money, marriage: anything with a whiff of the old, of ordinary humanness, is now suspect and deemed superfluous. A decade or so into its existence, Auroville undergoes its version of a cultural revolution.

A DEFENSIVE CROUCH

JOHN TELLS A STORY TO a friend during Auroville's cultural revolution. He says that a few years earlier, when the conflict was just beginning, he took a trip to New Delhi. While there, he met with Daniel Patrick Moynihan, the American ambassador to India. Moynihan is a towering political and diplomatic figure, a former adviser to presidents Kennedy and Johnson, now back in the United States as a senator representing the state of New York. He's also an acquaintance of John's father's; it's possible he and John know each other.

In John's telling, he found himself alone with Moynihan in a room at the American embassy, a modernist edifice in the diplomatic quarter of the capital. Moynihan asked John where he was living and what he was doing these days. John mentioned Auroville, and Moynihan's face dropped. He went silent. He pulled a file out of a drawer, placed it on the table between them, and left the room. The file contained documents on a secret American government program to feed LSD to people in Auroville. John tells his friend that the CIA has been running an experiment in the community.

"I guess that's what's going on in Aspiration," John says, raising his eyebrows. "That explains the craziness down there; that's what we're going through." The friend isn't sure if John is serious or joking. Either way, the story provides some indication of what John thinks about the direction Auroville's revolution is taking.

As always, the center of action is Aspiration. It is from there, in the community kitchen, below the thatch roof and under those watchful portraits of the Mother and Sri Aurobindo, that the new, increasingly radical phase of the revolution unfurls. Plans are hatched, traitors are denounced, and visions of a reinvigorated Auroville are summoned. The language is lofty, often abstract. It's little surprise that it seems to draw from the idiom (and, occasionally, demagoguery) of the French Revolution.

"One by one, we break down the walls, we crush our imbecilities and our egos which separate us," writes a French resident of Aspiration. "We eliminate our conditionings and our traditions which imprison us. With blows of laughter, with block blows of mockery and smiles, with even blows of conflict and bitterness, we come closer . . . together. We get down to the core of it. To the marvelous lake where we are already ONE. Ineluctably ONE. Cell by cell."

Sometimes the results of all this zeal are comical. For a time the residents of Aspiration decide that politeness, ordinary civility, must be discarded. Men and women refuse to greet or thank each other. "Please" and "You're welcome" are rejected as artifacts. Other initiatives tread a fine line between the farcical and sinister. A head-shaving movement gains popularity. Men and women (they will eventually number around ninety-five) sit on stools outdoors in Aspiration, accompanied by groups of laughing, jovial friends. Their heads are lathered up and shorn with a razor. For some, this is a gesture of solidarity, a physical mark of togetherness—like a badge of the revolution. Others find the whole thing creepy. It summons images of fascism, and they feel coerced into joining.

One morning a Frenchman named Jean is walking along a dirt path in Aspiration. He's a teacher, one of the courageous Aurovilians who keeps offering

classes out of his home. He's carrying a vial of homeopathic medicine, and he's making his way to a young man who lies writhing in a nearby hut with a painful boil. Three men, also French, step onto the path. "Where are you going?" they ask Jean, blocking his way. *"Ç'est finis"* (It's over), one of the men says. *"Ça suffit avec ton trip d'écoles, de médecins, et de couples"* (That's enough of your trip of schools, doctors, and couples). *"Ç'est finis,"* they repeat.

Jean recognizes these men as stalwarts of the revolution; he's unimpressed by their threats. He pushes them aside and treats the young man, and after a couple of hours the boil bursts and the pus oozes out. Later, Jean is denounced at a community meeting. People say he lacks loyalty to the Collective; one man accuses him of practicing "black magic." This is the type of language Aurovilians now use on each other.

"We were a little bit like the Taliban," one of Aspiration's revolutionaries will say years later. He tells me about marching through communities with his comrades, targeting those they considered impure or insufficiently committed. "Anyone who didn't agree with us, we crushed," he says. "I was young and ignorant; I was against things and I didn't know why. To be honest, I didn't know what I was doing. I was part of the Taliban simply because that's what was in the atmosphere at the time."

One of the first officially recognized victims of China's Cultural Revolution was a teacher. On August 5, 1966, a group of tenth graders at the Beijing Normal University Girls High School, in the heart of the Chinese capital, began violently attacking their instructors. They were responding to demands by the Party leadership for a "thorough criticism of academia, educators, journalists, artists, publishers, and other representatives of the capitalist class."

The students seized a group of five teachers, sprayed ink on them, hung boards marked with red *X*'s on their necks, threw boiling water over them, and hit them using nail-spiked clubs. They accused the teachers of being "counterrevolutionary revisionists." After several hours of torture, Bian Zhongyun, the school's first vice principal, passed out and was thrown into the girls' bathroom. She was later taken in a garbage cart to a hospital across the street and, at the age of fifty, declared dead. She was the first of around one hundred teachers killed that month in just the western part of Beijing. Millions died in the following decade of terror. This was all in the name, to quote a popular revolutionary slogan, of "eliminating the four olds": old ideas, old culture, old customs, old habits.

Of course things never get quite so bad in Auroville. Nonetheless, one of the main arenas of conflict during the community's cultural revolution is in education. After Last School ceases operation, pressure builds on individuals such as Jean to shut down their home schools and "liberate" children. Jean and his wife have set up a blackboard and some tables and chairs in a large thatch hut outside their home, in the community of Douceur (sweetness). Seven or eight children come regularly for classes—mathematics, French, a little science—and a handful attend more sporadically; Auralice is in this latter category. When the radicals come by and ask Jean to shut down his school, he tells them, not politely, to get lost. He simply doesn't understand how Auroville can be built if its children don't learn basic skills.

Pressure builds on children, too. Some of Jean's students are forced to hide their books and pencil cases under their T-shirts as they go to his house in the mornings. This is particularly true for children who must pass through Aspiration; Auralice, who comes from the relatively relaxed atmosphere of Kottakarai, doesn't encounter as much opposition. But one day a friend of hers is stopped by a group outside the Aspiration kitchen. They mock the friend and say she's wasting her time, and they try to get her to stop going to Jean's classes. She asks them, "You people know how to read and write, you know mathematics. How is it fine for you to know but not for us?" A revolutionary answers, "That's all part of the old world, it's a mental construction. You won't need any of it in the new world."

Jean is in his forties. He's older than many of the radicals, and he's seen more. His home was occupied during the Second World War, his mother was killed by a soldier, and he remembers watching newsreels in which Nazis burned books and Goebbels railed against old culture. As the temperature of Auroville's revolution rises, he starts having a horrible feeling of déjà vu. "*Putain, on ne va pas revisiter ça!*" (Damn, we're not going to relive that!), he thinks to himself. One morning, sensing that something is about to happen, he pushes a rusty metal wheelbarrow to the buildings that formerly housed Last School. He enters the library, where some four thousand books lie unattended on curved shelves, and he removes around fifty, piling them into his wheelbarrow and taking them home.

A few days later, a handful of Aurovilians are sitting around a table in the Aspiration kitchen. Their conversation turns to education, and then to Last School and its library. The problem, someone says, is that we remain stuck with a foot in the old world; maybe those books are the shackles that bind us to history. Soon a group of about twenty-five is making its way along the narrow path that leads to Last School. They enter the library and start pulling books off the shelves. They throw the books outside, pile them into an empty concrete pond near the school's entrance. Someone lights a match. A bonfire. A cleansing fire.

The flames quickly gather momentum, climbing to around ten feet. A man remarks that these books are good kindling indeed. Everyone is cracking jokes; the mood is cheerful and bantering, but the intensity rises, reaching what some participants will later describe as a frenzy. People are sweating as they run in and out of the library, occasionally bumping into one another. Books are pulled off shelves without reason or method, their fate decided haphazardly. Sometimes a book gets saved at the last moment when a participant offers to adopt it. In this way, many of the comics—Astérix, Tintin—are rescued, as are a few science-fiction titles.

Victor Hugo, a paragon of the French establishment (perhaps they've been force-fed him in high school), is consigned to the flames. A woman picks up a novel she's read about a kid in New York; she remembers that the kid was miserable, had such a hard life, and she hated the book. So she tosses the book into the fire. Works by members of the Ashram, and most having to do with philosophy or sociology, are also condemned. Religion is mercilessly culled. A woman finds herself holding a leatherbound Bible; it's an elegant edition and she wonders if she should burn it. Soon it, too, crackles.

This goes on for a few hours; about four hundred books are burned. Evening arrives and cinders rise golden into the advancing darkness. The flames die out, and the group returns to their homes. One of them lives next to Jean, who's been standing outside his hut watching smoke on the horizon. When Jean sees his neighbor, he rushes over and confronts him, maybe grabs him by the collar. The neighbor is also in his forties; he, too, has experienced the war. "How could you be so stupid?" Jeans asks him. "The others are just kids, they don't know what they're doing. But you've lived through so much, you understand the symbolism of this. How could you do it?" The neighbor seems sheepish; he knows what he's been part of. Then he turns defiant. "We had to do something," he says. "Action is better than inaction."

Some of the worst actions are against the Neutrals. During this phase of the revolution, the Collective's antipathy toward the Neutrals descends into out-

right vilification, even cruelty. Auroville's radicals are unsparing of moderation and any attempt to stay outside the fray. One teenage daughter of a Neutral is told to stop playing tennis on community courts unless she's willing to renounce her father. She protests and says she wants nothing to do with these adult quarrels; she doesn't even understand them. An American man explains the situation to her: "You see, it's like a game of basketball. One side has to win, and one side has to lose. You have to choose sides; there's no option to stay in the middle."

A determination grows to evict Neutrals from Auroville land. The battle for territory, until now directed against the CFY, has turned inward. One morning Amrit is sitting in his house in Certitude. By now, he's gone from being a key protagonist of the revolution—the person whose visa problems provided one of the earliest sparks—to a public villain accused of siding with the CFY. Amrit is on a cane mat on the floor of his meditation room, a small red-tiled chamber lit by a single bulb. His eyes are closed and he's singing devotional chants. He hears voices from outside. As the voices grow louder, Amrit realizes that a mob—he will later reckon its size at about one hundred—has come for him. Someone tries to open the locked door of his house. "You

don't have to come out," a man says, "but I'm telling you that the community has decided you have no place in Auroville and you have to go. We will come here every day until you leave."

Amrit feels the hatred of the mob; he knows that he's helpless against so many, and he remains sitting in meditation, without a word. His refusal to respond seems to exasperate the intruders, who start banging on his windows. They smash a few plant pots, breaking the fired clay against the veranda. A chant goes up: "Howard, coward! Howard, coward!" Still, Amrit—who has only recently changed his name from Howard—refuses to open his eyes.

The mob seems disoriented by Amrit's silent resistance, and it dissipates. They come back the next day and start repeating their demands that he leave Auroville. Amrit is meditating again, but this time he responds. "I'm here because the Mother put me here, and the only way you will get rid of me is by dragging out my dead body," he calls from his room. One member of the mob shouts, "He's a suicide freak, he wants to kill himself!" Another says, "Yes, do it, do it, you're better off!"

After a while this group, too, departs, moves on to the homes of other Neutrals. But Amrit is left shaken, and searching for a way to register his indignation. He thinks of Buddhist monks in Vietnam who self-immolated to protest the war. He knows that the Mother was against suicide, but he believes she would be less disapproving about the Japanese tradition of hara-kiri, which is committed not out of despair but in a spirit of self-sacrifice. He goes to the house of a friend, another Neutral, and asks for a bottle of petrol. He returns home and lays out his only kimono, a mottled blue-and-white one he bought in Japan. He composes notes for his family, and letters to newspaper editors, explaining the situation in Auroville; he wants the world to know. Then, at the last moment, he has a thought: Killing himself would only give the fanatics what they want. Amrit's stubbornness kicks in. He will remain in Auroville, a proud, defiant Neutral.

Years later, Amrit speaks to two of the people who were in the mob. They're his neighbors now, and they've undergone a measure of reconciliation. Amrit mentions the day they showed up at his house and tried to throw him out. They say they don't remember; they insist they weren't there. "You know what probably happened," one of the neighbors finally says. "We probably don't remember because sometimes when people do things like that, they aren't really themselves. It wasn't really us at your house that day."

Everyone struggles to locate their true selves on this fractured landscape; everyone must orient themselves, determine where they stand and what they stand for. Most Aurovilians, it should be said, are not radicalized. The outbreaks of extremism are more sporadic than systematic, generally confined to a fringe (though highly vocal) contingent. The majority of the community tries to get on with life: planting, digging, baking, raising children, nurturing the Mother's dream. But civil wars are all-consuming. One man will later compare Auroville during this period to Vichy France: life is a series of delicate moral negotiations and compromises, the imperatives of personal survival (or at least social viability) pitted against the urge to do what's right. This man will paraphrase Edmund Burke's famous dictum that all that's necessary for the triumph of evil is for good people to do nothing.

On a sheet of yellow paper, John scribbles his prescription for the times.

"Read Sri Aurobindo," he writes, in what appear to be notes for an essay, or perhaps talking points for one of the community's ubiquitous meetings. "Were everyone here to pledge in all seriousness to spend an hour a day, or if not possible, half an hour, to read Sri Aurobindo, in one month Auroville would have moved further forward than it has in ten years. This is the solution for all of Auroville's problems." It's a naïve proposal, so like John in its guilelessness. But it sums up his—and Diane's—response to the state of affairs. This is how they navigate their Vichy: faced with an aggression and malice that are entirely alien to their nature, they retreat to fundamentals.

They are living in a new house. The friend who lent them his place near Auroson's Home needed it back, so they've gone to the community of Slancio ("run" or "jump" in Italian), where they're now staying in another borrowed home. It's larger than the last one, with a pond and a planted inner courtyard, and an upstairs loft where Auralice hangs out and plays with a white rabbit with pink eyes named Nijntje. The rabbit is eaten by a mongoose and Auralice is distraught. John and Diane console her; they say that the mongoose had a good meal, and these are the ways of the world.

They aren't political. John and Diane's engagement with the revolution is characterized by evasion and deflection, a turning away rather than an overt rejection. They go further inward during these troubled times, toward an extreme privacy and a hermetic seclusion. One by one, Diane rejects all her attendants, until only John remains. She never leaves the house anymore, and she won't allow visitors. When John goes out, he mostly avoids people, often looking right through acquaintances. Somehow, somewhere along the way, he has shed his initial ambivalence about Satprem's dictates. Now when John gets sick, he, too, refuses to see a doctor. He has infections on his legs but won't consider antibiotics. He has lingering stomach ailments and he's losing weight, but he won't take medicine for what's presumably the usual Aurovilian parasitical infestation.

Two friends visit John from America. One of them, Judith, is the artist who first told him about Robert Lawlor and Auroville, at Le Pavillon, in New York. Judith and Bob arrive in Pondicherry, and they aren't sure how to find

John. But they know the man, know his tastes, and so they stop by an expensive antique store. Sure enough, the shop owner directs them. They take a taxi out to Auroville, and John meets them outside the house; he speaks to his friends for a while, but he won't invite them in. He says Diane doesn't want to have anything to do with the past, and he gives an impression of feeling the same.

Judith and Bob go back to New York concerned; they think John seems depressed. I have no doubt that he is, and Diane, too. They have much cause. But I think of their increasing seclusion as a kind of defensive crouch. The psychological pressures of the moment are immense, and John and Diane persevere by clinging ever more tightly to the one thing they know is true: their yoga. I can't help wondering if events could have played out differently, if they might not have withdrawn so much from life, and ultimately reality, in a less charged atmosphere. Then again, their fate was probably charted when Diane fell—or at least when Satprem wrote his open letter about the fall, thrusting them into the maelstrom of Auroville's conflict.

Satprem is in the hills. He's settled into Land's End, his colonial bungalow with views onto a foggy promontory. A small group of associates, many of them former Aurovilians, works with him to publish the *Agenda* and live in the neighboring bungalow, which they call Happywood. He goes for walks in the forests, long meanders among the mimosa and eucalyptus, where he sees barking deer, bison, and giant Malabar squirrels that leap as if flying from tree to tree. He has a favorite rock in a swampy clearing, and he sits on it and smokes Charminar cigarettes. He's always dressed in blue; it's the color of his beloved ocean and also, he says, the color of someone doing deep inner yoga. Satprem is working on his own transformation now, trying to push forward the cellular process initiated by the Mother.

He writes—a lot: books, diary entries, and especially letters. Satprem writes many letters. He sits at a wrought-iron table covered with a thick cement slab, and he writes from morning to evening with a blue pen that he keeps in a gold box. Some of his letters go out to the notables whose support he's been culti-vating. He writes to the industrialist JRD Tata about a corruption and darkness trying to prevent the Mother's new world. He writes to Indira Gandhi, warn-ing that his enemies are capable of anything, that his own life is in danger, and asking her to use her influence to protect the *Agenda*. In another letter, Satprem admonishes CPN Singh, the governor of Uttar Pradesh, for spending too much time on religious riots, natural disasters, and visits of international diplomats. Those are but minor swells in the currents of time; Satprem assures Singh that the *Agenda* will truly register on history.

Much of Satprem's correspondence flows to Auroville, too, in the form of open letters or notes to individuals. In this way, he keeps abreast of the conflagration he helped ignite. Satprem's responsibility for the excesses of the revolution will subsequently be a matter of considerable debate. At times he appears noncommittal, like an indulgent uncle who understands without explicitly condoning. Satprem refers to the book burning as a "*débordement*" (overflow), adding that youth must have its fling. On other subjects, notably the Neutrals, he is unequivocal. Ever the Manichaean, he denounces the Neutrals as CFY agents and traitors and, in one particularly scathing letter, "slugs who sided with neither one nor the other [and] left their trail of sticky and spiritual slime to embellish the situation."

Among the Aurovilians Satprem writes to is Diane, although his corre-spondence with her has become more sporadic. She continues to seek his guidance, asking repeatedly for his estimation of when the Hour might finally arrive. She beseeches Satprem for a word and wonders why that stream of notes that so sustained her has run thin. But Satprem's attention is elsewhere now; he has bigger battles. He writes to Diane patiently, as to a child, that he's very busy, that the work—the Work—is demanding. Speaking one day to an associate, Satprem adds another explanation. He says he's changed his mind about Diane. He's come around to the view that her body may not, in fact, be a fit vehicle for the transformation. The associate will remember the tone in Satprem's voice when he says that. He sounds disappointed, a little annoyed. Satprem seems to feel that Diane hasn't been receptive enough.

Satprem has asked Diane to share her dreams with him, and she continues to do so, even as his correspondence dwindles. There is one that she writes down, but that I suspect she never shares. In her dream, Diane finds herself with Guruji—whose company Satprem has interdicted—and she gives him a red lungi. The priest puts the lungi on, and Diane looks upon him and thinks he's very handsome: youthful, his skin smooth, his hair golden. Guruji offers to initiate Diane into his sacred knowledge. She agrees enthusiastically, pointing at her heart and saying that's where she keeps the Mother. Guruji sits on the ground in front of her and says, "We start now." He takes Diane's right hand and starts kissing it passionately, running it over his face as he proclaims, "Shakti! Shakti!" (an expression of feminine power). Diane takes her hand to Guruji's eyes and scratches at them roughly, not angrily but ardently. This feels good, a release. But then all of a sudden a man standing by the priest—perhaps a student or a disciple—screams, "She has been influenced by Satprem!" Guruji abruptly ceases his initiation, and he pushes Diane's hand away. She is unhappy, but also relieved. When she awakens in the morning, she's tired.

219

At 10:50 p.m. on the night of December 8, 1980, Gillian Walker is in her apartment at the Dakota. She's just returned from a long day at the office of her family therapy practice when she hears ten shots outside. Someone got killed, she thinks to herself. A friend telephones to say she heard on the radio that John Lennon was assassinated; the assassin fired five bullets. "No," Gillian says, "it was ten, I heard it clearly." Later, she finds out that she heard an echo for each shot; Lennon was killed in the stone foyer entrance to the building.

Over the following days, the area around the Dakota is filled with grieving fans. They congregate in the park, in an area that will come to be known as Strawberry Fields, and they crowd the streets, crying and singing. Their songs filter into Gillian and Albert's apartment. People's minds turn to family at times such as these, and Gillian broods over her brother's absence. She's heard reports from Judith and Bob about John and Diane's growing isolation, and she's convinced that they're into something bizarre. She believes that her brother is stuck in India against his will, that Diane has ensnared John by appealing to his sense of responsibility and decency. Gillian even imagines that Diane threw herself intentionally from the Matrimandir to keep John from leaving.

She writes a letter to John in which she accuses him of trying to be a saint. Later, she will characterize this letter as manipulative. She tells her brother to stop playing the martyr and return to where he belongs. John writes back quickly, his tone jocular but also emphatic. "I look after Diane because I love her, get satisfaction from doing it, and owe her much," he writes. "If I were anywhere toward saintliness—an admittedly respectable family traditional ambition—then I would be at the bedside of someone I didn't like, which surely must be the case of you and some of your patients."

If there's a silver lining to their seclusion, it's in their growing closeness. Gillian is right that John and Diane are cut off, but they are not alone. After all the restlessness—Diane's flirtations, John's wanderings and notions of returning to America—they are living together. Auralice, now eight years old, has stopped sleeping at the neighbors' and has moved in with them, too. For the first time since Diane's accident, they are family again—a very particular kind of family, no doubt, but nonetheless family.

John adopts a new name. Henceforth, he writes to his baffled parents, he will go by Janaka. He says this is his "Indian name," and with them he continues to sign off as John. He gives a whimsical explanation for the change. As he rides around the area on his bicycle, he says, Tamil children call out, "John Walker, John Walker." Mangled by their accents, it comes out as "Janaka, Janaka." He's always had a thing for wordplay.

But there's more to this new name. In Hindu mythology, Janaka is the name of an ancient king. The king is childless and implores the gods for a baby. One day, while plowing the fields, he comes across an earthen casket, and he opens it to find a girl—"a radiant baby, a child of the earth," in John's description to his parents. The king adopts the girl, names her Sita, and brings her up as a princess. When she's older, he marries her in a lavish ceremony to Rama, one of the most revered figures in the Hindu pantheon. "Great was the rejoicing," John writes to his parents. "Let's hope the story comes true."

One morning Auralice goes out to meet some friends and she develops a fever. She comes back home early, but the door is locked. "Mama," she calls from outside. "Mama, I'm sick." Diane is alone upstairs and she can't reach the door. John has gone out, to run an errand he's said, and he's been gone for hours. As time extends, Auralice sick outside and Diane stuck inside, Diane gets more and more worked up. She starts screaming from her mattress, telling Auralice not to worry, that John will be back soon. She keeps reassuring Auralice, but the way she repeats herself, and the urgency in her voice, betray her own anxiety. Auralice sits on the ground and rests, patiently waiting.

Finally John returns, sweating on his bicycle, and Diane screams at him, "Where were you? Where *were* you?" He unlocks the door and lets Auralice in. He goes upstairs and assuages Diane, then he comes down and makes sure

Auralice is all right and he starts cooking. That night, over dinner, they come up with a plan: henceforth, Diane will always have a key, attached to a rope so she can throw it out the window. Order is restored. But Auralice is reminded of the volcanoes under Diane's calm exterior—and she's left, too, with an awareness of her mother's reliance on John, and of the way their lives are now so tightly bound. This relationship is nurturing, but it's also a fragile codependence; a blow to one could fell them both.

Some of the revolutionaries start saying John is a Neutral. They know he still has friends in the Ashram and Pondicherry, and there's his past association with Guruji (even though he and Diane have stopped visiting Rameswaram). Mostly, John lacks the right temperament. He's too nuanced for the times—"wishy-washy," as a man who suspects John's allegiances will later put it to me.

One day John stops by the office of an Aurovilian Frenchman who works as a contractor. He wants the contractor's help, maybe to fix a leaking roof or a cracked wall. But the contractor doesn't like John's "vibration." He feels there's an air to John, a certain darkness, and that John is clearly "not on the side of the divine." The Frenchman recoils from this negative energy and wants nothing to do with John. Later he tells me, "John was a man who knew he had a force, and he was willing to use it. I was very aware that he had a definite power." The contractor adds that he thought of John as a "kind of male witch."

John is spared the worst of the treatment meted out to Neutrals—no violence, no efforts to force him from Auroville. Partly, this is no doubt because of his association with Diane: her revolutionary credentials are impeccable. But another Frenchman, also one of the radicals, will later suggest an additional reason. He tells me about a time he was having serious financial difficulties. He saw John cycling around, and John asked what was wrong. When the man told him, John pulled five thousand rupees out of his bag and handed it over—"just like that," the man says, "he called it 'the Mother's gift.'" So, I ask the man, was

John a noble Neutral? He replies indignantly that there's no such thing. Still, it's hard to entirely vilify a person when you're taking his money.

I have always distrusted radicals and revolutionaries, never had much patience for wide-eyed schemes that aim at sudden rupture or dramatic transformation. Growing up in utopia is a good way to make you an incrementalist. It's not so much that the utopian ambition inevitably fails; we all have dreams that refuse to materialize. The problem is that utopia is so often shot through with the worst forms of callousness and cruelty. Human beings—individuals, families—are mere sideshows in the quest for a perfect world; they are sacrificed at the altar of ideals. Robespierre said that you have to break some eggs to make an omelet. Mao warned that a revolution was not a dinner party. These were hard, hard-hearted men. Maybe I'm too soft, but I feel that I've seen these maxims in action. I've lived them, and I could never subscribe to them.

It's the early 1980s, and I'm nine or ten years old. I'm playing with a couple of friends in the sports ground at Certitude. My family—now including a younger brother named Vikas—still lives in Pondicherry, but we no longer have our hut on the plateau. A group of radicals came by one day and told my parents we'd have to give it up unless we planned to live full-time on the land. "We don't need your Pondicherry boots stomping all over us," one Frenchman said to my father.

Still, we keep driving out, maintaining our connections, and on this day I'm bouncing a ball against a wall with my friends, and we're exchanging stories about girls, and I'm complaining about how much homework I get at school. My Aurovilian friends' lives don't include homework, and I envy them for that.

Two people walk by, down a path bordered by eucalyptus trees. One is an elderly Indian man dressed in flowing white robes, the other a younger white man in shorts, with a tightly cropped beard. We recognize these men; the adults of our world call them Neutrals. We stop bouncing the ball and we follow them. We trail for a while, snickering, hesitant at first, and then as they leave the sports ground, into the open, we grow bolder and start catcalling. We shout their names in mocking, scornful voices; we run up until we're right behind them, and when they turn around, we retreat, sneering and jeering. We get some twigs and throw them at the men, and pebbles, too. Sometimes they look at us over their shoulders, but they keep going. They seem to hope that if they ignore us, we'll disperse.

Finally, the younger man in shorts turns around. "Why are you doing this to us?" he asks one of my friends, in a loud voice. There's rage in his question, but also pain. "Why are you doing this? I've known you since you were this small and pissing in your pants," he says, holding his palm down facing the road, as if to indicate the height of an infant. This really gets us going. We start laughing hysterically, whooping and shrieking. We take so much pleasure in the discomfort of these men.

It's an ugly scene, and whenever I think of it now, when I consider my role, I feel deeply ashamed. They were Neutrals, and we were bullies. I'm not trying to absolve myself of any responsibility, but I do wonder: What was it in our world, in the ethical context our adults painted for us, that made it seem acceptable to chase these men like prey down a dirt path, as the sun set behind the eucalyptus and over Auroville's red land? What happened to the moral compass of my town, this inspired, idealized project dedicated to human unity?

Decades later I meet the man with the tightly cropped beard. I ask him if we can get together to speak for this book, and he invites me to his house. He serves me tea and shares his memories; his cat sits in my lap and she scratches and draws blood. We talk for a couple of hours, and when we're almost done, I tell him there's something I want to share. I say I haven't been able to look him in the eye for years. I speak of my shame, and of my need to apologize.

The man looks puzzled; he doesn't remember. I remind him about the time we chased him, and still he doesn't remember. He laughs, though it's a tight, mirthless laugh. "There was so much of that," he says, and he looks away from me, as if into the distance. "I can't possibly remember it all."

He tells me of neighbors who spat at him, of people marching into his home at night and demanding he leave town. He describes a steady whittling away of his rights as an Aurovilian—his food, his water, his laundry, his ability to visit public places such as the Matrimandir. "To tell you the truth, I started seeing myself a little like a Jew in Nazi Germany," he says. "I was anxious about my safety, worried all the time that they would come for me. I started sleeping with a knife under my pillow. They took everything; I told them that the only thing missing was a Star of David.

"So no," he says. "I don't recall that day. It's all a bit of a haze." We shake hands as I leave, and now when I see the man around town, we nod at each other, sometimes we exchange greetings, and I find it easier to look him in the eye.

"We were young and beautiful and we had so much energy," Joss, an Australian green worker, also labeled a Neutral, tells me. "We could have done anything. But somehow, there was a failure, a breakdown. I don't blame anyone. I never say they did things to me; we did them to each other. But what I always think about is what that breakdown meant. What if the better versions of ourselves had triumphed? We could have all marched forward and accomplished so much. Sometimes I have quiet discussions with people. We sit around, still shocked, and we look at each other and ask, 'What was all that about? What could have been if we'd just worked together?' We had the universe in our hands."

PART III

There is no happiness like this happiness: quiet mornings,
light from the river, the weekend ahead. They lived a
Russian life, a rich life, interwoven, in which the
misfortune of one, a failure, illness, would stagger them all.
It was like a garment, this life. Its beauty was outside,
its warmth within.

—James Salter, *Light Years*

The same thing that makes you live can kill you in the end.

—Neil Young

RAVENA

IN THE SUMMER OF 1957, the Walker family took a trip through Europe. They sailed from New York across the Atlantic, probably on the *Queen Mary*. From the teeming docks of Southampton, they drove east to Dover and caught a ferry for Calais. They worked their way down the Continent by sleeper train and hired car, through France, Germany, Austria, and then on to Florence and Venice. John was fifteen years old. It was not his first time in Europe, but this visit seems to have left a particular impression.

In Venice, they checked into the Gritti Palace, a fifteenth-century Gothic palazzo, the finest hotel in town, where they stayed in two rooms above the Grand Canal. Walker Sr. knew everyone; travel for the Walkers was always a mix of family time and professional obligation, social engagements arranged with an eye toward identifying new talent or a promising acquisition for the National Gallery. Dinners with counts and countesses; parties with wealthy industrialists who might be persuaded to donate their collections.

One morning Walker Sr. told his family to prepare for a day trip; they were in for something special. In a chauffeured car, father in front, children and mother in the back, they drove south toward the town of Ravenna. They made their way through marshes and swamplands, along the country road that led to that former capital of the Western Roman Empire. It was in Ravenna that Julius Caesar gathered his troops and crossed the Rubicon in 49 BC to march on Rome. It was to Ravenna that Flavius Honorius, one of the last Roman emperors, fled during the fifth century as the barbarians ransacked what remained of his kingdom.

Later, Ravenna became an important administrative and commercial center in Byzantine Italy. The city's brilliant mosaics, the most impressive examples of Byzantine art outside Constantinople, were created during this period. It was to see these mosaics that the Walker family drove down on a hot, sticky August morning.

The fields surrounding Ravenna were golden with the summer harvest. The town was quiet, virtually abandoned, its cobblestoned streets blissfully free of the tourists and touts that crowded Venice. The Walkers parked the car near the Basilica of San Vitale, a squat octagonal church in the city center. The building was drab and unimpressive on the outside, but inside was lit up with bright, colorful scenes from the Bible and imperial life. Green-and-blue-flecked images of Jesus and the Apostles. Two haloed Roman emperors. Winged angels and a white lamb, also haloed, etched into a starred night sky.

The family toured the church in silence, their necks craned, gaping at these masterpieces. Walker Sr. didn't speak; he only motioned at details with his walking stick, and his children didn't ask questions. Art in this family was to be contemplated, bathed in, its appreciation less a matter of study than intuitive experience. A few steps, stop and gaze; a few more steps, gaze some more.

After visiting the basilica, they had lunch in a trattoria on a side street. Parents ordered red wine, and the children were allowed some, too, diluted with water. The mosaics were on everyone's mind, and now, at last, Father began speaking of them, a mini-lecture that encompassed their history, their influence, and their spiritual significance. He spoke of the relationship between art and religion, about how the mosaics were an aesthetic representation of faith and devotion. He reiterated his long-held belief—or was it hope?—that the aesthetic and the spiritual, so expertly fused in that church, offer our only respites from human transience.

They finished their wine, settled the bill, piled into their rented car, and drove back to Venice. The trip lasted six or seven hours. A pleasant outing, a cultural expedition on a hot summer morning. Nothing unusual for this family.

But what really happened that day in Ravenna? What was it in that basilica, under those vivid mosaics, that lodged in John's teenage mind? He would carry it into adulthood, around the world, to South India, and it would come to define the last chapter of his life.

Twenty-eight years later, 1985, and John is living with Diane and Auralice in Pondicherry. He has left his father's world—that life of luxury travel and high culture, moneyed art collectors, European nobility—far, far behind. John is forty-two years old, Diane thirty-five, and Auralice twelve. They are living in a whitewashed three-bedroom apartment, across the street from a boisterous Ganesh temple. The temple is adorned with colorful statues and it's noisy, horns and cymbals and drums, especially on weekends. An elephant named Laxmi, the temple mascot, walks the streets, accepting donations and offering blessings in return. Her forehead is lined with ash, and the bells around her neck ring out, echoing through the apartment.

They have been living in Pondicherry for around six months. They have come to get away from the ongoing strife in Auroville; and they have come, too, for the relative comfort of the city. Diane needs hot water to spur the circulation in her legs, and it's easier to receive daily visits from her masseur in town. They have rented this apartment from a friend of a friend, and they have developed something of a routine. Auralice cycles to school in the mornings, a French lycée near the park; she likes to ride without holding her handlebars, a practice that Diane frowns upon. John goes to the bazaar and does the shopping; he concocts a procession of soups and juices in the ground-floor kitchen. He's busy, often overwhelmed. Sometimes in the evenings he manages to slip away for some time on his own, but he's always back for dinner.

Diane stays upstairs, in a sparsely furnished bedroom attached to a terraced garden. She never comes down, but she and John exercise together every day on the spiral staircase—vigorous, fruitless efforts to coax her legs back to life. She writes letters and embroiders colorful butterflies onto dresses for Auralice and vests for John. She reads Sri Aurobindo, and after dinner, Auralice reads to them from leatherbound copies of the *Agenda*. This is how Auralice practices her French.

It's been nine years since Diane's fall, and she still has no mobility and no feeling below her waist. An Aurovilian man visits one day; he's one of the rare people allowed to see her. "Why do you refuse to come out?" he asks. "Why not just move on, get on with things?" He dares to broach the idea of a wheelchair. This time, the topic doesn't incite Diane's fury. She just says, calmly, "Satprem has assured me that if my consciousness is right, I can get up and walk out of here."

John still visits Auroville regularly. He remains dismayed by the conflict, but he's deeply attached to the geography. He misses the forests, misses the wide-open spaces and what he describes to a friend as "the thick velvet stillness of the land." He and Diane talk often of moving back, but it's not clear how, or to where. They're tired of borrowed, temporary homes.

On June 30, 1985, John visits the Ashram for his birthday. He brings a handful of jasmine and places it at the base of the Samadhi. His hair is combed back and he's dressed in a white kurta. As he sits with his legs crossed and meditates, an acquaintance from Auroville, a Dutch woman named Marika, sees him from across the courtyard. Marika lives in Forecomers, the community set up all those years ago by Robert and Deborah Lawlor. The canyon is vast, the land uninhabited, and Marika feels the area needs more people to watch over it. She's heard that John and Diane want to move back to Auroville, so she waits for John to finish his meditation, then she approaches him. "John, don't you want to come to Forecomers?" she asks. "We need people who are into the yoga. We need people who want to build the real Auroville."

John doesn't say much; he nods. But about a month later, Marika and her American husband visit John and Diane in their apartment, and they tell them about a large, empty plot of land owned by Auroville, bordering the canyon. John and Diane express interest. It's true that they are tired of Pondicherry. The city is no longer a peaceful enclave; it has developed like the rest of the country, grown more prosperous, and with the prosperity have come crowds and disorder. They would love to get away from all the construction, the honking buses and cars, their noxious diesel fumes. The temple festivals grow ever louder, and Diane worries about the increasing traffic and Auralice's safety on the way to school.

There's another reason that they're considering moving back. Faced with continuing unrest in Auroville, the Indian Parliament has recently passed an Auroville (Emergency Provisions) Act, which temporarily handed control of the community to the government. The act is only provisional, it hasn't translated into a complete cessation of hostilities, and the CFY is challenging it in the courts. Nonetheless, a government administrator is now based in Auroville, watching over things, and greater state oversight has reduced some of the conflict and alleviated some of the revolutionary fervor. John and Diane have a sense that life in Auroville is less likely now to be defined by violence and extremism.

Shortly after meeting with Marika and her husband, John takes a sandy back road out to Auroville on his motorcycle, a newly purchased blue Rajdoot. It is, quite possibly, his first visit to Forecomers since those early days, when the Lawlors still lived there. The barren moonscape is gone, replaced by trees everywhere. A decade and a half of green work has brought Auroville's red soil to brilliant life.

He stands at the edge of the canyon and marvels at the transformation. He takes in the birdsong (there didn't used to be birds in the canyon), the porcupines, the crawling reptilian monitor lizards that stretch as long as a man's arm. It's all so beautiful! He looks down and notices red dust between his toes, and a layer wrapped around his ankles. He feels invigorated—like Antaeus, he thinks, the legendary Greek son of Gaia, the earth, who is strengthened every time he touches the ground.

There is a circularity in this visit to Forecomers, the first place John ever set foot in Auroville. It's a kind of homecoming, and a thought comes to him. He would like to build a house for his family—for Diane, for Auralice—by this canyon. He would like a family home. But not just any old home. John wants to build a majestic house, a work of art; and also, like those churches he saw in Italy, he wants something holy, that would fuse the aesthetic and the spiritual. This house will be an offering to the divine, a material embodiment of their yoga. He will call it Ravena—a Vedic word that signifies a "cry of the soul," but clearly, too, a reference to that Italian town.

He walks the land, and a large brown hawk circles overhead. He gets on his motorcycle and the hawk follows him to Pondicherry, tracing his return journey, swooping down at the outskirts of town. Back in their apartment that evening, he tells Diane of his idea for the house, and also about the hawk. They agree the bird was a providential sign; and so, back to Auroville.

He throws himself into this new project. He asks a Frenchman named Divakar, a friend of Diane's, to be the contractor for the house. John meets with an engineer, who produces some initial designs. He visits his prospective new neighbors. John assures them that he and Diane intend to keep to themselves, and that they will cause no disturbance. Most are enthusiastic about the move, although a few mutter about John's life in Pondicherry and his links with Guruji.

The engineer helps John develop some cost estimates, and then it's time to turn to his parents. He writes to his father about wanting to move back to Auroville, and of his desire to build a house. Although he knows that most of his life in India is impenetrable to his American family, John hopes that this undertaking—artistic, devotional—is something his father will understand.

He says that his house will be "the manifestation of an aspiration towards an ideal." "Art should be the expression of the Divine in life and through life," he writes, quoting the Mother. "This manifestation of beauty and harmony is part of the Divine realization upon earth—perhaps even its greatest part."

Along with such lofty ruminations, there are more mundane, practical considerations. The building John has in mind won't be cheap; he estimates the whole thing might cost $50,000, and he asks his father if he would be willing to fund the project. John assures him that the money can be channeled through a foundation in the United States, thus allowing for a tax deduction—all perfectly legal, since Auroville, not John, will own the building. He promises to keep detailed accounts, down to the sugar used in the construction workers' tea.

Walker Sr. replies with questions. Can his lawyers see Auroville's constitution? If John can't own the house, can he at least take out a long lease on it? Walker Sr. is still struggling to grasp how things are organized in this place. The situation remains that they aren't very organized. Even after all these years, there are few systems and protocols. Most resources are still technically owned by the CFY, and any new assets—such as a small piece of land John proposes to buy alongside his house—are reposed in a number of loosely organized trusts managed by Aurovilians. The community is administered (somewhat) by a ten-member Executive Council of residents, which has limited authority and an unclear mandate. Mostly, people continue to repose their faith in "divine anarchy."

John writes back to his father that trying to enter into any kind of legal agreement with Auroville would in his opinion violate the core principles of the community. He assures Walker Sr. that the house will for all practical purposes remain in the family; he (and his heirs) will always be able to stay in it. "I can conceive of no eventuality which would necessitate a lease such as you mention," he writes. "I understand and appreciate your concern but it is without cause." In lieu of a constitution, he sends the Mother's Charter, though he's dubious—no doubt justifiably—that an American lawyer would know what to make of it.

Walker Sr. relents. He will send the money, ideally in installments of no more than $10,000, so as not to arouse the suspicions of the IRS. He complains about Ronald Reagan and delays in proposed reductions to the estate tax.

John replies with gratitude. "For years I have hoped that you would accept and encourage my being here," he writes. "A filial need that this letter fulfills."

The land where they plan to build is wild. There's so much work to do before the family can consider moving in. Jackals howl at night, owls haunt the mango groves, and gangs of smugglers roam the gullies of the canyon, their bullock carts carrying bottles of illicit booze, creaking under the moon. Sometimes the gangs fight each other; one man has his arm chopped off.

The still-simmering conflict with the CFY often plays out around the canyon, too, as do battles with the shadowy, violent watchmen. An Aurovilian woman who lives in the area is attacked in the cashew fields outside her house by a group of men armed with sticks; she needs five stitches, including some on the head, at JIPMER hospital. Corrupt police drive around in jeeps, pressing false charges to intimidate Aurovilians. One of John's new neighbors is forced to attend a police hearing on concocted charges. Seeing one of his accusers in the station, the neighbor asks, "How can you possibly justify doing things like this?" The accuser, who styles himself as a follower of the Mother, replies, "She works in mysterious ways."

So the land needs fencing, needs protecting. John hires a twenty-year-old Tamil man named Narayanan Samy to work as a gardener and watchman. Narayan (as he goes) lives with his widowed mother in the village of Edyanchavadi. His family is poor, he's been doing odd jobs around Auroville, and he sees in John—and in John's reputation for generosity—a chance to work his way up in the world. Narayan moves into a hastily built hut that will double as a storeroom for the construction site.

Then there's the perennial question of water; Ravena needs a well. A water diviner is summoned from one of the villages. He holds a neem branch above the ground, and at a certain spot the stick turns so fast that, John later recalls, the man's hands are bruised. Soon a team of bullocks comes out; they are connected to a metal drill, and they go around in circles, their owners exhorting them with whips as the drill bores into the hard earth. Water is struck early, at just under twenty-five meters, and it flows copiously. That diviner knew what he was doing; he has discovered an underwater river. It's another providential sign.

The dirt track that leads from Pondicherry is widened, so that construction materials can be transported. Convoys of trucks start heading toward the canyon: fifteen loads of bricks, ten of sand, and ten of gravel. All of this happens to the consternation of the neighbors, who have been assured that John is building a humble home. They protest and John visits them, smiling and earnest, a flower tucked behind his ear. He promises to try to minimize traffic, and he says he won't bring electricity to the area; he intends to run the whole house on solar power. John explains his and Diane's quest, and what they are trying to do in Ravena. The house they are building, he says, will be a divine offering; he quotes from the Mother and Sri Aurobindo.

At least one of the neighbors is unimpressed. He finds John dogmatic, and John reminds him of Auroville's revolutionaries, a believer who wields the teachings as religion. This is probably uncharitable, and diametrically contrary to the accusations that John is a Neutral. Such are the perils of refusing to take sides: distrusted by all.

The footprint of the mansion, about thirty-five hundred square feet, is cleared near the canyon. John has a notion for the house, he shares it with Diane, and she paints some watercolors to visualize it. They share these paintings with a couple of Aurovilian architects, two Italians who have been involved in the construction of the Matrimandir, and together they begin creating more detailed designs. What emerges is an expansive two-story structure, envisioned as one of the largest private construction projects ever undertaken in Auroville.

Unlike so many of the modernist buildings in the area, Ravena will have a distinctly classical, Renaissance look. John wants rounded corners, layered cornices, a façade adorned with a panel of flying geese and a setting sun. The bottom floor will have colorful stained-glass windows, and the high ceilings will be supported by an array of wooden beams, using a local technique known as Madras terracing.

The reverberations of that other Ravenna are unmistakable. Parts of the interior will be painted in the same distinctive emerald green that colors the mosaics. A central courtyard will open to the sky, bringing to mind the high cupola of the Basilica of San Vitale. And most strikingly, the house is arranged as a series of interconnected octagons, the same shape as the basilica.

There is, too, another echo from John's life. The church at Portsmouth Abbey, the Catholic boarding school John attended in Rhode Island, is also an octagon. The church is an exquisite, floating structure, modeled explicitly on the basilica. John doesn't mention these echoes to anyone (as always, he's secretive), but in building this house, he's drawing deeply from his past.

Around the time he's conceiving this mansion, John writes to a close friend from Portsmouth Abbey:

Your letter came spanning twenty-five years and almost as many thousands of miles to find me out in this out of the way corner of the globe and to make dance before me memories resurrected. What these 25 years have been for me about—looking here, there, the craziest places, trying to find out what is behind it all, a little like trying to catch your own shadows. For some years now, I have been putting the past back behind, thinking if I maybe could truly get into the present, I would have the key, get the answer. I had it down nicely, this part. And then comes your letter.

Somehow, I feel we are still very much together, all this class of '60 which on a sunny day some 25 years ago stood together on the green of that field, talked at and then precipitated into that decade for which we supposedly had been prepared. Were we not, this class of '60, a little like the decade upon which we were on that graduation day loosed? There was about us, as there was about the '60s, something of magic, of mystery, of promise unique—or at least so I like to think.

He is reading Kahlil Gibran, *The Prophet*. The prophet says, "Your house shall be not an anchor but a mast. It shall not be a glistening film that covers a wound, but an eyelid that guards the eye." This mansion is a grand—perhaps grandiose—project. Its construction is likely to take at least a couple of years, probably more. That's too long for John and Diane. Now that they can envision a home in Auroville, they're in a hurry. John tells someone he can't take another day in Pondicherry. Diane writes to a friend of how she longs to roll in the red soil again, and how much she wants Auralice to grow up in the Mother's world. In Auroville, Diane writes, "I get to break out of this prison."

They come up with an interim solution. They decide to build a small hut a short distance from the main construction site. This hut comes up quickly, in around six weeks, and consists of a single modestly proportioned floor, with a wooden loft that's accessed by ladder. Granite pillars support a thatch roof, and the ground is covered with a cheap cement floor. There's no electricity; water is extracted from the recently dug well by windmill.

On the evening of February 21, 1986, John, Diane, and Auralice load their possessions into a couple of taxis in Pondicherry. It's the Mother's birthday, and the streets are crowded with white-robed pilgrims. John and Diane are tired of these crowds; they cramp the yoga.

They arrive in Ravena in fading light. Narayan, the newly hired gardener, has cleaned the hut and stands outside waiting. He sees John lifting Diane out of the car, one hand under her head, another under her legs, cradling her as he carries her to their new home. It's the first time Narayan has seen Diane and he wonders, *What's wrong with her? Is she unwell?* But then he notices she's smiling, laughing a little, and when John introduces them, Diane is friendly and says, in broken Tamil, *"Vanakkam, sowkiyama?"* (Hello, how are you?)

A week later and the first concrete pour, for the mansion's floor slab, takes place. A bullock cart drags in a diesel generator and a cement mixer with tiny squeaking wheels. Some sixty workmen assemble, and a wedding cook, so that the crew is kept nourished and energized with hot tea softened by twenty liters of milk. Someone breaks a coconut and lights incense; a priest performs a puja to bless the construction. Two hundred and fifty-eight bags of cement are mixed with sand and gravel, passed from worker to worker in steel pans, then poured into wooden shutters. The cement mixer is noisy and vibrates across the canyon.

The concrete pour lasts twenty-seven hours. It continues through the night, under the harsh glow of tube lights, and is finally complete at 10:00 a.m. on February 28, which also marks Auroville's eighteenth anniversary. What a day for Ravena to manifest!

Ravena is their chance for a new beginning. It offers a reprieve—as new beginnings often do—from the severity of recent life. "I loved the desert best of all places and I think I always will," Diane writes to a friend. "But now I am thirsty for green grass and little canyon brooks to wade through and flowers and trees and blue birds and myself—like them—without ego, and then more that cannot be said." Is she finally allowing herself to live a little? Is she unburdening herself of her divine obligations?

They lead a very human existence in that hut. It's a time for family, for simple domestic pleasures. Diane sits on the floor, leaning against bolsters, while she chops vegetables on a wooden cutting board; John hums and cooks in the narrow kitchen. Auralice feeds carrots through the kitchen window to a newly

acquired pony, a brown mare named Tulsi. After dinner, the three sit in the living room and Auralice shows John and Diane the latest steps she's learned in her Bharatanatyam dance classes.

Diane reads the *Mahabharata* to Auralice, and Auralice is distressed by the violence. She cries, and Diane hugs her. "I'm sorry you're crying," Diane says, "but you need to know about these things, you need to understand about these forces in the world."

They adopt a cat, a yellow male they name Big Boy. A baby squirrel falls from the thatch roof and they wrap it in cloth and make a nest for it in a cane basket. They spend hours in the garden together, where John plants cucumbers, tomatoes, lady's-fingers, marigolds, pink and orange zinnias. The garden also includes a section of Ayurvedic herbs: tulsi, aloe vera, turmeric, and the leafy datura shrub, with thorny pods that contain dark seeds used as remedies for skin diseases. Diane has heard that the datura seeds can be highly toxic, but she loves the plant's trumpet-shaped white flowers.

Auralice sleeps downstairs, in a small room by the entrance. Diane and John mostly sleep side by side on two mattresses on the floor of the living room, though some nights they go upstairs to the loft. Getting Diane up the wooden ladder is a tenuous affair; John carries her while carefully maintaining his balance. One time Diane tells Auralice that John wants a child, and she says that when she's healed, they may have a baby together. Auralice is old enough to know how these things work; she's skeptical.

But she feels their closeness, feels the settledness of their lives. Sometimes she watches as John carries Diane down to the canyon around sunset. When they return, Diane is nestled in John's arms, and they're smiling and softly laughing. They share private jokes and John tells stories in a low murmur; he constructs his fantasy dithyrambs, and Diane giggles. She giggles again in Ravena. They are in the moment, together, and the present is all-enveloping. It's hard to imagine a past or a future.

But the future is always around the corner. In Ravena, even amid all the easy domesticity, their yoga reaches a new level of ardor. The project of building this house seems to reinforce their spiritual ambition, tapers it toward a new extremity. Ravena is an amplification of their yoga; it represents another effort to infuse matter with the divine, much as they have been doing with Diane's body.

Their seclusion intensifies still further, so that only a few close friends and people directly involved with the construction are allowed to visit. They—and John is now very much part of this—deepen their experimentation with food and diets. Diane sends a note to Satprem expressing a desire to hasten her trans-

formation through fasting. She says she wants to "defy" her body, and Satprem replies that fasting does indeed offer tremendous potential. He cautions, too, that it can be dangerous.

"Pas de médecins!" (No doctors): Satprem's old injunction to Diane takes center stage, now a battle cry for all three of them. Diane has frequent urinary-tract infections and ulcers on her legs, probably from poor circulation, but she refuses antibiotics. Two friends carry X-rays of her spine to Bombay, where they consult with a leading neurologist; they return with encouraging news, but Diane won't meet them. These convictions extend to Auralice, too. When she catches a bad case of amebic dysentery, they treat her with Ayurvedic medicine and garlic juice. Auralice's stomach pains ease and Diane is triumphant: See, who needs allopathy? Once, Auralice is ill and she sees a doctor on her own, and he recommends a blood test. Diane refuses permission but Auralice goes ahead with the blood test anyway, without telling her mother; as always, she feels guilty.

John has a bicycle accident, and he suffers a deep leg wound. Limping and bleeding profusely, he pushes his cycle to the sports ground in Certitude. A young medical student from JIPMER, a South African named Siva who hangs around town, is playing basketball. When he sees John's bloody leg, he tells him he better take some antibiotics and get a tetanus shot. John laughs; he's not interested in pills and injections. Finally, he agrees to apply a wrapping and an Ayurvedic ointment, but he pulls the bandage off after two days.

His long-running stomach ailments worsen. He has pain, bloating, and he's losing weight. He's increasingly emaciated; his long face stretches out, his mouth drawn like an old man's. One day a friend brings John a box of anti-parasitical medicine, and to the friend's surprise, John actually considers taking it. But Diane reads in the accompanying pamphlet that the medicine has been known to cause cancer in mice, and she throws the box away. This is precisely why she avoids medicine: the cure is worse than the disease.

Another friend suggests that John should see a homeopath for his stomach. John agrees, and they go by taxi to Pondicherry. As they're getting out of the car, John gets a distressed look on his face. "Something's happening, something's happening," he says. A long white worm is emerging from his shorts, crawling along the back of his thigh. The friend, remembering his college biology class, grabs a twig and pulls the worm out intact. It's about a foot long. The friend stores it in a cloth bag. "You've got serious stuff in your stomach," he tells John. "Worms like that will eat all your nutrition, you've got to do something about it." John says he's on a diet that will solve the problem, and they never speak of the worm again.

It's difficult to know what to make of this moment in Ravena. In many ways, it's the most rooted period of their lives. For John, especially, Ravena offers a new sense of definition and purpose. He has drifted for so long. Now he's in his early forties. Will his life amount only to a search, a dilettantish trust-funded journey that moves around a lot without ever reaching a destination? This house has the potential to be John's masterpiece. In Ravena, in his yoga there with Diane, I think John finds the gift of faith.

Yet Ravena is also a prelude to the end. Alongside all the warmth and quietude, there's a streak of foreboding, and of *weirdness*. This streak is like an ominous marbling that runs through the texture of their lives. Their finest hour leads directly into their darkest.

"We were so happy there," Auralice tells me years later. "I know it's hard to believe, I know it sounds impossible. But there was nothing terrible or depressed in that hut, no gloominess. We were such a tight-knit little unit, and everything felt like it was finally working out. There was just no way to imagine what would happen."

"The principle employed for building a house hereabouts is much the same as the method of remembering dreams," John writes to his father. "You sit very quietly and wait. Then you catch a fragment of what is to be, of the dream, and slowly you pull it down to earth and reality—carefully, not to tug too abruptly, as it will dissolve in your hands and you will be left under a pile of rubble. Little by little, scene by scene, it will play itself out. The carpenter and mason appear when wanted; the roof fits its walls; the walls, the foundation. And after some time with a click you can close the door behind you and dream another dream. The trick is not to get attached, not to tug too hard."

He's always been a dreamer. Predictably, the project starts spinning out of control. Teakwood for the house ends up costing $10,000, twice what John expected (there's no question of substituting a cheaper wood). Tiles come in at $2,000, and cement at $1,500, both substantially above budget. Then there's steel, at $200 per ton, which John has somehow forgotten to factor into his calculations. The original estimate of $50,000 rises to $90,000.

It's a big ship to steer, and there are many difficulties along the way. The checks from Walker Sr. don't always cash in time, yet still some thirty-five laborers must be paid. It rains, unseasonably, and trucks get stuck in the mud. The workers huddle idle in wet bundles outside the storeroom, smoking bidis and sipping tea (and *still*, they must be paid). A well collapses and has to be re-bored. Problems, problems, problems. The truth, John confesses in a letter to his father, is that he often lies awake at night, "troops of figures marching noiselessly and disorderly through my head." Sometimes he wonders if he should just quit—"take to the high Himalayan hills with begging bowl and saffron robe and call it all illusion."

"This, of course, is a solution," he writes. "But the true solution—as I understand it—to the Problem is not escape from life but fulfillment of life, and this house is towards that. It is an opportunity to create something of beauty and harmony in matter (cement, wood, steel and especially earth) and to make this creation an offering that maybe can call down from beyond high Himalayan hills an answer."

Walker Sr. feels stretched in his own finances. He's tired of the high taxes in England, and he isn't pleased with his son's profligacy. With one check, he includes a letter in which he expresses the hope that this mailing will end his "obligation" to the project. John reacts defensively. "For over two years now I have been trying to communicate to you how I saw this house," he writes.

"Like some infatuated teenager, I put before you what were my deepest feelings, my highest aspirations. Ah Pa, what a sad ending. Have we become a race of accountants?"

Wealth, John tells his father, quoting Sri Aurobindo, "belongs to the Divine and those who hold it are trustees, not possessors." He writes of the austerity in which he, Diane, and Auralice live. No coffee, no sweets, hardly any clothes, no movies, no restaurants, no vacations: a self-abnegation he is certain no one in his American family could ever bear. He's distressed and clearly pained by the separation between him and his parents and sister.

And there's something else, too, perhaps also contributing to John's distress. He mentions, as if in passing, that he's not been well. He says he has a fever, and his leg is in pain. He writes that he's supposed to be resting.

One day he takes a walk out to the construction site with Auralice. His mind is swimming and he's anxious. He notices an orange butterfly among green leaves. Its brightness is a striking contrast to the oxidized red of the soil. He remembers that his father once told him of a butterfly he saw as a young man in Italy, how its fluttering lightness lifted a stubborn depression. Now, suffering under the strain of his construction project, a thought comes to John: Butterflies don't worry, so why should I?

He tells Auralice of his anxieties and she gives him some advice: Just ask your father if you should continue or abandon the project. If he says stop, then stop; if he says go on, then do that. "She simplifies nicely," John writes to his father. "Like orange butterflies."

In the open space between their hut and the emerging mansion, four women in colorful saris stand under the sun and pound against the ground with poles attached to flat wooden bases. They are beating a mixture of lime and water, smoothing it to a paste. The mixture serves as mortar for the construction.

The ladies do this all day, swinging steadily, up and down, from morning to

evening. They sing Tamil songs as they pound, choruses about gods and cour-
tesans. Auralice sometimes joins them in the pounding, and in the singing, too.
In this way, she improves her Tamil.

The "pounding ladies," as John calls them, are paid a couple of dollars
a day. He writes to his father and explains their work, describes the chants
that carry over the construction site and into their hut. "I hope your trip
back to England on the Concorde was comfortable," he adds. "I would not
like to think that my ladies pounding lime and singing songs is paid for by
inconvenience to you."

He sits at a wooden desk in the loft and writes another letter. It's 2:00 a.m.
Auralice is downstairs in her bedroom, and Diane is asleep behind him, the
drama of getting her up the ladder done with. John's desk is lit, dimly, by a
motorcycle lamp attached to three overworked solar panels. A fan, attached to
the same panels, keeps mosquitoes at bay. Earlier, when John first connected
the panels, the fan ran backward, but he fixed that with a few turns of a
screwdriver. He's proud of his electrical work; this project is bringing forth
hidden abilities.

Outside, the windmill creaks. Crickets chirp and an owl calls out, "To
who? To who? To who?" "Being wise, he of course knows the answer," John
writes. "But he has been given the work of asking this question, which he does
faithfully and continuously, from sunset to sunrise."

"I wish that I could have written to you with greater depth describing
the turns in the road and the vistas that open on this pilgrimage of mine," John
writes. "But partly because I miss what's happening until it's long gone past, and
partly because I feel you would in any case prefer not to know, I let it go on by
unnoted.

"I am up early because for the last so many hours I have been in my head
talking to you, trying to make you see that it really is alright, that there are
worse and even more foolish sons than me. Pa, if you have ever done anything

for me—and you have done so much; one more thing, please—read *Savitri* with an open mind and heart. Everything that to me matters, towards which I strive, is here expressed in a language than which I know no finer. Pa, if you and Ma could derive from these lines some sense of the clarity of purpose they have given my life, then for once I could have given you a present worth giving."

The moon outside is bright, a pirate ship sailing through the clouds. John looks through an opening in the thatch toward the silhouette of his mansion, its outline defined against an illuminated sky. "I love this house and I want to finish her as carefully and consecratedly as I can," he writes. "I'm not doing this for myself or Diane, or even Auroville, but for that which holds it all together. This house is our offering and I wish for it to be—and it will be—supremely beautiful. You tell me what else is worth doing with one's lifetime?"

Walker Sr. is seventy-nine years old, and increasingly, he feels the years. His childhood polio has resurfaced; he has pain in his left leg, and trouble walking. Gillian writes with concern to John, suggesting he may want to come back and see his parents. She says they miss him. John replies that he can't leave Auroville right now; it would be like taking Mowgli out of the jungle.

His father and mother still holiday during the winters in Florida. They rent the same house every year on Jupiter Island, a wealthy hamlet in northern Palm Beach County, home, among others, to Prescott Bush, Averell Harriman, and, later, Michael Jordan and Tiger Woods. It's a two-story, tile-roofed white stuccoed structure called Spindrift. John, disparaging of his parents' lifestyle, calls it Spendthrift.

Walker Sr. sits in the garden one February morning. He's in a starched cotton shirt and red pants. A glass of iced tea is on the table in front of him, and a typewriter, and in the typewriter there's a sheet of paper with green Jupiter Island Club letterhead.

"I cannot thank you enough for your letter," he writes to his son. "I have read it twice and intend to read it again. It told me so much about your thinking. I admire you on your pilgrimage. May it have a good ending. But no matter, better to have gone on it than to have stayed here quietly. At the end of my life I realize that there is nothing worthwhile except love and compassion and the search, which I have not made, for reality."

Mortality is on his mind. But whose?

THE NATURE OF WANTS

SATPREM AWAKENS AT SIX IN the morning; he's in blue pajamas. It's cold outside, the forested hills of Kotagiri thick with mist. He freshens up at a sink in the bathroom and then sits on a wooden stool at his wrought-iron table, and he takes coffee with milk and sugar, and toast with butter, maybe a few slices of papaya. After breakfast he reads the newspapers, and at 8:00 a.m. he heads back to the bathroom for a bucket bath, with water heated by an electric geyser, and then he returns to the table and pulls a set of cream-colored curtains and writes with his blue pen that he stores in his gold-colored box. He writes until lunch, a meal of chapatis, dal, an egg boiled for three minutes, and three spoons of curd mixed with basmati rice. The lunch is cooked by a maid named Rani and served by her brother Joseph, who also works as a gardener.

Joseph clears the table and prepares tea. Satprem writes until 4:30 p.m., after which he goes for his daily walk. He wears blue leather shoes, except when it rains, when he puts on rubber boots, also blue, and a blue raincoat. He's outside for about an hour—half an hour of walking, half with a cigarette on his favorite rock—and then he returns to the bungalow and washes his face in the bathroom, changes into warmer clothes, often a blue sweater. He sits with Sujata in front of a stone fireplace and sips slowly from a glass of Ruby red wine. Joseph lights a fire with wooden logs, fifteen tons of which are annually delivered by lorry and stored in a godown behind the house. After dinner Satprem and Sujata sit on the carpeted floor of his bedroom and trade stories, mostly about their dreams and visions. Satprem goes to sleep alone at around nine thirty; Sujata sleeps in a separate room.

The days pass at Land's End in this way—days into months, years, repetitive and steady, their consistency a salve against all the turmoil that has afflicted Satprem since the Mother's death (and, indeed, for most of his life). Things aren't perfect in this retreat. Satprem complains about real estate projects in the hills, and about disturbances caused by a group of Sri Lankan refugees the government has settled in the area. He's sixty-three years old in 1986 and suffers severe pains in his neck and upper back, which he attributes to the difficulty of trying to achieve the cellular transformation. But overall, life in Kotagiri has structure and a sense of purpose—a feeling that things are falling into place, and that the foundations for the *Agenda* are being firmly established.

The *Agenda* is typeset in a room near Satprem's, on a Compugraphic machine imported from France. He names the machine Mohini, after an enchantress in Hindu mythology. Mohini is operated by Satprem's Aurovilian associates who live in the neighboring cottage. They work seven days a week, entering letters and typographic codes via a keyboard attached to a small black-and-white monitor. They load a filmstrip with two fonts—New Aster and Baskerville—onto a fast-rotating metal drum, and the machine directs a flash of light through the film for each letter, and in this way, with a series of clicks, proofing paper is illuminated and the *Agenda* is born. The machine has two eight-inch floppy drives, and the associates are diligent about backups, but sometimes the electricity goes out midpage and they lose their work and have to begin again.

As always with Satprem, the process is cloaked in secrecy. He remains convinced that the Ashram is spying on him, that agents and dark forces are out to block the *Agenda*. "We were like Santa's little elves up there," one of his associates will later tell me. "We'd just be working away, all of us, working in this secret location. Nobody was to know anything about where it was, including my own wife. It was all very CIA, very hush-hush."

So much rides on maintaining this veil. "Everything hung in the balance," the associate adds. "It all rested on the *Agenda*. The new world depended on our work. It was as though we were publishing Gutenberg's Bible."

Meanwhile, some fifteen hundred miles to the north, another, less symbolic battle is playing out. On the broad avenue of Tilak Marg, in the heart of New Delhi, a special constitution bench of India's Supreme Court is in session. Inside a large wood-paneled room, amid the dark and chill of November, five judges in black robes sit on a platform behind a long wooden table. They have gathered to address a crucial question: Should Auroville be considered a religious project? Sitting in front of the judges are members of the CFY, whose depositions hold

that followers of Sri Aurobindo and the Mother are indeed part of a new religion. To their right, in a separate set of wooden chairs, are residents of Auroville, who vehemently oppose this position; they argue that Auroville is a spiritual, not religious, project.

This is what Auroville's revolution has come to. That provincial family squabble—a disagreement over a Japanese American man's visa, a conflict over a thatch hut in a remote corner of South India—has risen to the level of a dispute with constitutional ramifications for the entire country. Even as the revolution has subsided within the community, the CFY's challenge to the Auroville (Emergency Provisions) Act has been winding its way through India's legal system. Among other objections, the CFY argues that Articles 25 and 26 of the Indian Constitution prevent the government from intervening in the affairs of a religious organization. It's taken some time, but the matter has now come before the Supreme Court, which must decide what precisely constitutes a religion, and what the difference is between a spiritual and religious project.

The hearings last nearly a week. The parties arrive at nine thirty in the morning, climb the long steps that lead under the court's imposing dome, and make their way along a busy hallway to a room behind wooden doors. Two of India's finest lawyers argue the case. Soli Sorabjee, an eminent jurist and future attorney general, argues the case for the CFY. Fali Nariman, one of the country's most famous constitutional lawyers, has been brought on board Auroville's side with the assistance of JRD Tata; he works alongside government attorneys.

References are occasionally made during the hearings to conditions on the ground—the violence, allegations of financial impropriety and immoral lifestyles—but most of the discussion is more conceptual, concerned primarily with the constitutional aspects of the case. Aurovilians cite several passages from the Mother and Sri Aurobindo, who always warned about the perils of turning their philosophy into a religion. But one lawyer on the Aurovilian side will remember feeling concerned that many aspects of the community—its collective meditations, ubiquitous photos of the founders, incense burning and other rituals—are indeed suggestive of religiosity. A judge comments, in something of an aside, that just because the founders say the community shouldn't become a religion doesn't mean it actually isn't one.

There are questions about whether Auroville is a sect (and on the nature of a sect's relationship to religion), and debates over the meaning of the word *yoga*. Aurovilians argue that yoga is a method or science rather than a religion. The judges appear skeptical of this distinction, but they are more receptive when Auroville's legal team points out that the community has received the backing of UNESCO as a "cultural township," and that the CFY's own admission policy speaks of membership "without any distinction of . . . religion." There are, also, questions about the Matrimandir: Isn't it a temple? One of Auroville's lawyers points out that a city doesn't stop being secular simply because it contains a temple.

The judges appear to be grasping for a way forward, trying to define the contours of the word *religion* and how it can be distinguished from similar notions. A breakthrough is provided by Kireet Joshi, a former member of the Ashram who now lives in New Delhi and serves as an adviser on education to the prime minister. He's another ally of Satprem's and has been central in advancing Auroville's interests in government circles. One night, Joshi will later recall, he has a dream in which he sees a parchment inscribed with an explanatory formula. Religion, philosophy, and spirituality all aim at the same thing, he realizes. The difference is that religion aims at it through rituals and ceremonies, philosophy through what he calls "ratiocination," and spirituality via a change of consciousness.

This formulation is presented in court, and Joshi hears the chief justice exclaim, "That's it!" The verdict is soon delivered, and it goes Auroville's way. The judges concur that the government is within its rights to intervene (though one justice, in a minority opinion, rules that "Aurobindoism" itself, as opposed to the town of Auroville, could be classified as a religion). The CFY will henceforth have no say over the community's affairs, and all of Auroville's assets—its land, its buildings, any bank accounts—will be transferred to a new entity that will be managed by the government in conjunction with Auroville's residents. It's a major, perhaps decisive, victory for the community's long-running insurrection.

Satprem, who has submitted a legal brief in support of Auroville, is in the back seat of a car when someone tells him about the victory. They tell him, too, that the Supreme Court quoted the *Agenda* in its judgment, and he's thoroughly pleased. The *Agenda* is now being released at regular intervals—first in French, and then slowly, after a series of legal travails, in English. Satprem is determined to spread the word, and he sends an associate to America with a mission to have the *Agenda* disseminated there (the thirteen-volume set receives a tepid response; publishers want to know why the conversations can't be condensed into a single book). America, Satprem feels, is in a state of barbarity. He believes that the ghosts of Watergate and Vietnam still hang over the country, and he denounces Henry Kissinger, whom he characterizes as the biggest devil since Hitler. Satprem is convinced that the United States wants the *Agenda*, urgently needs it—even if the country isn't yet aware of its own needs and wants.

But despite progress with the *Agenda*, and ample financial support, things have started to sour at Land's End. Like a traveler who keeps running only to meet his own shadow, Satprem finds himself after a few years struggling with old demons. He's having nightmares about real estate developers; he's convinced that a large hotel will soon be erected in the surrounding tea plantations. His need for seclusion has increased, too, grown into a phobia of all but a most trusted inner circle. As Satprem's renown spreads, Kotagiri begins attracting a stream of pilgrims who've read his books or the *Agenda*, and who come now in search of insight and illumination. They wait for him when he goes walking, or they jump the wire fence around the estate. Satprem hides in his room and instructs others to tell the visitors he's away; he obsessively asks Joseph, his gardener, to patrol the perimeter and look for holes in the fence.

His physical sufferings, the agony in his neck and back, which he attributes to his body's ongoing transformation, also worsen. Satprem tells someone that a divine force is bearing down on him, and that the human body isn't equipped to handle such formidable power. The process is excruciating and there are days when he can hardly walk. He starts writing while erect, standing at the fireplace. Sometimes he stays still, ramrod straight, the slightest movement unbearable. Other times he moves loosely from side to side, legs and arms spreading out like a marionette's, and he says that the force is moving through him, directing him. At moments such as these he quotes from a poem called "The Drunken Boat" by Arthur Rimbaud, one of his favorite authors, another tortured, restless soul. In the poem, a ship's whole crew has been killed by Native Americans, yet the ship sails on, freely and without direction, over rivers and oceans.

After some time, Satprem decides to leave India, to find "Mother's Island." He and Sujata sail the South Pacific, visiting a string of tiny islands—Wallis, Futuna, Alofi, Tahiti, Rurutu—in search of a place more unspoiled and isolated and, most important, more secret. But soon they return, devastated and disappointed, disgusted by the mercantilism of the region's tourist economy: all the whiskey and beer, the millionaires' yachts, and the pigs that Satprem says are more numerous in the Pacific than humans themselves. Yet again, Satprem is dismayed by the unconsciousness of humanity. He has vivid, pining dreams of the Mother; he has never felt such hopelessness, even when he was in Mauthausen.

His relationship with Auroville turns fraught during this period, too. A group of Aurovilians decides to organize an exhibition on evolution in the community. The exhibition includes around twenty panels, including one that depicts different stages of evolution—from fish to primates, followed by man, and then a question mark, representing whatever higher form of life might be attained through the yoga. Somehow, through a convoluted series of errors and misunderstandings, and a slide show that never quite comes together, the exhibition fails to include a mention of the *Agenda*. Satprem hears about this omission and he's incredulous. In Kotagiri, he bangs his hand in rage against the fireplace. He sends a letter to the community, writing that an Auroville in which an exhibition on evolution can exclude the *Agenda* is an Auroville where the Mother no longer has a place. Therefore, he announces, the time has come for Satprem to bid adieu.

The episode hastens an already-developing split among the community's remaining revolutionaries. Satprem's admonishing letter renews the ardor of some; they double down on their conviction. A few even concoct a purity test, planning to go around town and ask people if they agree that a good Aurovilian should place the *Agenda* at the center of life. But there's less appetite for this kind of fundamentalism now, and most Aurovilians, including many former radicals, recoil. The purity test never takes place.

One day a Frenchman who has been close to Satprem, but now finds himself doubting some of the edicts, confronts another Frenchman who is still a true believer. "Come on," the first man says. "You can't force the *Agenda* down people's throats." The second man replies, "Yes, we will! It's our *Little Red Book* and of course we can force it on people."

This growing schism culminates in predictably theatrical fashion, when Auroville's dwindling band of hard-core Satpremites effect a dramatic late-night decampment from the community. They have been working out of a shed near Aspiration, preparing and distributing copies of the *Agenda*. One day, they rent a van, pile it high with books and other objects from the office, and drive away, destination unknown. The next morning a man comes by and finds a handwritten note taped to the entrance. The note says that the *Mother's Agenda* has left Auroville. The man pulls out a red pen, circles the message, and writes, "Not possible."

I'm on a soccer field in Auroville when I hear about this late-night caper. My family has now moved back to the community. My parents have been tracking developments from Pondicherry, and they've seen that things have cooled down, that Auroville's revolution is easing. We've spent a few months driving around the plateau on my father's motorcycle, looking for a place to build, and now we're living in a new house on a peaceful stretch of land adjacent to one of Auroville's largest forests. Our construction project has coincided with Ravena's. In fact, my father helped John organize the teakwood for his mansion; they sourced it jointly, from a government auction in Central India, and so the roof beams in my new home and Auralice's emerging one have a common provenance.

Another reason my parents have decided to return is because a new school has now opened in Auroville. A group of teachers—including the Frenchman Jean—has renovated some tile-roofed buildings in Center Field and transformed them into classrooms. They call the place Center School, and I gather there every morning with around twenty-five friends, and then in the afternoons we have an organized sports program in Certitude. I'm at this sports program when I hear the story about the van that left Auroville in the middle of the night, loaded with copies of the *Agenda*.

Our soccer coach, a Frenchman named Patrice, hasn't shown up. Patrice has always been kind with me; he seems gentle, with a soft sense of humor, but I've heard people say that he's one of the heavies, a loyal Satpremite and a radical. Now, as my friends and I wait around on a sandy playing field, bored, other teachers come up and tell us that Patrice has left Auroville, and so we won't have sports today. Later, I hear some of these teachers talking among themselves about the departure, and they seem relieved. The community is ready to move on.

I'm so happy to be back in Auroville. I like my new house, and I revel in the freedom, physical and emotional, of life in the countryside. I cycle the dirt roads with my friends, we hang out at the Matrimandir, and on New Year's Day and other special occasions we attend dawn bonfires in the amphitheater, playing loudly—and irreverently—as the adults of our community pray for a better world. I go for walks with my brother in the forest near our new house. We go over a hill, across a thin wooden bridge, and then, on the other side, make our way under a thickening canopy to a deep pit that fills with muddy water when it rains. Snakes slide into the pit, carried in by streams or while hunting for frogs. We watch from above as they slither and coil around one another, desperately trying to get out.

I'm happy in school, too. The adults of our world are newly determined to make up for the lost years, and hardly anyone hassles kids anymore about getting an education. My friends and I take a yellow bus every morning to school, our classrooms are equipped with blackboards and chalk, we have textbooks and basic lab equipment, and the teachers even assign us homework (though not much, and we don't have tests, and we're never graded). I have good friends in my class, including Auralice, who sits facing me, and sometimes we play footsie under the table, although she will later swear she doesn't remember this. It's all kind of . . . *normal*. There's a sense of wonderment in the community, a dazed astonishment that those crazy years may really be over.

But the normalcy goes only so far. One day I'm in a math class with a teacher named Pierre. He's at the blackboard, and as he's writing on it, an animal walks in, a little furry dog—except it's not a dog, and we soon realize it's a jackal. Pierre sticks his leg out and tries to shoo the jackal away, and suddenly it lunges at him, digs into his shin, and draws blood. As we all scurry out, make for the exits, the jackal jumps at a kid, an English friend of mine, and bites him, too. We shut the door and stand outside, and all the teachers assemble and try to figure out what to do. They conclude that the jackal is rabid; it's now lunging at a window, leaping off the ground and throwing itself against the glass, foam spraying all over the place as it smashes its snout. Finally, a teacher volunteers to go into the classroom with a big wooden stick. He enters, confronts the rabid jackal, and bludgeons it to death.

Pierre and my friend each get seven shots at a medical center in Pondicherry, and they will be fine. This is how life goes in Auroville. Things have cooled down, but *normal* might be a stretch. My town is still wild and enigmatic, there's always excitement and a bit of menace—and I love it.

I've taken up tennis and I'm at the Certitude sports ground one evening, playing with a couple of friends. The light is getting bad so we stop, and while I'm packing my belongings, I see a man leaning against a eucalyptus tree. It's John. He's tall and thin, and I think he seems alone, kind of aloof. I will remember him as gaunt—but, of course, memory is always colored by our knowledge of what comes later. John cycles away, toward Ravena, and this will be my only physical memory of him. I will have no recollection of seeing Diane, although I know she looked upon me and held me several times when I was a baby.

What do John and Diane know about all the permutations that are taking place in Auroville's governance—the parliamentary acts and court cases, the late-night departures that shuffle the community's balance of power and influence? *What do they care?* They are deep into something else now. They've wagered on another game.

"Faith holds me," Diane writes to a friend. "I want very much to grow out of this little person, so I am exercising and preparing for that. I would like for the story of Mother to end in a beautiful and joyous manner. I don't like fairy-tales with unhappy endings. For me, they are *not true*. So, necessarily, it means Her story is not over yet."

On a rainy morning in July, John is cycling on a dirt track near Ravena. His mind is on gardening, on the vegetables and flowers blooming behind their hut. He meets a friend and she tells him that she's despondent about the community's conflict and its lingering divisions. She's thinking of moving to the Ashram. "But the Ashram is the past, this is the future," John says, gesturing over the sweeping red land, soft after the rains, and the puddles of rainwater on the land that reflect gray clouds.

A group of Tamil laborers digs nearby. "Are they planting more trees?" the woman asks. "No, seeds," John says with a wry smile. He tells the woman he has many seeds—his mother sends them from America, he's flush with them, and he offers to share some with the woman. He says that planting seeds will soothe her anxieties, distract her from Auroville's troubles. "Dig in the soil and have your problems fall away," he tells her.

He rides off and thinks of the nature of wants. The trick, he knows, is to want nothing, expect nothing. Return to basics. Zen Buddhism calls it the original face. "Every time a thought arises, throw it away," say the great Japanese monks. "Thoughts are like clouds; when the clouds have cleared, the moon appears. That moon of eternal truth is the original face." In this way, taking recourse in seeds, focusing on soil and the life that it gives, John (and Diane) seek to rise above the mundanities of revolution, conflict, and human divisions—and their own destinies.

John, in a letter to his father:

As to your admiration of my having risen above human transience, my admiration is with you for knowing even how to spell the word. I, not knowing, have copied it from your letter. As to having risen above it, I wish it were so, for were it, then indeed I would have got a major turn in the road behind me. High time to end this wrong fixation, this absorption in the transient—pinned like a butterfly by desire and ego to this copy book catalogue of reality that we live.

DATURA

IT'S 1:20 A.M. ON MAY 6, 1986, and John, forty-three years old, wakes abruptly from a troubled sleep. Yesterday was his mother's eighty-first birthday; he's forgotten it! He sits at his desk and writes a quick letter, on a card adorned with a painting of a colorful turkey. He's four and half hours ahead of England, where it's still her birthday. He imagines harnessing his wishes to a "beloved gobbler," who will swoop across the continents and raise a timely toast. The imagined gobbler clears his throat and winks at John; it's a tough assignment, but he promises to try. The gobbler puffs out his chest, filled with the importance of his mission.

"I wish I could give you for your birthday something from here which I love," John writes. "But how can one send a sunrise or the coconut palms that frame the sun rising, or the song of the birds that sit in the palms or the soft breeze that blows through their fronds? Or maybe, a crate of mangoes—but the border people would not let them through, even if there were mangoes, which this year there do not seem to be as the rains came so late that the flowers on the trees were washed away. And no flowers, no fruit."

But if the mangoes have failed, other crops hold more promise. On John's desk, by the birthday card he's writing, sits a small packet contain-

ing more seeds—sunflowers his mother has sent him. He and Narayan have found a spot for them in the garden. The packet says that the sunflowers may grow as high as fourteen feet. John writes, "I plant the seeds tomorrow and await in wonder what will happen."

When it happens, whatever it is that happens, the time is one o'clock in the morning in early June—just about a month, to the hour, since John emerged from a fitful sleep and penned his belated birthday letter. Auralice is awakened by Diane. "Auralice, Auralice, something has happened to Janaka!" she shouts. "Go quickly, get Narayan." Auralice runs out in the dark, frightened of snakes but more frightened of whatever is going on in the hut. She finds Narayan asleep on a wooden rope cot outside the storeroom. "Come quickly, come quickly," she says in Tamil, a little out of breath. "My mother is calling you."

Narayan rubs his eyes and runs over to the hut. "What happened, Ma?" he asks. Diane is on her mattress, and she's crying. She points to the bathroom and says John's in trouble, she doesn't know what's going on. Narayan finds John in white pajamas, on his back on the red cement floor. His arms are palm down by his hips, as if he's trying to push himself up.

"Janaka, what happened?" Narayan asks in English.

"Hello, Narayan," John says in a flat voice. "I fell down, I can't get up." He's calm, and distant, as if removed from the situation. Narayan picks John up, one arm under his shoulder and one around his waist, and carries him out to the living room. He puts John down on the mattress beside Diane. "Fell down, Diane," Narayan says, and now when she sees that John is disoriented and too weak to sit on his own, she's scared, and she starts crying harder.

Diane asks Narayan to find Divakar, the French friend who's been helping them build Ravena. Tell him we need help, she says. Narayan jumps on his green Atlas bicycle and pedals through the canyons and forests, with just a small light powered by a back-wheel dynamo to show the way. The road is sandy, and every time his wheels get stuck the dynamo stops and the light falters. He, too, is scared of snakes. He gets to Divakar's in forty minutes, sweating even though it's early morning. He calls and Divakar comes out, groggy and shirtless, with several barking dogs. Narayan gives him Diane's message, and Divakar nods his head meaningfully; he says he'll come first thing in the morning.

Narayan returns to Ravena, and John and Diane are asleep on their mattresses, and Auralice, too, in her room, and Narayan thinks that maybe the whole episode is over. The next morning, John seems better. The left side of his body is a little numb and he's tired. But he can move, he can even stand on his own, and his mind is clear. Divakar comes over, and John asks if he'll take him to Pondicherry, to see Diane's masseur. The masseur's assessment is that John is overtaxed by the situation in Ravena: the construction site, all the workers, the salaries, the load of Diane's condition. The masseur advises rest. This will pass.

But it doesn't pass; and it isn't over. John suffers a series of attacks after that night. He seems to grow thinner by the day. One of his legs, maybe the one he injured in that bicycle accident, swells up and causes him severe pain. He drags his feet, and some days he has trouble walking. Fevers come and go. Of course, they do not consider seeing a doctor.

The situation grows increasingly difficult. Who will take care of Diane? John is too weak to lift her, so a team of four or five Aurovilians comes together. They help by day, and Narayan takes over at night. He moves his cot outside their hut, and Diane calls whenever she needs the bathroom. This happens at least three times a night. Narayan picks Diane up, places her on the makeshift toilet connected to a bucket, and steps out until she calls him back in. Later, he cleans the bucket.

Diane hates all of this. "Why do we still have to do these animal things? Why can't we transform ourselves?" she asks one of her Aurovilian attendants as he carries her to the bathroom. The attendant tells Diane that there's nothing wrong with being an animal; these are our bodies, and we have to take care of them. But Diane hates relying on others. The only person she trusts is John.

There are good days, and there are bad days. On bad days John is exhausted and he can barely move. He's in a lot of pain and loses interest in food. On good days, it's clear to both of them that this is just another trial, a further tribulation they must endure together, part of their yoga. The Mother has her reasons; she must. And, who knows? Maybe some kind of salvation lies on the other side. After all, they've been waiting a decade: it's been ten years since Diane's fall, ten years of hard, diligent, faithful work. At least—at last—things are moving.

Work on the mansion continues. The bottom floor is completed, and walls start rising for the upstairs. Beams are sawed and polished for the ceiling, and vermiculite insulation prepared to protect the building from the sun. In letters home, John alludes only obliquely to his illness; he focuses on accounts. The trucks keep coming in with materials, and he's alternately apologetic and defiant about his continuing need for money. His cost overruns, he says, are nothing compared to those run up by I. M. Pei on the East Building, an extension added to the National Gallery in the late 1970s, at a cost of $93 million.

June 21 is Auralice's fourteenth birthday. She throws a party in the incomplete mansion. Six or seven girlfriends come, and they bring their ponies.

The girls do tricks together: riding while standing, sitting under the animals. They swim in a small concrete pool filled with overflow from the water tank. Diane doesn't attend, but John does. He's wearing a white dhoti and he hobbles, maybe with the aid of a walking stick. Auralice is worried; John seems really unwell.

A month after that party, the upstairs roof slab is laid, in a twenty-hour concrete pour that extends through the night. Now the shell of the building is complete. Despite all the difficulties, something magnificent is materializing. "Me, I'm not worried as to when the house is ready," John writes to his father. "More of a question is will I be ready for the house when it is ready for me."

It hardly rains that summer. The canyon dries out, and a hot wind blows from the coast, sweeping away layers of sand that cover the hard red earth. Birds and animals—mongooses, rodents, rabbits—are famished. They come closer to the hut, nervously looking for pools of water or human discards.

Things take a turn for the worse in late July. John suffers another attack at night, and this time he passes out. When he comes to, he's vomiting bile, and he's cold and dizzy. An Aurovilian arrives the next morning to help. He finds "two crippled bodies, in a mini-chaos of things and animals to tend to, with meals to prepare, and the main site to look after as well." The situation seems increasingly dire. The friend takes Auralice out of the home that night, to a movie playing at a community center.

Now John is in bad shape. He sits on the back porch in a recliner, watching the animals and feeling the sun on his skin. His attendants carry him out, carry him back in for the bathroom or meals, and then out again—back and forth like that, several times a day. One attendant will later recall, "We would just move him around like a stuffed animal; we'd prop him up on a chair and he would smile."

He seems to float in and out of consciousness. Despite Diane's entreaties, he stops eating; everything he takes in comes out anyway. The right side of his face suffers painful twitches. He mumbles, "I am lost, I am lost," and he cries out, "Help! Help!"—until someone comes and holds him, hugs him tightly. Diane insists they must remain open to the Mother and her force, they must try to understand what's happening, why this is happening. There must be a reason. John simply says, "Nothing works."

In the midst of all this, Narayan comes down with a stomach condition and falls unconscious on the ground by the construction site. The doctors say he needs an operation. Diane gets a heavy fever and shivers under five blankets. Then Auralice comes home with a bad case of tonsillitis; she can barely swallow, and Diane has to drip orange juice into her mouth. "There appears to be an accelerating propensity towards disintegration or defeat in the situation," writes one of their attendants in his diary. He feels "the grab of death, like claws."

A man who visits them during this time finds himself questioning the Mother's intent. "Why all this, Mother, why all this?" he cries out. It's hard to believe this is all part of something bigger. One morning even Diane has a crisis of faith. She lashes out at the Mother, demands to know why she and John have to undergo yet more torture. In despair, she reaches out to the one person she thinks may be able to offer guidance: Satprem.

She writes Satprem a letter, but he's a difficult man to reach. All correspondence is now being routed through one of his confidants in New York. Diane writes a frantic note that someone sends to the confidant. A reply comes soon from New York, asking for further clarifications, which are duly provided. Finally, more than a month after Diane's original letter, a note arrives from Satprem himself. It contains just one line: Satprem says that he loves them.

John vomits a worm. This one, too, is about a foot long, and it comes out with the bile. Diane has read—or heard—that these kinds of worms can go to the brain, cause neurological symptoms. The situation has been so opaque, the cause of John's distress so unclear, that the worm actually cheers Diane up. "At last we know what Janaka has!" she keeps saying.

An Ayurvedic doctor is called in. He arrives by scooter and examines John. He suspects an infection in the kidneys; maybe the infection has risen to the brain. Or it could be the worms. Or something else. He speculates on a variety of potential causes, including tertiary-stage syphilis. The doctor has a nice smile, a comforting voice, and he's calm and confident. He believes the situation is remediable, and that John can be healed.

Diane prepares a syrup for John made from *bhallataka*, an Ayurvedic medicine used to treat worm infestations. "By its use," write the ancients, "a person lives for one hundred years, free from old age." It leads to a "robust physique, strong like iron, . . . exceedingly charming personality, mental happiness, enormous strength." But the medicine can also be toxic, and it seems only to make things worse for John, who hates its taste anyway. He discontinues the treatment.

A homeopath comes; he professes to be puzzled. Diane's masseur visits regularly from Pondicherry, presses and prods both their bodies, tries his best to extirpate whatever it is that seems to be consuming John. He pleads with them to go to the hospital, but they refuse, and none of their attendants insists that they see a doctor. Later, this will be a sore point for John's family in America. How could the community just stand by? they ask. How come no one intervened and got him help, or at least informed us so we could intervene?

At some point over the summer, Auralice, overwhelmed and worn-out, asks her mother if she can move out for a time. Afsaneh, an Iranian woman who lives on the other side of the plateau, has offered Auralice a place to stay. Diane is reluctant, but finally she accedes to her daughter's wishes. "Remember who your mother is," she says. "Remember who loves you the most." A couple of times a week, Diane sends a blue bag of food for Auralice. One time it includes an acerbic note for Afsaneh: "Thank you. Now she has a real mother."

Siva, the South African medical student from JIPMER, is playing soccer in Auroville one afternoon. Despite John and Diane's wish for privacy, word has spread around town that something is going on in Ravena. A man tells Siva after their game that John is unwell, and that he should consider visiting.

Siva is reluctant; he knows how they feel about doctors. But the friend insists, and so they drive down to Ravena together, where they find John and Diane at home. It's still relatively early in John's illness, and things don't look too bad. He's weak but he can stand, and he isn't in much pain. Nonetheless, Siva is taken aback by how much weight John has lost. Siva asks if he can help, but they immediately turn him down. "No, no, no doctors, no medicine," Diane says. John adds that they're doing things their way, using natural remedies, and he doesn't need anything.

Siva doesn't insist. He's been around Auroville a while. He knows that many people are skeptical of conventional medicine. He's seen a woman almost die of malaria when she refused treatment. A boy with bone cancer had to have his leg amputated below the knee because his parents delayed medical consultation. A woman lost her finger after an infection from a small cut turned gangrenous. So Siva tells John he's only there as a friend, not as a doctor, and if there's anything he can do, now or in the future, please contact him. "I know how to get in touch, and I won't need to," John says, smiling. He seems in good spirits.

Siva visits several times over the following months. John and Diane are standoffish initially, but slowly they grow more comfortable with him. They know Siva spends a lot of time in Auroville, that he's for all practical purposes a member of the community, and they seem to trust him. Siva always emphasizes that he respects their wishes; he's not trying to change their minds.

In the later stages of John's illness, as his pain increases, Siva offers him oral morphine. John always turns him down. John's attitude combines elements of Catholic martyrdom with Eastern fatalism. He tells Siva that this is his cross and he can bear it. He says that whatever happens, it's part of his destiny, his shared journey with Diane, and it would be a betrayal to take shortcuts by trying to control the direction of that journey. "My body, my life, my choice," he says over and over. Only once does he give in; Diane is out of the room, John is having a particularly bad day, and he pleads with Siva in a whisper to slip him some morphine.

Siva is the only person with medical expertise allowed into their lives in those final months (indeed, in those final years). I catch up with him decades later to see if he can shed some light on the mystery, to help me understand what was going on. Siva has moved back to South Africa in the intervening period. He's joined the ANC, become a successful businessman, a member of Parliament, and a crusader against corruption.

Probably, Siva tells me, we will never know exactly what ailed John. At the time, he considered many potential diagnoses: tuberculosis, an infection (possibly from the injured leg) that spread to John's brain, a urinary-tract infection that moved up to the kidneys and turned into sepsis, a bleeding ulcer, maybe cancer. This last possibility was always dismissed by Diane. She would ask, "Where's the lump?" John had difficulty urinating, but when Siva suggested that he go to the hospital and get his prostate checked, John laughed. "I'm not letting you people stick your finger up my bum," he said. Like many others, Siva tells me about John's gentle humor; he's impressed by the way John maintained it even through his tribulations.

"I didn't understand it very much at that time, but now I'd look at their situation and I would say that they were naturalists," Siva tells me. "They had a belief that all medicines were small poisons, and when you take them, you are taking poison into your body. They had the belief that nobody should try to live forever because you're breaking a natural cycle. What is to happen must happen; they thought that medicine was fighting against nature."

I ask him what he thought about these beliefs as a medical professional. Did he think John and Diane were irrational or crazy? Did he feel he should just drag them to a hospital? "To an extent, I did," Siva says. "But I've become more mature as a doctor now, and I know that to intervene is sometimes going against people's wishes." He talks about cancer patients he's seen who have rejected treatment, and about Jehovah's Witnesses who refused blood transfusions, even for their children. Who's to say what's right and wrong, sane and insane? He's learned over the years that sanity is contextual; he tries to avoid labeling people or their beliefs.

He adds that, even back then, when he was still a young medical student, he was already open to different systems of belief. He'd lived in India long enough to know that some things defy explanation. In the villages, he'd seen men pierce themselves and walk through fire. How does one explain that? And Siva also had a personal experience. A few years before visiting John and Diane, he contracted a serious case of hepatitis. He fell into a coma and was transferred to a specialty unit in Madras. Medicine had exhausted its options; everyone thought he would die. Then one day an Ayurvedic healer came to the hospital and the doctors let her give Siva a rolled-up concoction. Two days later, he awoke from his coma.

"It shook me and I learned that I had to believe in other things," Siva tells me. "Medicine and science can't solve everything. Working in India taught me that sometimes you need another frame, call it spiritual or whatever, to understand things. That's what John and Diane believed; that was the path they were following. I felt bad for them, I thought this wouldn't end well. But who was I to question the path they had chosen?"

In August, John writes what will turn out to be one of his final letters to his father. "Dear Pa," it begins. "Got your letter yesterday and want to assure you rightaway [*sic*] that my fever is gone and my leg is better. It was silly of me to worry you."

John's reassurances are false. And other things about this letter are incongruous. Instead of John's usual sloping scrawl, it's written on a typewriter and riddled with spelling errors. The note is perfunctory and has none of John's usual lyricism; it's focused on his need for money. "As for my financial position the bequest of aunt Bee has been pretty much used up," the letter says. "I just received my bank statement in which they credit me with $2000. I'm not sure if that's the intire [*sic*] income for the rest of the year or not, but Schroders could tell you."

This letter will engender considerable resentment among John's family. They will always believe that it was written not by him, but by people around him who wanted to keep the funds flowing, even while John was dying and the family remained uninformed. It's hard to know what's really going on. John's right side is now all but paralyzed—he couldn't handwrite a letter—and there's little doubt that he would want construction to continue. The most likely scenario is that the letter is written by someone else, but with John's concurrence. Nonetheless, it will feed a lasting bitterness toward John's friends in Auroville, and toward the community itself.

"My brother was dying," Gillian tells me later, standing at the counter in her basement kitchen in the Dakota. "My brother was dying and no one did anything about it. They just wanted more money; that's all they cared about. Is that what you call a community? Is that the yoga? I'm sorry, but it was disgusting. I'll never get over what happened there."

October comes around and at last the summer breaks. Monsoon clouds cross the Bay of Bengal, carry with them a cool, thick humidity. The first showers arrive, and the canyon returns to life. Slender streams and waterfalls flow down its sides, merging to form a central current that carries the summer's debris (dried-out branches, roots, dead leaves) to the ocean.

In the hut at the edge of the canyon, they battle an infestation of white ants. The ants swarm in from the forest, escaping their flooded nests. Narayan sweeps and scrubs; he gathers a seemingly endless supply of musty ant eggs and throws them into the rains. There are treatments for this kind of infestation, powders and solutions that work. But they're made of chemicals, so obviously not an option.

John's skin has turned gray. He has deep circles under his eyes and his heart palpitates and his chest heaves. He lies on his mattress on the floor, often facedown because it helps him breathe. Diane spends much of the day by his side, wrapped in a scarf, Big Boy, the yellow cat, purring in her lap. John moans, and she cries. She calls out to the Mother, and she writes furiously in a notebook, scribbling prayers and mantras that she hopes may perform miracles.

On October 8, she sends another letter to Satprem:

I am writing to you with anguish in my heart. Things are not going well with Janaka and he shouts that he can't go on but I keep calling Mother. I call and I call but it's as if there's nothing there. I know that can't be true but it goes on and on and Janaka's condition gets worse and worse. Now his head is no longer clear and his body is in constant torture.

I had this dream, like you, to work together for Mother, in true love—I love Janaka and Janaka loves me—to create something together. What do you see Satprem? Where is the force that could cancel all this disorder that wants to destroy the body? What can I do?

Around this time, Auralice makes what will prove to be her last visit to the hut. She finds John on the floor, moving in and out of lucidity. When he sees her, he seems to come back from somewhere, and he smiles, though it's more like a grimace. He tries to raise his head, and he starts shouting, "Auralice is here, Auralice is here. Have we cleaned her room?" Auralice knows he's putting on a reassuring front, trying to make her feel at home. She and Diane calm John down; they say the room doesn't matter. Diane is clearly distracted, but she attempts to give Auralice some attention. She scolds her daughter for having cut her hair short, like a boy's. "All that beautiful hair gone!" Diane says, and she blames Afsaneh for letting Auralice do it. The whole scene is too much for Auralice. She gets on Tulsi, her pony, and leaves Ravena.

A few days later, with John's condition having deteriorated further, Diane finally agrees to let a doctor in. The doctor is a young Bengali from the Ashram, and he comes out to Auroville in a jeep equipped with oxygen cylinders. He checks on John and concludes immediately that the situation is grave, and that this man needs to be shifted to a medical facility. A van arrives soon after and John's attendants lift him into the back. As he's being loaded, Diane says, to no one in particular, "If he's going, I'm going also." She makes no effort to join him in the van. John is taken to a clinic by the sea in Pondicherry and put on respiratory support.

Now Diane is alone in the hut, and five days after her last letter to Satprem, to which she has received no response, she writes another message for him. This time, she manages only two lines: "Satprem, we cannot go on like this anymore. Where is Mother's force for us?" She asks one of her attendants to send it urgently as a telegram.

John struggles through the night and dies the next morning, October 14, at 9:50 a.m. He's forty-four years old. It falls to a man called Oliver, a close friend of John's and one of their attendants, to drive his motorcycle to Ravena and give Diane the news. She's sitting upstairs in the loft when Oliver arrives. She's got her hands on a statue, the brass Krishna with a missing ruby eye that my father gave her many years ago. Almost before Oliver can get the words out, she pulls the statue to her chest and says, "Yes, I already know. My father died on the same day." In Diane's universe, there are no coincidences.

She seems calm and focused. Clearly, she's been anticipating the news, and she knows right away what she wants to do. She tells Oliver that she must follow John, that he's waiting for her, and she asks for his help. She wants Oliver to get some kerosene so that she can set herself alight. When Oliver refuses, Diane asks him to throw her into the canyon. Oliver says he can't do that either, and Diane grows angry. She accuses him of cowardice, of standing in the way of her and John's destiny. "You don't understand, it's not that I'm sad or lonely," she says. "I just need to go with him. I need to follow him."

Diane is a strong woman; her convictions are severe, and her will is formidable. Oliver is in a daze from the loss of his friend, and he tries to buy time. He tells Diane they need to think about it, let's talk some more. Don't rush, he says, don't do anything in a hurry. He'll come back in three or four days and then they can decide together. Diane keeps insisting, and Oliver always demurs.

Now, faced with his refusals, Diane's calm cracks; the storm begins. She starts shrieking. She screams, "No, Janaka, no!" It's a piercing cry, raw, like the sound of a wounded animal. She removes her earrings and bangles and hits her denuded arms against the wooden floor of the loft.

A motorcycle pulls up outside and Diane panics. She knows that people will come, that they will try to take care of her and save her. She doesn't want to be saved. She wants only to be with John. She calls Narayan and asks him and Oliver to carry her out to the back and keep everyone at bay. They place her in the garden, alone near a bowl of fruit. Oliver goes to tell the visitors, two of Diane's friends who have heard about John's death, that she doesn't want to see anyone.

When Oliver comes back to the garden, he notices that Diane is smiling. Then he sees discarded banana peels and a half-eaten apple on the ground. Also, he sees broken stems from the datura plant and scattered seed pods around her. Oliver understands at once what she's done. She's taken the datura seeds and stuck them in the fruit and eaten them. She's poisoned herself.

Memories of this time will be blurry, not entirely consistent. Everyone's under a lot of pressure and they will remember different things. Divakar arrives; he makes his way to the garden and sits with Diane. He doesn't see any bananas or apples. He will remember Diane in an armchair by the Ayurvedic herbs, begging him to help her die, and when he refuses, she reaches out in front of him, lunges at the datura, and starts shoveling seeds by the fistful into her mouth. "I have to rush," she says. "He's already gone, he's expecting me."

She isn't crying and there's no drama, no second-guessing. "It was clear that speed mattered to her," Divakar tells me years later. "There was no fear, no sadness. It was like shifting from one house to another. Imagine seeing your child drowning: You jump in to save him or her, there's no time for questions about the meaning of life and death. It doesn't make it simple or easy; it's just that there's no time to think or talk about it.

"In retrospect, yes, maybe it would have been good to talk a bit, to make a more thought-out decision," he says. "But she didn't have that time. There was a sense of being taken into a tunnel, like you have no choice. They couldn't let go of each other; they held on so tightly."

In *Savitri*, the eponymous widow follows her husband, Satyavan, into the underworld and argues with the god of death to release him. The god refuses, telling Savitri that she's a mere mortal, nothing against the immutable laws of life and death. But Savitri is defiant. She says she represents the god of love, who is more mighty than Death. She tells Death that she and Satyavan need to be on earth to complete their work (a "sacred charge"). Declaring that they are "God's messengers beneath the stars," she emanates a brilliant light and undergoes a divine transformation. Death relents, and man and wife return to earth, having conquered the laws of matter; they share the fruits of their knowledge with humankind.

Auralice is at school, a new place near Aspiration that I also attend. It's past lunchtime but the food still hasn't shown up, and a group of about forty hungry kids is gathered in a clearing, under the shade of trees. They hang out around black stone tables, teasing one another and talking about their teachers. Some of the boys play soccer.

Eventually, a teacher comes out and tells the kids that there will be no lunch that day. The van that usually brings their food from the community's central kitchen had to go to Pondicherry instead, because John Walker has died. The van was needed to transport his corpse. This is how Auralice finds out. She doesn't even know that John was taken to the hospital.

She will not remember much after that. She will dimly recall a woman, another teacher, coming up to her, maybe putting her arms around her—though maybe not—and telling Auralice she should come home with her, stay with her until all this blows over. Auralice will remember sitting on the back of that teacher's moped driving past the turnoff to Ravena, thinking of her mother, wishing that she could be with her, but then wondering if Diane would want her around. She almost tells the teacher that she wants to go home. But the moped turns away from Ravena, and the moment passes.

Auralice will always wonder, What would have happened if she'd gone to Ravena that afternoon? Could she have saved her mother? Diane always told her to listen to her inner voice, to trust what her deepest self already knew. Premonitions and intuitions are real, Diane would say. Auralice will always wish she'd listened to her inner voice that day.

Narayan is in the back of the hut with Diane, and tears are running down her face. "Look, Narayan, look what I have done," she tells him, pointing at the empty datura pods. "How much longer do you think I have to live?"

Narayan starts crying, too, and says, "How can you ask me this? You and John are everything to me. I'm just a boy. What will happen to me?" He feels abandoned. Diane tells him there's a box in the house with her gold jewelry and some money in it. He can take it all, she says; use it to get married and build a life.

One of the visitors who arrived by motorcycle makes her way to the back garden, and she sees what Diane has done. She hugs Diane and tries to convince her to get to a hospital, to have her stomach pumped. The friend says that Sri Aurobindo and the Mother were against suicide; killing yourself, they taught, can make reincarnation difficult. Diane says she isn't worried. With all the hardship she's undergone, she's pretty sure they'll understand.

"Think of your daughter then," the woman says. "She's only fourteen. What will happen to her?" But Diane is implacable, determined about her fate and apparently resigned to Auralice's. She says Auralice will have to go to Belgium and stay with her grandmother—Diane's mother—until she's sixteen and legally an adult. "I managed after I lost my father," Diane says. "I lived under my mother's control until I was free at sixteen. She'll be fine."

She talks about John and their shared destiny. She says she has to go quickly, so she can join him. Her eyes are starting to roll in their sockets and her speech is unsteady; the poison is taking effect. The woman asks Diane again to think of Auralice. Maybe she speaks more emphatically, hints at an intervention. "Stay away from me," Diane says. "Stay away or I'll put a curse on you! I swear I will."

It's afternoon and Siva is playing basketball in Aspiration. He's heard about John's death; the news has gone around town. He wondered if he should visit Ravena, but he thought that Diane would probably want to be alone. And anyway, what could he do?

Oliver pulls up on his motorcycle. He walks hurriedly to Siva and tells him that Diane has taken poison, and that they need a doctor's help. Siva isn't surprised—he had a feeling she'd try to kill herself if John went. He doesn't want to go, but Oliver is insistent, clearly distressed, and so they drive to Ravena together, through the muddy, slippery canyon roads, splashing the monsoon puddles, under a canopy that's still dripping from recent rains.

By now, a crowd of some thirty or forty people has gathered outside the hut. They mill around, praying and meditating, a few whispering, What should we do? What can we do? Inside the hut, a smaller group, six or seven Aurovilians, is in charge. When Siva arrives, they say that Diane doesn't want a doctor. They insist that he must respect her wishes and ask him to remain outside.

Siva sees that Diane's pupils are dilated, and that her breathing is shallow. Her body seems to be moving spontaneously in uncontrolled jerks. Datura is a hallucinogenic. Sometimes she smiles or laughs, as though she's on a trip and having pleasant visions. Siva tells the gathered group that it's not too late to save her. JIPMER has an entire ward dedicated to poison cases, but they need to get there fast. They tell Siva again that this is Diane's decision, and what's happening is part of her yoga. They ask him once more to step outside.

Diane starts going in and out of consciousness, and anxiety builds in the crowd. A Frenchwoman asks about liability under Indian law. In France, she says, you can be held criminally culpable for standing aside while a person dies. A murmur goes around. Now someone says that Diane has decided she made a mistake and wants to be saved. They need to intervene.

They turn Diane upside down and shake her. A person sticks a finger in her mouth, but nothing comes out. "Milk, milk, get some milk!" another person shouts out urgently. Her mouth is forced open and milk poured down her throat. A man calls out for castor oil, and another has heard that salty coffee can induce vomiting, so they try that, too. They press Diane's stomach and gurgles come out of her mouth, bubbles of liquid that run down her chin and neck, and onto her clothes. Soon she's soaked, and a woman pushes through the crowd and tries to change her top. Diane resists and fights back, but the woman looks her in the eyes, tells her she's messy and she's just trying to help.

There's a moment of lucidity; somehow, Diane understands what this woman is trying to do, and she sticks her arms up and lets the woman put a fresh shirt on her.

Four or five hours after Diane has taken the datura, people call Siva back into the hut. They ask him to help, and he's incensed. "Now you're asking me to do something?" he says. He knows it's probably too late, but he tries anyway. He sticks a pipe into Diane's mouth, attempts to flush the poison out. Milk and water come gushing, and they seem to be coming from her lungs. She's still alive, but later, Siva will conclude that Diane possibly drowned before the poison got her.

Evening arrives and the gray monsoon light turns milky blue. The crowd's apprehension builds; they decide to take Diane to the hospital. And so she's loaded once again into a van for JIPMER, where she swore she would never return, which she said was worse than a concentration camp. Divakar is distraught as she's driven away. He promised her that he would never let them take her back, that he would protect her from hospitals and doctors. But he's powerless in the face of this panicking crowd. "It was plunging her again into that horror," he says later, a disgusted look on his face. "That cutting into her, that violence."

In the van on the way to the hospital, a man tries mouth-to-mouth resuscitation. He breathes and breathes, but Diane grows steadily more unresponsive. For years afterward, this man will have strange dreams and visions, what he refers to as "mini-hallucinations." Later, a doctor will tell him that he probably ingested some of the datura while breathing into Diane's mouth.

They get to JIPMER in about twenty minutes, but she never makes it to the poison ward. She's pronounced dead in Emergency. A senior doctor, one of Siva's professors, comes around and reproaches him. You know that you could have saved her, she says. You know this wasn't a complicated case. How could you just stand around and let her die? The professor is angry, and Siva is worried. His exams are coming up, and this professor might be grading them.

"Madam, you don't understand, I was helpless," he tells her. "You don't understand these people. They are different. They have different beliefs."

Their bodies are placed alongside each other in the mansion, off a central octagonal courtyard. This is the first time Diane has been in Ravena; she enters as a corpse. They are laid on a table on sheets of ice, surrounded by flowers and incense. John's jaw has slipped open and it's held together with cloth. Diane is wrapped tight in white fabric, like a mummy. She has come like that from the hospital because the doctors insisted on an autopsy. One more humiliation for that battered, beleaguered body: Diane has been sliced open and dissected, her innards examined under a microscope.

The funeral takes place the evening after they die. A few friends and construction workers from Ravena dig a pit with shovels and crowbars. They sprinkle a layer of salt at the bottom, to keep away rats and other mammals. A couple of Aurovilians climb into the pit, and two teakwood coffins are handed down, laid on the moist salty earth. Narayan leans in from above and places a gold chain on John's coffin, and Diane's bangles on hers. Someone adds a gold-framed portrait of a blue Krishna; it was their favorite painting. People throw flowers, and the pit is filled with earth.

No one says anything, there are no prayers or chants. Everyone will remember the quiet. Auralice does not attend the funeral. She refuses to go; she remains at Afsaneh's house.

A day or two later, Afsaneh finds Auralice crying in bed. She's in a thatch hut in a dark room, on a mattress on a concrete platform. She's wet with tears and her body is trembling and shivering. "Why did she leave me? Why did she leave me?" she says, sobbing and wailing. She lashes out at John; she's furious with him and blames him for taking her mother away.

Afsaneh crawls into bed with Auralice. She lies on her side and scoops Auralice into her arms, pulls her into her body, as if to envelop her in a womb.

"Don't cry," she says. "Don't cry, I'll be there for you. I'll always be there for you." Auralice sobs and sobs in the dark hut, her body shaking uncontrollably.

She remains at Afsaneh's house over the following days and weeks, but it's clear to everyone that this can only be a temporary arrangement. Larry is now back in Auroville—he returned two days before their deaths—but he feels helpless and underequipped to handle the situation. The adults of Auroville wonder what to do with Auralice. Who will take care of this girl? Who will raise her now?

Auralice won't talk about any of this. If other kids bring up the deaths, she gets a tight look on her face and walks away. She refuses to engage. Every night, as she's going to sleep, she cries and clings to Afsaneh. Once Afsaneh asks if she wants to visit Diane and John's grave, and Auralice shakes her head emphatically. "No!" she says, and leaves the room. Afsaneh never again brings up the subject.

I will come to know these barriers. They are like walls between Auralice and me, and then walls that run through our marriage and our family. There are places we don't go, things we don't—can't—talk about. I suppose one of the reasons I wrote this book was to break down those walls.

It's October 2003 and Auralice and I are in Central Park. We're sitting on a stone mound near Strawberry Fields, watching a group of people playing soccer on a lawn. It's an unseasonably sunny day, and we've taken the opportunity to have a picnic. Auralice is more withdrawn than usual today. She's barely spoken to me since the morning; I feel as if she's somewhere else.

A kid comes into view on the asphalt path below us. He's around ten years old and he's on a skateboard. He falls and hits the ground, hard, and he starts bleeding from his arm. He sits there, stunned at first and then crying. A man and a woman, presumably his parents, run over. They crouch beside the boy and run their hands through his hair and pour some water on his wound. They lift him by the shoulders, get him back on his feet, and the mother kisses him a few times on the face and the father runs his hand along the boy's forehead, and then they walk away, the father holding the skateboard and the kid in the middle as the three of them hold hands. Now the boy is laughing. Auralice turns to me and she has tears in her eyes. She tells me that today marks seventeen years since John and Diane died. She leans her back into me, facing away, and as I put my arms around her, she says, "Why did they leave me? Why did they leave me?"

I'm stunned. How could she not have told me? How could she not have talked about what's been going on since the morning? Our relationship is still young, and I'm just getting used to her silences. I find them frightening, as if there are places I will never be able to touch, depths that I (and perhaps Auralice, too) can never reach. I should have known on that day that we would end up moving back to Auroville—that we would be plunged into this unfinished business together, those two tragic deaths by the canyon, and their long aftermath that would shadow us, wherever we were and whatever we had built in our lives.

FECKLESS

GILLIAN WALKER IS IN THE office of her family therapy practice, on Lexington and Seventy-Eighth Street. It's around noon and she's at her desk, in a leather-upholstered chair. The phone rings and it's an old friend of John's, a woman who has visited Auroville and stays in touch with people there. "Did you hear?" the woman asks. "John's dead."

Gillian grips her desk; her knuckles go white. She calls her husband, Albert, and then she calls her parents in England. Maybe she tells them the news on this call, or maybe she simply says, "I'm coming, wait, I have something I need to tell you." She takes the Concorde to London. By chance, the family's neighbors from Fishers Island are on the same flight, and she tells them about her brother. Their son was a friend of John's, grew up sailing and cycling around the island with him, and they're shocked and they hug Gillian. A few months later, their son will die in a plane crash.

Gillian's parents meet her at the airport and they drive together to their home in Amberley. There aren't many tears, nor words. This is the Walker way. And really, no one knows quite what to think. They haven't seen John in over a decade, his life has been a black box. All they know, the only information Gillian's been given on that phone call, is that John may have died of a kidney infection. "Well, that's treatable, why didn't they do something about it?" she asked the caller, and the caller said something about yoga and Ayurveda.

A service is held in a Catholic church outside Amberley. It's presided over by Cormac Murphy-O'Connor, who will later rise in the Catholic ranks to become the archbishop of Westminster. The church is small, and the intimate service is attended by around fifty people: uncles and aunts, cousins with whom John and Gillian grew up and shared a world as children. They're down the road from Arundel Castle, their uncle's estate, where they spent time during their summer holidays.

After the service, at a reception at her parents' home, Gillian finds herself in a corridor alone with Murphy-O'Connor. The priest asks about her brother and wants to know more about John's time in India. What can Gillian say? She doesn't know much about what John was up to in Auroville, but she tells the priest about something that's been happening in her apartment in New York. For some time now, she's been waking up to the smell of incense. She doesn't burn incense; only John did that. She can't explain it. And she feels the need to tell Murphy-O'Connor one more thing. In her opinion, what John has been doing in India has all been a kind of sacrifice, his death a very Catholic martyrdom. "You know," Gillian tells the priest, "in his own way, my brother was a saint."

October is cold and damp in Kotagiri, and Satprem is in agony. The nerves on his upper back are inflamed, and now his spine seems to be affected, too. His mind dwells on suffering—his, humankind's, the planet's—and he thinks and writes about mortality and the constraints of the physical body. Most days his faith is strong; he's fixed on the Mother, and he remains convinced that these constraints are surmountable. Death is still a lie, the yoga an instrument of overcoming. But some days the suffering is overwhelming. On October 11, 1986, three days before John and Diane die, Satprem makes a single-line entry in his diary: *"Je ne sais plus"* (I don't know anymore).

One night he has a dream. He finds himself in a large hall next to a grand piano covered with a shawl. He's always loved music. In his youth, he aspired to write with the same abandon that one plays an instrument; he had a poster of Beethoven in his room, inscribed with a proclamation that the composer was his god. Now, hungrily, like a starving man, Satprem pulls the shawl off the piano and begins playing a Beethoven sonata. The piano is elegant, with white ivory keys. But the sound that comes out is awful; as Satprem plays, all the notes are off. He awakens with a thought running through his head: he no longer wants music.

It isn't clear if Diane's last two notes ever reach Satprem. The news of her death merits only a glancing entry in his diary. On October 17, he briefly notes her passing, a parenthetical between more lofty musings on the human condition. He wonders how long he can continue with his yoga; he writes that he endures his suffering only for the sake of the world, and that he is searching for an exit from the inferno of existence.

A couple of months after their deaths, one of Satprem's admirers in Auroville writes, asking him to help her understand the events in Ravena. He sends a short note in reply. He says he shares her pain and he's sure that the Mother and Sri Aurobindo have wrapped John and Diane in their compassion. He adds that each person must arrive at their own interpretation of their deaths. He has nothing further to say; he wants only to focus on his Work.

Diane never told her family in Belgium about her fall; her mother and sister don't know a thing about the decade she spent paralyzed. She's only sent them photos of herself from the waist up, a hand over her broken jaw. But for some time, they, too, have awoken to the smell of incense in their house in Sint-Niklaas. Like Gillian, they can't account for it. Who can explain how these two families, so different and far apart, each about to suffer a bereavement, experience the same omen? Diane's sister will later say that the scent of incense was like a warning: she knew that something wasn't right.

Still, they are astonished when they hear the news. Like John's family, they're furious, and they cast about for villains. Both families need someone to blame. Diane's mother goes to the media, convinces a newspaper to run an article about how her daughter was mesmerized by a community in India, and now her granddaughter is trapped there. She tells the reporter that Diane fell under the sway of a Parisian woman referred to as the Mother, and that she followed a leader named John, who was extremely skinny and forced his followers to fast. In her version of events, Diane died of exhaustion after being led into fasting by John.

The article includes a picture of a gaunt Auralice, like some kind of hostage, and a stunning but sad-looking young Diane, in a sari with a string of jasmine in her hair. "Auralice must come back to Belgium as soon as possible. She should never fall victim to the communal atmosphere over there," the grandmother is quoted as saying. "My daughter Diane left for an Indian commune fifteen years ago to never return. She must have been totally confused. That should never happen to Auralice!"

I'm in Singapore when I hear the news. Singapore is one of the most normal places in the world: systematic and regimented, free of deviants, of people pushing limits and following extreme paths. Singapore is a utopia in its own way, but in a way that's the opposite of Auroville.

I'm on a short holiday with my father and brother, and my mother calls. When she tells me John and Diane are dead, I'm looking out from our hotel room onto a road, all those busy shoppers, ordinary, untouched lives consuming on a sun-dappled afternoon. I'm twelve years old. What do I understand about death? What do I know of grief and tragedy? All I know is that my friend will now be very sad.

But then I see Auralice a few days later, back in Auroville. She's at my house with Afsaneh and they're swimming in a pool outside my room. Auralice is in a leopard-print swimsuit, and she doesn't look sad at all. Again: What do

I know about grief? But I do know that Auralice on that afternoon seems—if not quite happy, then at least untouched.

Grief is like fame. We expect individuals to be transformed by it, to occupy a room in a different way, as if the experience of tragedy is somehow physically altering. But Auralice isn't bigger or shinier, or more crumpled or wrinkled, or different in any way that I can see that day. She looks just the same, and she plays in the pool, bouncing in the water under a gray monsoon sky, sometimes even laughing.

On November 18, 1986, about a month after John's and Diane's deaths, Auralice writes a letter to Gillian. She writes it on blue paper, in the looping handwriting of a teenager. I will find this letter decades later, in Gillian's green folders. It brings tears to my eyes every time I read it. I cry for Auralice, the woman who is my wife and the mother of my children. Mostly, I cry for that fourteen-year-old girl caught up in all this adult madness, these impulses and convictions that have led to such a dark place.

"Dear Gillian," the letter begins:

I'm writing to you from Auroville. Right now, we are making a
parcel with all of John's things to send to you. We will be sending
it as soon as someone from here goes to America because the mail
here is not always so safe. It's been a month now since John and my
mother died but I'm still very sad, I guess you must be too.

The building of the house goes on. The land and the house are
very beautiful—I think—and I would like very much to live there
in a while. Before that, I would like to go out of Auroville for a few
years, everything has been too sad for me here.

Auroville is a small town, a village really, and the notoriety that attaches
itself to Auralice is claustrophobic. People whisper that John and Diane died
for the Mother, calling them divine warriors. They hazard opinions about sins
Diane must have committed in a past life, and about a malignant karma that
might now carry over to her daughter. What this girl needs is human compassion; what she gets, mostly, is grandiose metaphysical speculation. In this way,
Auralice's fate repeats that of her mother, whose personal tragedy was hijacked
by theories and narratives.

Auralice tries to shut it all out. She keeps walking away whenever the
topic of their deaths comes up. She grows increasingly isolated, and she starts
skipping school. She needs an exit, and it arrives in the form of a reply from
Gillian, who invites Auralice to come stay with her family in New York. "I was
so angry with Auroville, but I could never blame this little girl," Gillian will
tell me years later. "I knew she was like a daughter to John. I knew John would
want me to care for her."

She arrives at JFK on a cold February morning, after her first flight alone.
She's led through customs and immigration by an air hostess dressed in a
Caledonia tartan skirt, and she carries a suitcase filled with John's trinkets.
Gillian and her eldest daughter, Rebekah, are there to greet her. They take a

taxi together, through Queens, over the Triborough Bridge, the river partly frozen below, and then along the park, till they reach the Dakota. A new life begins.

That first night in the city, the family is invited to a neighbor's for dinner. The neighbor's apartment is an opulent duplex, one of the largest in the Dakota. He's a wealthy entrepreneur, a larger-than-life-figure in New York society, and among the guests is Sean Lennon, the son of Yoko and John. The neighbor has heard Auralice's story and offers to help in any way he can. She has no idea how to take him up on his offer.

The transition from that hut bordering a South Indian canyon to the Dakota is almost unimaginable. There are expensive artworks on the walls of Auralice's new home, and sometimes she runs into the building's famous residents in the elevator or the central courtyard; mostly, she has no idea who they are. She has no context. Auralice is more impressed by the washing machine and running hot water. She takes a photo of herself in front of a double-doored refrigerator and proudly sends it to a friend in Auroville.

Gillian has committed to providing Auralice with an education, so they take a tour of the city's private schools. They visit the Rudolf Steiner School, on the Upper East Side, which Gillian thinks Auralice might appreciate for its alternative approach. They sit in chairs while the teachers ring bells, and Auralice rolls her eyes, and she and Gillian break out in giggles; Auralice doesn't want any more of this New Agey stuff. Finally, she enrolls in the Calhoun School, on West End Avenue. The other kids dress better, and they're richer and smooth in that Manhattan private-school way. Paul Simon's son, who also lives in the Dakota, is a classmate; Auralice develops a crush on him, but he barely notices her. She doesn't know how to apply makeup, and she's lacking the mandatory vaccinations. She struggles with standardized tests, which require her to understand how a touchtone phone works. There are no touch-tone phones in Auroville; there are hardly any phones at all.

She's needy and insecure, profoundly homesick. Every evening she waits by the door for Gillian to come home, then she throws herself, sobbing, into Gillian's arms. The family takes a holiday in Florida and Auralice stays in bed much of the time, bawling. This isn't easy for Gillian's family, especially her three children. Auralice and Rebekah fight. Albert tries to be welcoming, but he's never had much sympathy for John's undertaking in India, and now he's not sure what to make of this new arrival in their lives. A massive adjustment is required from everyone.

Auralice must navigate Gillian's fury—against Auroville, and against Diane. Gillian will always say she was careful in front of Auralice, that she tried not to show her anger and distaste for the world from which Auralice emerged. Gillian is a wise, compassionate woman. But she's human, in despair herself, and her feelings slip through. Auralice will grow up in two estranged and apparently incompatible worlds.

It will take years, and a lot of rehabilitation. Gillian is a respected therapist, and she's well positioned to introduce Auralice to Manhattan's therapy culture. Auralice resists initially, so Gillian tells Auralice she's hiring an academic tutor, and the tutor doubles as an undercover therapist. Slowly, patiently, the tutor nudges Auralice toward recovery. Auralice becomes part of the family; this story is tragic, but it's also about generosity and healing. Auralice will always say that Gillian and her family rescued her. "They took me in, like a wounded kitten, and they gave me back my life," she says. "Who knows what would have happened to me without them? Gillian saved me."

In the midst of this rocky transition, the family takes a drive one morning down to Canal Street. Among the many ways Auralice has landed ill prepared is with a lack of winter clothes. So they all pile into a taxi and head downtown to buy her some. Auralice gets carsick on the way and vomits out the window. She's miserable and starts crying; she's a sullen little girl. Then, suddenly, the car slams to a halt. A truck is blocking the road and a few workmen are arguing around it, shouting at one another in a foreign language.

Auralice breaks into a grin. Gillian is puzzled and asks her what's going on. "They're cursing in Tamil!" Auralice says. "It's so disgusting, I can't tell you what they're saying." She's positively gleeful. At last, something to hold on to.

Nineteen eighty-six is a rough year for the family. John's passing in October is followed a couple of months later by the sudden death of David Maysles, Albert's brother and partner in filmmaking. Gillian's work takes her into the bowels of New York's AIDS epidemic. She visits hospitals filled with emaciated young men, and she finds herself in dimly lit rooms counseling their grieving, shocked relatives. Death is in the air.

One day the woman who called Gillian to tell her about John's death invites her to a séance. She says it's an opportunity for Gillian to communicate with her dead brother. The séance will be held a couple of blocks from the Dakota, in an apartment on Seventy-Second Street, between Columbus and Amsterdam Avenues. Two devotees of the Mother and Sri Aurobindo live in the apartment; the man has been to Auroville, he knows about Diane and John, and the woman is reputed to be a psychic.

Gillian doesn't believe in such things. In fact, they infuriate her; she's had it with Aurovilians and their superstitions. She decides to go to the séance anyway, not with hopes of speaking to her brother, but to teach these people a lesson. This is exactly the kind of unscientific mumbo jumbo that killed her brother, she thinks.

Gillian walks down the street on a winter evening, then up a flight of stairs to a small second-floor apartment. Four people sit around a table, and on it there's a sheet of oaktag with handwritten letters, an improvised Ouija board. The hosts light some candles, and some incense from Auroville. They dim the lights, and the woman who is said to be a psychic goes into a trance. Her hand starts moving around the board, apparently of its own volition, sliding from letter to letter, spelling out words.

There will be varying accounts of what takes place that evening. The friend who invited Gillian feels that John comes through and speaks to them. According to the friend, he doesn't talk about his death. He says he was Monet in a previous life. This makes sense to the friend: just like Monet, John had a long, thin face and big, spidery hands. And also, he was sensitive and creative.

Gillian will remember things differently. In her recollection, she poses a series of tests for the Ouija board. "John, I seem to have forgotten the name of our nanny," she says. "Can you please remind me?" The psychic's hands remain still. "And what about that dog we loved so much as kids? Can you remind me of its name? Can you tell me anything at all about it?" Again, the hands remain still.

After about half an hour of this, Gillian gets up to leave. She's polite and thanks her hosts for inviting her, but she can't help making a comment on the way out. "Well, that's strange, isn't it?" she asks. "How strange that my brother doesn't know all these basic details about his life."

She tells me this story years later, and she laughs, a dry, sarcastic chuckle.

"It was my little revenge," she says. "I was so angry with Auroville, you know, these fakers who messed up my brother's life. I thought I'll have fun with them, I'll really humiliate them. And it was fun. They were so irresponsible. I thought they were feckless. *Feckless* was the word I always used.

"Feckless, you know," she says again. "I remember John writing about the death of Aurolouis, talking about how it's fine because he'll reincarnate and all of that. I just thought it was crazy, and so stupid. You don't leave a child by a pond unattended. I mean, I don't know what was in Diane's mind to do that. It seemed so hippie-dippie, the whole thing. The whole place was negligent. How could they have just let him die?"

She tells me this decades after their deaths, and I can still feel the incandescent rage, and underneath it, the anguish. "It was all so senseless," Gillian says. "Senseless and sad."

Gillian is at Fishers Island with her parents. It's been a few months since John's death, and she's alone with her mother in the yellow-wallpapered living room. They never talk about John anymore, and neither does Gillian's father. Her mother drinks a lot now, probably too much, but she's eighty-one years old and her only son just died, and what is she supposed to do? She's drunk on bourbon tonight. Night falls and the bay outside is lit up by the last ferries from the mainland. Maybe a foghorn sounds, that call that John once compared to a chant of "Om, Om, Om."

Gillian's mother turns to her and asks, "Was I a bad mother? I was a bad mother, wasn't I?"

Gillian replies, "You did the best you could."

Lady Margaret Drummond Walker dies on September 23, 1987, just over eleven months after her son's death. She's cremated in England and her ashes are buried on Fishers Island, in a small graveyard with a white picket fence set by a baseball diamond. Mother and son both dead, so close together, and Gillian and her father decide to build a memorial for John alongside Lady

Margaret. So a large slab of gray slate is laid into the island's shimmering grass, and a line from a Henry Vaughan poem is engraved into the stone: "They are all gone into the world of light."

John Walker Sr. is eighty years old in 1987 and his bad left leg is getting worse. He can hardly walk anymore; he gets around mostly by wheelchair. He buys a small apartment in the Dakota, to be near Gillian and her family, though he still spends time in England. A wealthy art collector from Los Angeles hires him as a part-time consultant, and this keeps Walker Sr. busy. He's lonely, bereft, and bewildered. His wife is dead; his son, too, and he knows virtually nothing about the circumstances.

He receives a letter from an Aurovilian thanking him for his donations to the community over the years. In a shaky scrawl at the bottom of the letter, he jots down his questions:

1. Death certificate
2. Where is he or his ashes
3. What did he die of
4. When did he die

This father is starved for the most basic information. He writes a letter to a woman in America who's connected with Auroville. "John Anthony's death was a horrid shock to his mother and me. We know very little about his life and no one at the Ashram," he says. "We will be grateful for anything you can tell us. Did he leave any papers? He wrote admirably, and I hoped he might leave something to be published. He must have had a few personal effects. What will happen to them?" He asks if it would be possible for the mansion, Ravena, to be named the John Anthony House.

Walker Sr. outlives his son by nine years. In October of 1995, he falls out of his wheelchair and breaks his bad leg and goes into surgery in Chichester,

England. It's a difficult procedure and he's eighty-eight years old. Gillian flies over, promises to gift him a half pound of caviar from Fortnum & Mason if he successfully undergoes the surgery, which he does. Walker Sr. eats the caviar and dies the next day. His ashes are buried alongside his wife and son's memorial, under the gray slate on Fishers Island.

The letters keep coming from Auroville, asking for money even after John and Diane are dead. Divakar continues to work on the project, uncompensated. He does this out of a sense of commitment to his friends, and a conviction that finishing the mansion is the best way to honor their memories. Those sentiments aren't shared by the Walker family. They ignore Divakar's letters and have no intention of pouring more funds into what they consider a murky situation. Divakar sends photographs, a statement of accounts, and repeated entreaties to the Walkers. Years later, he will tell me, "It was as if I wrote to the sky, and the sky didn't answer."

"I know that the family would have wished for John to have another life," he says. "I know they would not have chosen for him to be in India with an incapacitated woman. I felt like they had no idea what John and Diane were trying to do; they didn't understand it at all. I hated having to ask for money. Writing to them was like entering into a ready-made trap where you are defined before you can even speak."

Divakar taps his personal resources, a small savings instrument his mother set up for him in France. Slowly, the work comes together—plumbing, sanitary fixtures, stained-glass windows, a smooth wall plaster made of white cement and marble powder. Against all odds, the mansion is completed. Ravena is a spacious, harmonious creation, the kind of building that transports you to a different mood, like a cocoon. It is undeniably the masterpiece John always hoped for, one of the most aesthetic homes in Auroville. But now its creators are gone and no one knows what to do with it. The house is massive and expensive to maintain, something of a white elephant. There's talk of turning it into an alternative-healing center (no one seems to notice the irony), then that plan is dropped and Ravena becomes a guesthouse, a way station for visiting students.

Now the mythmaking that was attached to Diane and John transfers to the mansion. There are stories about ghosts and demons, about cries that purportedly echo from its corridors. One night the hut in which they lived—and died—catches fire. Its thatch roof bursts into flames, staining the night yellow and singeing the tops of surrounding acacia trees. A neighbor runs in to retrieve a red cylinder of cooking gas before it explodes. That cylinder is virtually all that remains the following day, and their last home is reduced to a couple of charred walls in the forest. It's a mysterious fire, with no clear cause; people say that the curse of Ravena continues.

The mansion becomes a place where people throw parties. I'm fifteen or sixteen years old when this happens. My friends and I have some wild times there; John and Diane must be turning in their graves. But even through these good times, I'm a little scared of that building. It has dark chambers, decaying overgrown gardens, and large bats that swoop around, like harbingers of a terrible fate.

One night a young guest from Alaska invites me to Ravena for a beer. We drink Kingfisher on the upstairs terrace, the air cool, blowing in from the canyon, and the man points down through the building's octagonal courtyard, to an illuminated small room with a closed wooden sliding door. The room is tiny, more closet than living space, and the man says he's heard it was meant to be John's. In this entire massive house, he says, only this little alcove was allocated for John. Every night, the man switches off the single light bulb in the room and opens the door. And every night, he tells me, he later finds the door shut and the light on. This man has heard so many stories. People say John and Diane were crazy, and that they both committed suicide. He's heard rumors that in following John, Diane was trying to conquer death and reenact the parable of *Savitri*. He says he doesn't dare approach John's room when the light goes on.

There's titillation in tragedy. I suppose I believed some of those stories as a boy, and maybe I wanted to believe them. The haunted madness of Ravena was an exciting corner in the map of my youth. Now I see things differently. The small room wasn't spooky; it was just John being John, trying as usual to have it both ways. An extravagant mansion and a monastic cell. The swan who always wanted to be a crow. I'm older and I don't believe in ghosts anymore, and even if I did, I wouldn't be scared of theirs. John and Diane were gentle souls; they wouldn't harm anyone (except themselves—and Auralice). And what is crazy, anyway? Crazy is a blunt concept. There are levels of intensity, degrees of deviation from the norm.

There's no doubt that John and Diane stepped pretty far out on the scale, that they pushed the boundaries of normalcy (another blunt concept). But I've spent almost ten years chasing this story, and I know that there were many versions of reality, many versions of the truth, that played out in my hometown. I'm not prepared to say which one was right. I'm not here to say anyone was crazy.

Decades after their deaths, I meet a woman in New York. She was a college flame of John's. I speak with her at the Colony Club, an exclusive women-only institution on Sixty-Second Street and Park Avenue. I'm wearing a shirt and jeans and the doorman stops me on the way in, says I'm not adequately dressed. He's standoffish, a little snobby, but I plead with him, and he lends me a jacket and tie. I fumble the tie and he laughs and helps me knot it.

The woman and I sit on upholstered furniture, under large arched windows, the whole scene bathed in the shine of privilege. She holds her back firm and her neck is long and she tells me stories about John. She was at Wellesley while he was at Harvard, and she remembers parties at the Casablanca filled with attractive artsy people, Edie Sedgwick in striking outfits dancing on tables and setting off sprinklers. There was a flamboyance to John, she says, a sense of drama and performance. He drank a lot; he would spontaneously propose to women; he gifted her a black charcoal Giacometti, a seminude that would probably be worth a small fortune today. Once she visited his home in Georgetown and attended a private talk given by Isaiah Berlin. She remembers a dinner there with twenty lavish baskets of flowers; each of those baskets, she says, cost as much as her flight ticket from Boston to Washington.

And then, the woman tells me, she heard John abandoned it all and moved somewhere strange in India. Someone said John committed suicide, and she's also been told that he sent a life-size naked picture of himself to his mother before he died. She asks me if those stories are true. I say the answer to the first one is complicated, and the second one isn't. I ask her how those stories made her feel. She straightens in her seat and says, "I'm glad I dodged that bullet." And sitting in that club, in my borrowed jacket and ill-knotted tie, encircled by New York society, everything that John was trying to escape, vanity of vanities, I think to myself, I'm sure he'd feel exactly the same. He, too, dodged a bullet. There are so many different versions of a good life.

Auralice stays in America, attends the University of Southern California, and then goes to graduate school at Columbia. I leave Auroville when I'm sixteen, spend two years on a scholarship in boarding school at Phillips Academy Andover, and then four at Harvard. We stay in touch during this time; we're friends, no more. We share an unusual background, and then an unlikely parallel path through the world. There aren't many people with our trajectory, that journey from Auroville to the heart of the East Coast establishment, and perhaps, as my parents will later say, it's inevitable that we will get married.

Is it inevitable, too, that we will return to Auroville? Auralice is of course propelled by her ghosts, even if it will take us years to realize that. I can't imagine her going through life without unpacking this mystery. But I think there's more to our return: other reasons, other propellants.

The summer after my freshman year in college I spend the holiday back home in India. It's 1994 and Auroville is a very different town from the one where I grew up. Much of what repelled or angered me as a child—the fanaticism, the cruelty, the fecklessness—has faded, and what remains are things

I love: freedom, a sense of opportunity, an awareness of a population that is, however imperfectly, attempting to build a better world. Maybe, also, spending time in places such as Harvard, the belly of the beast, all that ruthless ambition and materialism, has changed my perspective on Auroville's idealism, allowed me to better understand its value.

One afternoon I cycle over to the Matrimandir. The building remains incomplete—the revolution has taken a hard toll on the work—but the gardens are soothing and expansive, and I head to a patchwork of boulders and lawn on a mound looking over the structure. I sit on the lawn and a thought hits me; it hits me with the clarity of an epiphany. At least here they're trying, I think. At least they're trying to build something different. That moment, I am certain that I will ultimately return to Auroville to be part of this adventure.

Children of utopias, I've come to understand, are like exiles. We grow up with the promise, illusory though it may be, of an ideal society. We come into adulthood and we understand the impracticability of that vision, as well as the flaws of the grown-ups who offered it to us. Yet still we cling to the promise; a part of us never stops hoping, looking for a way back. It's hard to eradicate the vision of a better world once it inhabits your dreams. I think it was always inevitable that Auralice and I would return to Auroville.

There's an evening in the fall or winter of 2003 in Brooklyn. We're in a smoky bar on Smith Street. We've started early and we've had too many glasses of wine, and we're talking about the war in Iraq, and we're generally gloomy. A few more glasses and we find ourselves in an existential moment, questioning the tracks we're pursuing and dwelling on what feels like a stultifying sameness, a conformity of outlook and aspiration to all the lives in that room (ours included). Is this all there is? I see our reflection in a mirror on the wall, and I wonder if these forms we're inhabiting are really ours. I think that's when we have our first conversation about moving to Auroville. I know for sure we don't discuss Diane or John on this night; I guess we're naïve, but we don't seem to understand how they will be in our lives.

Some months later and we've done it—impulsively, it might seem, although really not at all. We live for a time in an apartment maintained by my mother, who is now divorced from my father. Then we select a location near a dam and a forest to construct our own house (although no one owns a home in Auroville; everything remains, as in the past, communal property). Building in Auroville now requires running a gauntlet of bureaucracy. Things are a little more systematized, the community has its homegrown planning groups, and those old tensions persist between John's "organicists" and "constructionalists." The planners initially resist our house, arguing that it doesn't adhere to the Galaxy master plan. We manage to push our proposal through, with some modifications, and we embark on the same project of building a home together that John and Diane did all those years ago.

We get a bouncy Labrador and we name her Laxmi. Our two sons, Aman John Anthony and Emil Larry, attend the community's schools, which are substantially more serious than the ones we had as kids. We go for walks around the Matrimandir, and jogs in the forests. I play tennis and Auralice goes to yoga classes. Most of the time, we're happily—insistently—living in the present.

But history will not be walled off; the past continues to infiltrate the present. One afternoon Auralice and I are walking with our sons in the foundation pit under the Matrimandir when a woman comes up and asks who we are. She informs us in a stern voice that only Aurovilians are allowed in this area. Auralice holds my arm to restrain my indignation, and she tells the woman our names. The woman looks at Auralice wide-eyed. "Ah, Auralice!" she says, and there's no question but that we're welcome in this place. Something in the woman's expression revives that old idea of Diane's sacrifice; we are standing, after all, in the very location of her fall.

Auralice has a car accident and suffers a deep cut on her neck, directly below her jaw. The injury is serious, and she's lucky to receive prompt medical care and the attention of an expert plastic surgeon. Nonetheless, she's left with a large scar, and it summons recollections—in Auralice, and others—of her mother's broken jaw. A woman asks Auralice, "Why do these things keep happening to you, over and over? What is it that the Mother is trying to tell us?"

I'm bitten by a dog. It's a domestic pet, a low-risk encounter, but someone recommends that I get rabies shots anyway, just to be certain. I hesitate, fearful of the disease but reluctant to get the shots unless they're absolutely necessary. Auralice, always less anxious than I am, insists I don't need them. I sit on our sofa and look at her, and for a moment I start thinking that she's trying to get me to avoid medical care, just as Gillian believes Auralice's mother did to John. It's a fleeting thought, it passes quickly, but nonetheless, these are the types of games Auralice's biography plays in our lives, and in our marriage.

One morning I go to the library in Auroville. I'm browsing aimlessly, and I pull a book off the shelves and flip through its pages. I find a piece of paper in the book. It's the handwritten last will and testament of John Walker. In the will, John declares Auralice to be his daughter, and he leaves everything to her. I give the will to Auralice and we tell Gillian about it. She cries. "I knew it," she says. "I just knew instinctively that's how he felt, and that's why I took Auralice in. I'm so happy you're telling me this."

People in Auroville always say there are no accidents. Mostly, I'm dubious; I know the universe is full of coincidence. But what strange cosmic twist, what roll of the dice and weird inexplicable happenstance, could possibly have directed that paper to my hands?

John's old friends Bob and Judith visit us a few years after we move back. This isn't the first time they've been in the area since they met John outside his house in Slancio. They've traveled in India on several occasions, driven along a highway that leads past Auroville, but their hearts were always heavy and they could never bring themselves to turn into the community. Now they know that Auralice is living here with her family, and maybe that makes it easier. They look us up and ask if we'll take them to Ravena, to see what their friend built.

We drive over late one morning in their rented SUV. We go through a forest, past a sprawling country home, and then along a yellow guesthouse with laundry hanging outside and a taxi idling in its driveway. India continues to prosper and grow, and Pondicherry is pushing past its boundaries, onto Auroville's once virgin soil. There's even an airport coming up across the canyon, and next to it a sewage-processing facility that emits foul odors.

We park outside Ravena, and we walk through the bramble around the shell of Diane and John's burned-down hut. We approach the grave, which is no longer merely a pit in the ground but a marble tomb inscribed with lines from *Savitri*. After our initial visit here, when Auralice crouched and cried over the unmarked burial site, she returned with a gardener and a couple of masons to build a more fitting memorial. She used marble left over from the Matri-mandir construction site, and Gillian helped choose the passage from *Savitri* (they selected lines from one of the last letters John sent to his sister).

We sit with Bob and Judith around the memorial, its marble turned mossy from recent rains, and they reminisce about John. They tell stories about how he always tried to escape his heritage, all his efforts at asceticism and self-abnegation. "He prided himself on physical suffering and self-denial," Judith says. "It was as if material things couldn't give him any real satisfaction. He just wanted to get some distance from his wealth and background." Yet at the same time, they say, he could never quite give it all up. They remember being in a car in England with John's parents shortly after his death, and Bob or Judith mentioned how John used to show them his family tree, boast about the centuries it stretched back and all the notables it included. Walker Sr. spun around in the front seat, astonished, and asked, "He did what?" The son he knew had always run away.

He was such a dandy, such a charmer. He would go to the beach in a white three-piece suit, a way of attracting attention and showing off his patrician background. Once he helped Bob and Judith buy a house on Long Island. He talked and talked to the owner until she lowered the price. "It was like watching a high-class used-car salesman, amazing!" Judith says. "He had his father's charm, he could really turn it on."

We laugh at these memories, Judith and Bob's affection for their friend still evident after so much time, then we lift ourselves off the grave and head toward the mansion. Ravena sits in a clearing, an imposing white building topped by a spacious open-to-air terrace. Its elegant cornices and wooden pillars are incongruous against the unkempt forest, as if a slice of Renaissance Europe has been transplanted to rural South India (which is close to the truth). I've been here several times over the years, but I notice for the first time that the building has few windows and is hunkered down like a bunker. I realize that this is another echo of Ravenna's cathedral, which is similarly closed off, as if to reserve all its beauty for the inside.

Auralice won't come into the house; that's a step too far. She waits near a parking shed while I introduce Bob and Judith to Jocelyn, a close friend of John's who now lives and runs an art studio in the mansion. I walk Bob and Judith around, pointing out all the octagonals, and then I show them the small room with the sliding door, John's man cave that my Alaskan friend told me was haunted. I take them into a bathroom that was intended to be Diane's. It has a narrow, sunken bathtub that would have been near impossible for her to get in and out of. People always say this is further evidence of John and Diane's removal from reality, their deep denial. Auralice will later disabuse me of this notion: the tub was actually intended to be a pond, and no one ever planned to bathe in it. So this is another of Ravena's myths.

We take a spiral staircase, made from the teakwood my father sourced for John, and we walk onto the terrace. We lean against the parapet, and I think of how John would have anticipated sitting up here with Diane and Auralice, looking over the red land, those dramatic crevasses that constitute Auroville's southern border. Today the forests hide the view of Forecomers canyon, but the sun is setting and the sky is purple, there's a breeze in the trees, and in the orange and magenta bougainvillea that spills over the parapet, and I feel that

for all the changes in this area, all the development, there's still depth and magic in this land. "It's so beautiful," Judith says. "This was clearly his life's work."

On our way out of the mansion we pass by a board containing a prayer of Saint Francis of Assisi, painted in John's handwriting. "It is in losing our lives that we shall find them," the prayer concludes. "It is in dying that we shall rise up to eternal life." We join Auralice by the car, and Judith says to her, "I'm so glad he found something. I'm so glad he met a woman he loved and who loved him. I think he discovered his purpose with your mom; he found someone he could build his life with." Auralice's eyes get glassy. I put my arms around her, and I tell them that's probably the nicest thing anyone from John's world has ever said about Diane. Bob says, "One thing about John, he knew how to get out. If he had wanted to leave, he would have. He would have just bought a ticket and left."

That night Auralice and I are sitting around the table after dinner. Our plates are empty, and the kids are on the other side of the room playing with LEGO. Sometimes the peaceful domesticity of these moments confronts me; none of this was foretold, none of it predictable. The odds were overwhelmingly against things working out like this for Auralice. When I think that way, when my thoughts turn to her past, that wild, extreme childhood, the contingency of everything we have hits me, and I feel overwhelmed, often filled with a sense of dread. I try not to, but I find myself dwelling on all that idle chatter about curses and karma. Living with Auralice, building a family with her, means constantly being aware of how fragile everything is. The wolf is perpetually at the door.

People always ask me how Auralice feels about this book. I always say, "It's complicated." Sometimes it's painful; we are rummaging in dark corners. And sometimes it's cathartic. When Auralice left Auroville as a fourteen-year-old girl so much remained unknown, and so much unprocessed. We are shining a light on hidden places, and we are doing it together. The process isn't easy, but at times I do feel it gives our marriage a certain ballast, a shared project. A man once told me, "The hardest thing in a marriage is really to look at each other, to step outside yourself and be curious about the other." I agree, I have failed so often, and I think that writing this book has helped me in that regard, and maybe made me a better husband. Auralice and I have spent many meals, many walks, many hours, together talking about John and Diane, tugging at the shroud that has long obscured her biography.

Tonight, while the kids are in the corner, alternating between bickering and lovingly playing, as brothers do, we discuss the day's visit to Ravena. We laugh at Bob's and Judith's memories of John and his fancy clothes, the way he liked to show off. "He was such a complex person," I say to Auralice. I feel that I know John now; I've read his letters, spoken to many people about him. I've been in his head, and he's certainly been in mine. "He had so many different sides," I say. "It just feels like he spent almost his whole life figuring out who he was. He sounds lost so much of the time."

I make the case, as I have before, that the worst times, the craziest periods of his life, were inseparable from the best. Ravena is the only moment when John doesn't seem lost. In those final months—until his very death: even in his manner of dying, in the way he stayed resolute in his convictions—he had an intentionality and determination that gave his life cohesiveness. I admire John's faith. I even find myself, despite its calamitous consequences, envying it.

"So few of us find that kind of purpose," I say to Auralice. "I mean, do you have it? Do I? I've been in Auroville almost my whole life, and I don't have even a fraction of the belief John did." What happened at Ravena was terrible. Who could deny that? But I tell Auralice that I can't help feeling that period of their lives was noble, even exalted. In Ravena, it all came together for them.

She doesn't say anything. She holds her head back and crosses her eyes, as if watching me from a distance. We've been together a long time, and I've known her even longer. I think I understand what this look means. The John I'm painting is not her John. Mine is an analytical construct, a character in a book.

The John she knew was flesh and blood: a man, a friend, a husband, a brother, a parent. I'll never know this John, and Auralice's reticence now indicates to me that she has something to add, an opinion she might share, but that she won't unless it's extracted.

"What?" I ask her. "What?"

"But he died," she says. "They died."

THE QUESTION OF BLAME

THE REVOLUTION IS LONG OVER and I'm sitting with Amrit in his house in the community of Certitude. Amrit is writing a memoir that he's shared with me, and we're discussing it. The book is an account of his life from his childhood in a Japanese American internment camp, to his struggles as a Neutral in Auroville, and then his subsequent reintegration into the community. It's likely to displease a few people, especially those who were close to Satprem, but I think it's an important work, and I'm telling him that now.

We're talking about history—Auroville's history, but also history more generally. Who gets to write it? Who will tell the story of this brave experiment in communal living? What version of events gets normalized, hardens into fact? These aren't abstract questions. There's no shortage of dreamers and searchers in the world, maybe especially in today's troubled, confusing world, and new people keep joining Auroville. By the early 2000s, the town's population numbers some twenty-five hundred people, including large representations from India (1,044), France (355), Germany (220), Italy (146), America (82), and Russia (64). These people are fleeing inequality and political tribalism, climate change and rampant consumerism. They rejuvenate the community and replenish its energy. But what do they know about its past? What do they know about how we got here, and why things are the way they are today?

There's little institutional history in Auroville. The past consists mainly of stories people hear around town; and those stories, as anywhere else in the world, contain a particular version. Auroville's history is the history of its vanquishers. There is a mainstream narrative—about a righteous revolution against the CFY, about the treacherous Neutrals and the treatment they received and deserved—and while not entirely false, this version leaves a lot out. True history is always multidimensional.

A woman who has been in Auroville since her childhood once told me, "We have the relationship of a construction site to this place. We've seen it come up brick by brick. We know where the cracks are and where improvisations were made." I think of Amrit's memoir as an architectural excavation. It questions the easy stories we tell ourselves (and the outside world). His book doesn't exactly contradict these stories, but it adds nuance to them—and that's a good thing.

"They were complicated times," I tell Amrit now, sitting at a table in his kitchen, two cups of tea between us. "They weren't black-and-white. I think most people knew that all along, but many acted as if things were black-and-white." I was just a kid; warriors in the revolution would no doubt tell me—have told me—that I don't understand the circumstances, the existential threat facing the community. Yes, there were excesses, they say, but the revolution saved Auroville; it's a miracle the community still exists. I take their point. I respect their sacrifices, their commitment and courage in standing up to a more powerful adversary. But if there's one thing growing up in this town has taught me, it's that too much commitment is often dangerous. It blurs judgment; it can even kill.

"They died for their beliefs," people say of Diane and John. I suppose this is true. You could just as well say they died *because* of their beliefs.

Amrit's troubles continued well into the 1980s. In 1985, after years as a social pariah, he was allowed to work again at the Matrimandir. He spent his days in the gardens, watering and potting, pruning roses. Sentiments had eased somewhat toward the Neutrals, but not altogether. After a while some people started objecting to Amrit's presence at the Matrimandir, saying that he was polluting the atmosphere. One day two Frenchmen visited his house and threatened him, saying he'd better quit working at the Matrimandir, warning of unspecified consequences if he refused. Finally, after about a year and a half of this, Amrit found another job.

In 1988, the Indian Parliament passed the Auroville Foundation Act, a follow-up to the Supreme Court's verdict in the case brought by the CFY. The act extended the government's earlier temporary legislation and set up a new administrative structure that combined broad state control with a modicum of self-determination. Although an imperfect solution—many people worried about effectively becoming a government department—the passage of the Foundation Act represented the culmination of Auroville's long revolution.

One of the immediate consequences of the act was a move to reintegrate the Neutrals. The government wanted a complete list of all Aurovilian residents. The Neutrals were residents in Auroville, but there was some debate within the community about whether physically living in Auroville was sufficient to qualify a person as an Aurovilian. In an article, a group of revolutionaries decried the "missionaries of integration" and "goodwill maniacs" who were pushing to bring the Neutrals back into the fold. They railed against "a staggering revisionism [that] replaced the historical truth" of Auroville's revolution. Eventually, bureaucratic expediency overcame ideological zeal. The final list of Aurovilians submitted to the government included resident Neutrals.

On October 3, 1988, Amrit marked his forty-fifth birthday by visiting Sri Aurobindo's room in the Ashram. He sat and meditated for a few minutes, then he stopped by the Samadhi on his way out. He left the Ashram to run some errands and outside a gas station, a young Aurovilian named Anna approached him with a wide smile. Amrit was surprised; people weren't usually so friendly to him. "How does it feel to be an Aurovilian again?" Anna asked him. "You have been accepted back into Auroville!"

Amrit felt himself reeling. "Anna," he said harshly, "I never was *not* an Aurovilian!" He told her that the Mother had accepted him into the community and he didn't care what anyone else thought. Anna was taken aback, and Amrit had to catch his breath. His overwhelming sensation wasn't one of elation or joy or even relief. It was disgust.

Amrit talks to me about this episode now, and as he speaks, I can see that he's reliving the era, and that the pain of Auroville's civil war is still raw. There are moments when I feel he winces, almost physically flinches. "The nightmare of the revolution was over, but it wasn't really over for me," he says. "For years I still felt so much hurt and anger. It was like a form of PTSD. To tell you the truth, I still have a hard time with my feelings toward the community. I believe in the Mother's dream, but sometimes I just feel like I don't want to have anything at all to do with much of what goes on around here. I'm so removed from everyday life."

He continues: "How could these people behave the way they did? How could they come to Auroville, claim they were here for human unity, and then treat people like that? It just made a mockery of everything. The shame is that it all started out so beautifully. When the Mother was alive, there was such a sense of togetherness, so much openness. The dream felt real. I still struggle sometimes to accept the way things turned out."

I ask Amrit why he thinks this all happened. How did the situation in Auroville go off track? Amrit is a mystic; he's steeped in ancient yogic practices, and his understanding of the world encompasses the supernatural. He gives me an explanation that includes the workings of the divine and demons, battles between good and evil forces, and an imbalance of light. I listen respectfully, but I find myself dissatisfied: this is not my frame of reality. Then he comes closer to the ground, and to what I take to be the heart of the matter.

"Things just became more and more radical, they spiraled out of control," he says. "I attribute this radicalization largely to Satprem. His letters and his contact with Auroville hardened attitudes. It gave the movement for independence from the CFY an ideological basis that it didn't have before. What I observed was that Satprem's paranoia transmitted itself to the whole community; there started to be this uptightness about things, this intolerance that was just very unpleasant. It was as if someone had stuck us all together, trapped us in a dark tunnel."

Amrit compares his own experience during the Second World War to Satprem's. "I was born in a camp, you know, so that usually carries a kind of karmic imprint," he says. "And it was the same with Satprem. I think Satprem's bitterness had to do with his experience in the camps. Of course the concentration camps were much worse, but what I'm trying to say is that there are two possible reactions to being at the receiving end of injustice. You can become bitter like Satprem, or you can become more idealistic and say, 'No, this must never happen again, we can't treat people like that anymore.' It shocked me when I saw all these people who were brought up in what I thought was a liberal democratic tradition doing all this stuff. I wondered, *How can this be? You people are supposed to believe in justice and decency and tolerance.*"

When John and Diane died, Amrit was employed in Pondicherry. He still lived in Auroville, but he spent most of his days away from the community, supervising workers at a small clothes factory; he was trying to get a bit of distance. Years had passed since he'd seen them, almost a decade since he'd massaged Diane's legs after she came out of the hospital. The news of their deaths was painful, but it didn't entirely shock Amrit. He'd heard about their entanglement with Satprem, and he'd long felt it wouldn't end well.

For Amrit, John's and Diane's deaths represented one more reverberation of the revolution, and of Satprem's role in it. "I rather blamed Satprem," Amrit says to me as we're having tea together. "I had already seen how he almost destroyed Auroville, and then I saw it again with John and Diane. He created an illusion, a kind of maya. He told Diane she was special, and that she had this special responsibility. I think it trapped her; it trapped them both. In my opinion, their deaths were the natural consequence of his influence."

I go to a bookstore in Auroville. This small place in a tile-roofed structure keeps a large stock of books by Satprem. He authored or edited at least sixty-one, including the thirteen-volume *Agenda*. They offer an unvarnished portrait of his many battles and internal struggles, and of his efforts to continue the Mother's project of cellular evolution.

I heard about Satprem throughout my childhood and early adulthood. He was a larger-than-life figure. I knew him as the father of Auroville's revolution, and his reputation was always fearsome. Despite my skepticism about such things, I was always a little wary of the spiritual powers he was said to possess, and of his purported ability to command occult forces. Like many of my friends (like, I think, most of our parents), I considered him dangerous, a powerful and fiery figure you wouldn't want to cross. This ability to inspire fear was one of Satprem's defining traits as a leader. It's why so few people, even those who knew better, who knew right from wrong, dared stand up to the extremists during the darkest days of the community's civil war.

I've read more of Satprem's books now, I've spoken to a lot of people about him. I feel that I know him better; I realize I was probably afraid of a caricature. Satprem was a complex, contradictory, brilliant, troubled, and yes, in many ways, *troubling* personality. I won't exonerate him of anything: appalling actions were committed in Satprem's name, and he was at the very least a silent spectator. But other aspects to his character were more salutary. Even Aurovilians who today doubt the man laud him for bringing the *Agenda* and its spiritual message into the world; they remain grateful for the impetus he provided to what the community still considers a noble struggle for freedom. A man who knew Satprem explained it to me this way: parts of a person can be highly evolved and in touch with the divine, even while other parts remain trapped in imperfection. To me, this duality simply sounds very human.

I'm at the store now to buy some of Satprem's books, and a Frenchman sits sweating behind a checkout table. He's one of the few remaining diehards in the community, someone who's never lowered the flag. He notes my pile of Satprem reading approvingly, and he complains that few people read the man as they used to. As he's adding up my bill, he asks, "I hear you're writing a book about Satprem?"

"I'm not writing a book about Satprem," I say, a little flustered. "I'm writing about John and Diane; I'm writing about my wife's parents. It's a deeply personal book. Though, of course, Satprem has to enter into it because he played such a big role in their story."

"But I hear you're writing about Satprem, and that you're blaming him for their deaths?"

"That's just not true," I say. I'm surprised to hear a note of apprehension in my response; even after all these years, I'm still scared of the man.

"That's good to know," the bookstore vendor says. "That would be really heavy. That would be too much." He shakes his head in relief, and I have a distinct sense that the relief is for me, for having avoided whatever dark forces or cosmic wrath I would invite upon myself if I were to write such a book about Satprem.

The question of blame—of responsibility—hovers over the deaths of John and Diane. In many ways it goes to the core of the endeavor Auralice and I have embarked upon. Why did they die? What—or who—was it that killed them? Blaming Satprem is too simple. It's like Gillian accusing Diane of trapping John; or Diane's mother suggesting that John guided her daughter into a fatal fast. John and Diane each had individual agencies. Fate happens to us, but we choose our pathways within its broad avenues. John and perhaps especially Diane were singularly strong-minded; I have no doubt that they willed their outcomes.

But there's no doubt, too, that their lives intersected with Satprem's battles, and with the revolution he fired up and in many ways directed. All my life, I've thought of their deaths as isolated tragedies, the sad but singular destinies of two individuals. Bad luck or madness, unwise choices or unfortunate destinies: these are the narratives that have presented themselves. Now Auralice and I know that, in addition to these personalized explanations, there was also a so-cial dimension. Diane and John were in so many ways collateral damage of a wider struggle and movement. And even more: their deaths were the perhaps entirely predictable outcomes of an age-old human longing.

Utopia sounds so good. Sweep away what is and build in its place a more perfect society. Like millions before them, John and Diane were looking for a better world; that search quickly grew complicated, as it always does. They got caught in the crash between their dreams and hard reality. It's an old story, played out across time, in virtually every revolution and millenarian movement, where human lives are treated as mere expedients on the journey toward a new world. Yes, John and Diane were victims of Auroville's revolution. They were also victims of the search for perfection.

A few weeks after that visit to the bookstore, I'm walking by the Matrimandir when I meet another Frenchman who also works at the store. He's heard about my conversation with his colleague. He comes up to me near the Banyan Tree, and he says he wants to tell me about something that happened to him; it may help me understand Diane's fate. A few years ago, he says, he was in a bad car accident. His leg was crushed below the knee, and he spent almost a year immobilized, de-pressed and sitting alone in a small room. He wondered if he'd be paralyzed for the rest of his life. Somehow, Satprem heard about his plight and sent two representa-tives from Kotagiri, who told the man that Satprem was aware of his condition and working on it. This message, the man now tells me, pulled him through. Satprem's attentions lifted his spirits and helped him heal, and now he walks again.

"What I wanted to say is that I just kept Satprem in my mind," he says. "I didn't need any letters or anything. I could have been paralyzed, but I realized it was a test, and I got through it. I thought of Diane and I wanted to tell you that, really, healing is all about one's personal receptivity; it depends on how open a person is. I don't know anything about Diane or how the accident affected her. But maybe it closed her off and created some barriers. I'm not saying it did; I'm just saying that what really matters is your own openness and receptivity. I was perfectly open and it made a huge difference for me."

I thank the man for sharing his story. As I walk away, he calls after me. "Everyone has their own karma," he says. "Who can say what's supposed to happen? But in the end, it's up to each individual, and we can't put everything on Satprem's shoulders. I was absolutely open, totally ready to receive—that's what saved me."

One morning in early 2006, a German doctor named Helmut receives a call at his Hamburg residence. The caller is an associate of Satprem's. She says that Satprem isn't well, and that he needs a doctor. She seems to know about Helmut—that he has recently returned to Germany after living for a decade in Auroville, that he's willing to go beyond allopathy and is well versed in alternative healing methods such as homeopathy and acupuncture. Helmut has read and admired Satprem for years; he's always wanted to meet him. So when the associate asks if he'd be willing to visit Kotagiri for a consultation, Helmut says yes right away. A few days later, he's on a flight for Bangalore, where a taxi awaits and takes him to Satprem's mountain refuge.

The first night at Kotagiri, Helmut has trouble sleeping; he manages only a couple of hours. The next morning he's led to the garden outside Satprem's bungalow. He waits a while and then Satprem walks out—slowly, unsteadily, an aged, wizened man, leaning on Sujata for support. Satprem stands at the top of a short flight of stairs, and Helmut is below them, on a lawn. Like everyone, he notices Satprem's penetrating blue eyes, and he feels an emanating force that he will later compare to the Niagara Falls.

They look at each other for a time, then Satprem descends the stairs and approaches. Helmut notices Satprem has tears in his eyes. Satprem asks, *"Est-ce que vous pensez que je suis fou?"* (Do you think I am crazy?)

Helmut, who speaks French fluently, answers, *"Non, vous n'êtes pas fou. C'est le monde qui est fou."* (No, you are not crazy. It's the world that's crazy.)

Satprem says he no longer understands the world in which he's living. As far as he's concerned, evolution should have stopped with the birds. "I don't get this species," he says, presumably referring to humans. Then he asks Helmut, "What are you searching for?"

Helmut tells him he's searching for beauty and truth. "Beauty I understand," Satprem says, waving a hand around the garden. "It's in nature—in the trees and the birds. But truth, that's a subject of academic debate."

"No, not the truth you get from reading books," Helmut says. "The truth you live, that you incarnate. That's what interests me."

Satprem turns to Sujata and says, "Look, he's really good." He uses the French word *gentil*, and Helmut takes this to mean that Satprem feels he is open to the yoga, that he understands what Satprem is trying to do in Kotagiri.

Later, Satprem tells Helmut about his ailments. He speaks of the terrible pain in his upper back and neck, and he says his body is being crushed by a weight of lead. He feels lightning in his ears, and a force moving up and down his body, bouncing from his feet to his head. Helmut takes Satprem's blood pressure and checks his other vitals. Nothing seems seriously wrong. He pulls out his needles and tries a session of acupuncture, but Satprem is too sensitive, and he reacts badly and pushes the needles away. Helmut has brought a device that emits infrared rays; he applies this treatment at the same acupuncture points, and Satprem seems to tolerate it better than the needles.

In many ways, Helmut is confounded. He feels Satprem is an advanced being, and that he's broken free of at least some of the laws that govern the human body. Helmut's medical arsenal, even the homeopathy and acupuncture, seems insufficient for the situation. "These were things that went beyond what I had learned or practiced," Helmut tells me later. "He had a different consciousness in his body; it didn't function according to the old laws. There really was nothing to cure, nothing I could do to relieve him of his pain."

Helmut senses that Satprem is a man in distress. He's lonely and isolated, and it's as though he's carrying the weight of the world. *"Mon corps est le chemin du monde,"* he tells Helmut (My body is the pathway of the world), and he repeatedly emphasizes the difficulty of the journey he's on. The problem, he says, is that the supramental force he's trying to manifest simultaneously attracts all its opposites. It's a wondrous, enlightened force, but it's also a hazardous one.

They spend several nights together in Satprem's room, under a handwritten sign that says *Mère Vaincra* (The Mother will triumph). Sometimes Helmut sleeps fitfully on the floor, but often they stay awake together, Satprem in a chair and Helmut on the ground, maybe on his knees and holding Satprem's hands. Satprem asks, "Do you feel this force that's going through my body, all this lead? Do you feel it?"

There's a cassette player in the room, and one morning at three Satprem asks Helmut to play Beethoven's Fifth Piano Concerto, also known as the *Emperor Concerto*. It's a pounding piece of music, with a delicate piano that seems desperate to flee dominating strings and horns. The music booms through the house at the edge of the cliff, darkness and fog outside, a fireplace burning inside. They sit there and Helmut feels as though Satprem is traveling somewhere, and he's taking Helmut with him.

Sometimes Satprem asks for a cigar. Once Helmut fails to light the cigar promptly, and Satprem loses his temper. He erupts, and Helmut sees a trace of the irateness that has been directed at many over the years. Mostly, Satprem is silent. He's too weak to speak much, and he doesn't write—or even read a lot—any longer. Helmut feels he's very concentrated, and inwardly directed. Satprem confides in Helmut that although the cellular transformation is certainly happening, well underway in his body, the road ahead remains forbidding. He says that ordinary people could never endure what he does. The only reason he's able to undertake this journey is because of the time he spent learning with the Mother.

Helmut stays ten days and nights in Kotagiri. He later tells me that they are the most intense of his life. He has recurring nightmares, dreams of skeletons in dark places. He feels that his proximity to Satprem unleashes a cleansing of his subconsciousness. It's hardly bearable, and as much as he admires Satprem and feels privileged to be in the company of this great sage, he's a little worried that Satprem will ask him to stay longer. He's not sure he could survive.

But that doesn't happen, and on Helmut's last morning in Kotagiri, Sujata makes him toast and wishes him a safe journey, and then Helmut catches a flight back to Germany. When he leaves, he feels that Satprem is doing a little better; he seems to have less pain and more energy. But a couple of months after Helmut returns, Sujata sends a letter saying that his visit has shown her the limits of medicine. Though she is grateful for his efforts, there has been no tangible result, and he will not be invited back.

On April 9, 2007, Satprem awakens and eats breakfast. While eating, he says, "Ma"—perhaps calling the Mother. A maid helps him to a sofa, and as he sits, she pulls the curtains so sunlight can enter the room. She hears two rasping sounds and turns around and finds Satprem dead, one eye closed, the other still open and directed at a photo of Sri Aurobindo.

He is buried in the garden, by a bush near a small Shiva lingam. Sujata dies about a month later and she's buried alongside him. A few months before dying, Satprem sent a note to a former associate. He wrote, "I have reached the goal."

EPILOGUE: BIRTHDAYS

IT'S FEBRUARY OF 2018 AND I find this hard to believe, but Auroville is turning fifty. Fifty years old, half a century! How did this new world, this blank slate for a reinvented society economy polity—how did the baby get to middle age? One thing is certain: for all our utopian ambitions, our determination to remake every rule, human and cosmic, we haven't succeeded in stopping time.

The community wears its scars, its rheumatic aches and pains. We've all been stuck in the bubble for a long time, and many of us share too much history, too much intimate knowledge of one another's imperfections. Some people complain that the original flame is dimmed, that Auroville's early idealism has been replaced by a tired bourgeois complacency. I suppose that may be partly true. But utopia is always a glass half-full or half-empty; its evaluation is always subjective. We haven't achieved everything we set out to (not even close), but I can't help feeling we've nonetheless achieved a lot. We're turning fifty; that's an accomplishment. Few intentional communities—now, or ever—have survived that long. The world militates against places such as Auroville, against anywhere that tries to play by different rules. We've held up pretty well against the assaults of conventionality and orthodoxy.

I'm proud of Auroville's schools, of an alternative system of education that has risen from the ashes of burned books and anti-intellectual dogmatism, that has sent so many children (Auralice and I included) to colleges around the world. I'm proud that despite our inevitable compromises and appeasements, we've nonetheless managed to create a society—or at least the embers of a society—that is somewhat egalitarian, and that endeavors to move beyond the materialism that engulfs the rest of the planet. I feel honored to be surrounded by men and women who have dedicated their existences to a cause, who have lived with intention and shown me, and now show my kids, that there are other things to strive for in this world than I me mine.

Fifty years. It's been a long, sometimes tortuous journey, but I feel privileged to have been along for the ride. I'm capable of forgetting this privilege; I lapse into occasional bouts of cynicism and negativity. Usually, all it takes to remind me of what Auroville has achieved is a walk through one of its forests: those winding red dirt paths, that green canopy of slender acacia, spiky palmyra, and leafy tropical evergreen trees. This geography is in my (and Auralice's) blood. It warms my heart—makes me gleeful—that Auroville's trees exist in defiance of all the planners' best efforts to build a concrete city. I think of the forests (and all that they contain: the snakes, the birds, the mongooses, the porcupines, and now wild boars, too) as an affirmation of life, an insistent declaration that preconceived human notions of what *should* be can never straitjacket or prevent what *will* be. These forests exist not because of utopia, but despite utopia.

For the longest time, all these achievements just simmered unnoticed. Auroville was happening, quietly emerging, a daily reality that no one beyond the plateau cared or knew much about. We lived here and we grew up here, and some of us died, but we weren't very interesting to the outside world, and the anonymity was liberating. No more. India and its cities keep swelling, extending their roads and train tracks like tentacles into once-remote corners of the country. Auroville today receives a large amount of media attention, and it's a magnet for curious tourists, who descend upon us in their buses, air-conditioned cars, and rented scooters. There's even talk of a national highway that might run through the community and swerve over Ravena's forest. In my nightmares, I imagine this highway slicing through the Forecomers canyon, emitting a fog of diesel exhaust that would spill over John and Diane's grave and seep into their mansion.

The visiting hordes drive me to distraction, and often to despair. They drive around doused in cologne and dressed in knockoff designer clothes, documenting every moment with cell phones and brightly colored selfie sticks. They run my family off the roads, stare at us curiously as if we're animals in a zoo. Sometimes I go for jogs and they come swerving around blind corners, three or four to a scooter, like invading tanks. They flag me down and ask where they can get pizza and croissants, or a caramel latte. With its international population and organic farms, Auroville now has something of a thriving food economy. We eat Italian, Korean, Japanese, Ethiopian, Israeli, and more. This is a far cry from the hardships of the past, and I guess it's a sign of progress. But the Mother never set out to build a culinary utopia.

Auralice thinks I'm a curmudgeon. She says that these tourists come because they admire Auroville, and because this town has something to show them and share with the world. She's probably right; especially in the context of India's ecological catastrophe, where water is often poison and the air a toxic smog, Auroville is something of a beacon. I should take more satisfaction from that. But still, some days I long to go back to the deserted vistas of my youth, to the endless flat fields and the openness we used to inhabit. One of the reasons Auralice and I left New York was because we needed more inner space: more room to think, to explore, just to be. A lesson we've both learned over the last decade or so is that inner space needs outer space. It's hard to grow as a person—or even to think clearly—amid the exigencies of urban sprawl. Sometimes I feel not so much a curmudgeon as an anachronism, a stepson of the age. Maybe the yoga we're meant to be practicing isn't compatible with the era of Instagram.

So this fiftieth birthday is upon us, and Auroville receives even more media attention than usual, and more people than ever swoop into town. I'm a little astonished by all the activity. New roads are cleared, installation art pieces set up along footpaths, a slew of cultural activities scheduled, and street signs added to forest tracks. Government grants pour in to the community, and it's as if the whole place is being cleaned up and dusted off. Movie stars and politicians show up with their retinues and gun-toting security officers. People I barely know—and who barely know Auroville—are talking on Facebook and Twitter about the community's anniversary. Among certain crowds, Auroville's fiftieth birthday is a can't-miss occasion, like a modern Woodstock or something.

Pretty much the only people who don't make it out to Auroville for the anniversary are members of the CFY, the group that originally founded Auroville. Some people in the community do suggest inviting them, as a gesture of healing. After all, it's been more than thirty years since the revolution ended, and a lot of water has run under the bridge. But then a petition goes around, and enough people still feel strongly about the bad old days, whose wounds remain raw; and so once again, in a replay of the revolution itself, the most uncompromising voices win out. The CFY is not invited, and this strikes me as a missed opportunity.

I consider leaving town, skipping the whole carnival. But I don't; I guess I feel just enough attachment to stick around. So I dodge the tourists and visiting dignitaries, do my best to stay away from the commotion, and try to go on with life. I take my kids to school, get groceries in our co-op, jog, play tennis, write, cycle the back roads. The one anniversary-related event I do go to is held on February 28, 2018, Auroville's official birthday.

Fifty years after the project's inauguration in a makeshift amphitheater on a sun-baked, empty landscape, the community assembles once again at dawn in the amphitheater, this time under the resplendent golden glow of the Matrimandir, which was completed in 2008. A bonfire has been arranged to commemorate the occasion, and it's the most sought-after show in town. Some seven thousand tickets have been distributed, and by the look of things, every single one of them is being used. The area outside the Matrimandir is jammed with motorcycles and cars. Volunteers in yellow vests move among the crowd, directing people and beseeching them to maintain the quiet.

I park my motorcycle under a tree, walk along a dimly lit path toward the amphitheater. I hang back a little, watch as people dart by clutching their tickets in the early-morning darkness. There's a pile of wood at the bottom of the amphitheater, under the marble urn that contains earth from 124 countries, and next to the wood is a large golden disk, like those that cover the Matrimandir. A crystal ball is in the center of the disk, and the ground is laid with flowers and flickering oil lamps. Most people sit on the steps of the amphitheater, and a few are in red plastic chairs, in a VIP enclosure cordoned off with rope. A dedicated VIP section seems to me to go against the spirit of things, but I suppose a few concessions to the ways of the world are inescapable.

The flame is lit at 5:15 a.m. Immediately the cell phones come out, an otherworldly mushrooming of blue lights that spans the round of the amphitheater. Camera shutters click and whir, overlaying the crackle of fire. A rooster crows in the distance, and nearer to us, a black dog starts howling. The dog runs over to the amphitheater, chasing a white one, and the volunteers in yellow vests rush to shoo them both off. The dogs move to the Banyan Tree, some twenty-five feet away, where they growl and bark.

I'm trying to concentrate through all of this. I'm remembering the bonfires of my youth—the silence, the focus, the integrity of those events. There's a lot of coughing and whispering in the crowd, and a group of tourists comes up behind me and one of them taps me on the shoulder. A woman holds her cell phone up, grinning cheerfully, and asks if I'll take their photo. She seems friendly and nice, but I snap, "This is supposed to be a meditation, not a tourist attraction." They laugh, look at me warily, and back off. I can see they think Aurovilians are an odd breed. I feel that I should feel something; I feel that I should be in the moment. But I don't, and I can't.

Then a speaker hisses, there's some organ music, and the Mother's voice rings out. She's reading Auroville's Charter; they're playing the original recording, which was broadcast from her room in Pondicherry at the community's birth. "Greetings from Auroville to all men of good will," the Mother says in her voice that simultaneously contains all the fragility and resilience of this project. "Are invited to Auroville all those who thirst for progress and aspire to a higher and truer life." She reads the Charter in French and English, and then someone else reads it in Sanskrit and Tamil.

To my great surprise, I feel shivers along my spine. A moment ago all I could think about was the aggravation of the ceremony and the tourists, the banality of the spectacle. Now I sense something altogether more meaningful and elevated. It's like a touch of the old intensity.

What is it that moves me so? I think it's something about the historicity of the moment: the sheer passage of time, that so much has played out on this land over the last fifty years. The Mother reads the Charter and I'm struck by her ambition, the audacity of her aspiration. I marvel at the way that aspiration has endured, battered though it may be. All the dreams, all the determination, all the resolute and at times blind faith. All the people who've worked so hard, who've sweated and bled on this plateau, who have overcome, and sometimes they've succumbed, and whose collective efforts have inched this project along. I'm moved by the way Auroville and its idealism have survived.

On my way out of the amphitheater, I see Frederick, Auroson's father. He's dressed in a yellow kurta. He's seventy-eight years old now and has a dreamy look on his face. I hug him and he hugs me; this is not how we typically greet each other. "We're still here," he says with a broad grin. "We're still standing."

There's a place in Auroville I haven't yet told you about. I've saved it for last. Maybe that's because the place is special, or maybe because it's the most dif-

ficult to explain. That's saying a lot: so much of what goes on in this town, has gone on, is difficult to explain.

Inside the Matrimandir is the Inner Chamber, the large meditation room conceived by the Mother. The Inner Chamber is fifty feet high and seventy-nine feet across. It's lined with white marble and circled by twelve white columns that point up to but don't quite touch the ceiling, as if reaching toward something higher. In the center of the room sits a massive crystal ball, imported from Germany, and during the day sunlight filters through an opening in the ceiling, creating a beam of light, like a saber, that runs from top to bottom.

Like many Aurovilians, Auralice and I go to this meditation space when we feel troubled, or when we need to center ourselves and figure out where we're heading, or whom we want to be. We also go there every year on our birthday; birthdays are good times to introspect. On my forty-fifth birthday, about a year and a half after Auroville's fiftieth anniversary, I drive over to the Matrimandir and go up a flight of stairs that enters into a large hall, a cavernous space filled with a subdued red light and the soothing sound of dripping water.

I ascend a curved ramp, a floating pathway that leads upward, toward the Inner Chamber. I enter the Chamber and sit on two pillows on the white-carpeted floor. I close my eyes and quickly lose awareness of the handful of other people in the room. It's easy to go deep inside in that space; the Chamber is utterly still, its atmosphere focused and charged.

I meditate for about forty minutes. Everyone has their own method for meditation, everyone has to find their own way. For me the process is just about going inward, watching the river of thought, following it as it courses through my mind, and body, but never letting the river stop, never getting attached to any part of it. So I sit in the chamber and the river flows, and as it flows, I see my sons, Aman and Emil, I see my wife, my parents, there's a brief moment when suddenly I remember an email I've forgotten to send, then I'm back with Auralice, I see her as an adult, as a child, riding a pony across the fields of Auroville, my stomach rumbles and I think of the lentils I had for lunch, I sense pain in my left ankle, which I broke when I was a kid, and now I can see myself falling on a dusty soccer field and breaking the ankle, then I'm back with my sons and Auralice, thinking of my birthday, how many years I've been with them, and how many more will I have, and then I think of this book, and I see John and Diane, John as a boy in Georgetown, playing with Gillian in the park, or at the National Gallery with their father, in a car, on a ship, and I see John standing in front of Ravena, and he isn't sick or limping, he's joyful and radiant, a soft smile on his face, gentle sweet John, gone too early, passed with Diane into that light, skeletons under the earth, poor unfairly suffering Diane, her dead infant on the ground by a pond of water, and those traitor legs dangling helplessly, and Auralice left all alone, shivering and crying in a bed, who could ever say she would end up on the Upper West Side of New York, and then back in Auroville, with a husband writing this outrageous story. This is how our river flows—this is how it zigs and zags, moving from image to image, thought to thought, things that matter and some that don't, but really, at the end of my meditation I always feel that nothing matters all that much, and that's kind of the point.

I leave the Chamber and head back down the ramp, and I exit the Matrimandir. I walk alongside the Banyan Tree, toward the amphitheater, where

I know Auralice and the boys are waiting. I'm calm and self-contained; this is what the Chamber always does to me. My mind is clear, as though it's undergone a cleansing, and I feel transparent, as if the world and its problems float right through me. I don't feel elevated or uplifted; this isn't positivity. I'm neutral, in the best sense of the word. You know I'm a skeptic, you know about my difficulties with faith. But something is going on in that Chamber, something beyond what I can figure out with my mind.

Birthdays can be complicated. It's easy to let the mind wander to the passage of time, to that transience that so preoccupied John's father (and John, too). As I approach the amphitheater, I see my sons running around, dark shapes in the advancing evening, and then I see Auralice on a bench, keeping an eye on them. The kids are a little wild, jumping and running up and down steps, clambering up a mound that contains the marble urn. I know these games can be dangerous, and they've certainly had their share of childhood injuries. Sometimes I get anxious, but not today. I'm confident that everything is all right, that it's all going to be okay—and even if it isn't, that's okay, too.

I join Auralice on the bench, and as we watch our boys together, I know we're thinking similar thoughts, that our minds are leaning in the same direction. Even after fifteen years of living in Auroville as adults, we still worry about raising them here. We wonder if we made the right decision in coming back. How will that decision play out in Aman's and Emil's lives? Will their unusual upbringing in this unusual town, with their family's unusual past, prove a blessing or a burden? Will they be inspired by the dream or dismayed by its shortcomings? Will they find their place in the world, or will they be misfits, exiles condemned to wander and never quite belong, always feeling like outsiders? And is it such a problem to feel like an outsider? I've often felt like one, Auralice, too, and I think probably also Diane and John. The sensation can be uncomfortable, but experiencing the world as an outsider also cultivates a form of insight and wisdom: a knowledge that there are other pathways and, if nothing else, the capacity to dream about different realities. Dreaming, the ability to imagine alternatives, is good for us—mostly, I think.

"They look so happy," Auralice says now. "They just seem so carefree running around!"

"Well, they have good lives," I say. "Think of all the freedom they have. There's still something special about this town. Of course they don't know half of what's going on, but kids can feel things. I think they have a sense of how unique this place is."

Auralice looks at me with surprise; I'm not usually so positive. I tell her about my meditation, and about the tranquility I'm carrying from the Chamber. She knows better than most that I haven't always been able to feel these things—that it's taken me years to break through my doubts, to turn away from the darkness I've often associated with faith. But now when I sit in the Chamber, the river flows, and I'm capable of getting out of the way. I tell Auralice that when that happens, I'm filled with gratitude—to Auroville, to the pioneers who built this place, and also to Diane and John. The way they lived has taught me so much about what it means to surrender. Learning about their stories and writing this book haven't brought me to faith, exactly, but they've shown me glimpses of a path that could lead there.

I start going on to Auralice again, as I have many times over the years, about how I think John and Diane lived with meaning, and that their deaths notwithstanding, they found purpose in Ravena. It's my birthday and I'm feeling good, and I've just been in the Chamber, and I tell her that I believe this story—her story, *our* story—has a happy ending.

"Look at us sitting here at the Matrimandir with our boys running around," I say. "Diane's grandchildren. She would be so proud. She'd be happy to see you here with your family. Think about how that would make her feel." I tell Auralice she's a survivor, like Auroville; she's come through adversity. She's wise and she's strong, and as a result, we—her family—are strong, too. I'm grateful for that, and I know that Diane and John would be gratified, though probably not surprised, that she's living here, and that this community still exists fifty years on.

Of course, she's silent. "Don't you think so?" I ask. "Don't you think they'd be happy for you, Auralice, and happy for all of us?"

This time, she takes half a step toward me. "Maybe," she says. "I don't know. Maybe."

The kids run over and complain that they're bored, they're hungry, and will we take them home? I ask for another five minutes but they're insistent, as kids can be, so we walk to the parking area and we get on our motorcycle and drive back to our community. We cook dinner together, a family meal, we drink some wine—it is after all my birthday—and then we go upstairs and Auralice and I help our boys bathe, dress them, get them into bed, and Auralice goes downstairs and I read to them, sing old childhood songs that they endure more for my sake, for the pleasure of my nostalgia, than their own. Increasingly, as they (and Auralice and I) get older, I find that they indulge our sentimentality. Allowing me to sing is their birthday gift to me.

I come back down and Auralice is on the couch and I ask her if she'd like to take a walk. So we return to the dam, our habitual retreat. We go under

the silver light of an almost full moon. Fireflies bounce in the darkness, and shadows of palmyras flutter on the ground. We sit on the embankment and listen to the crickets and the jackals, the rustling in the trees, and all the sounds of life upon this rescued, regenerated earth. A cow moos in the distance. We hold on to Auralice's *maybe*—all the possibility it contains, and all that might yet happen here.

ACKNOWLEDGMENTS

My first and overwhelming thanks go to Auralice and Gillian, for their time, generosity, and willingness to revisit deeply painful events. Nonfiction reporting and writing often feel like a form of exploitation, and I can only hope that in this instance, all my probing and prying, difficult as they may have been, were also accompanied by a certain amount of catharsis. I also want to add my thanks here to my sons, Aman John Anthony and Emil Larry, for their patience and support (knowing that their children and grandchildren might read this book was a source of sustenance); and to my parents, Dilip and Mary, who brought me to Auroville so many years ago.

Tina Bennett and Colin Harrison believed in this project from the start. They helped shape the project, and Colin, along with the rest of Scribner, gave me the gift of time. At WME, I am also grateful to Claudia Ballard (for picking up the reins so graciously), Fiona Baird, Camille Morgan, Elizabeth Wachtel, and Svetlana Katz. At Simon & Schuster, I am grateful to Wendy Blum, Zoey Cole, Sayantan Ghosh, Sarah Goldberg, Nan Graham, Sabah Khan, Ian Marshall, Katie Monaghan, Jaya Miceli, Emily Polson, Katie Rizzo, and everyone else who helped get this across the finish line and into the world. I am also grateful to Ed Klaris and Alexia Bedat for navigating me through some rewrites.

Acknowledgments

I owe a huge debt to the many Aurovilians, former Aurovilians, and Ashramites who shared their memories and experiences with me, even when they were worried at times about revisiting insalubrious events. I am humbled by their openness and by their trust that I would be impartial and fair. I hope I have lived up to that trust, though I fully anticipate that not everyone I spoke with will be satisfied with my interpretation of events. I can only say that I share their love and hopes for Auroville, and that, in my version of love, Auroville is stronger and more impressive for its ability to encompass different points of view and varying interpretations of the yoga.

There are too many among the hundreds I interviewed and spoke with to name here, but I would like in particular to thank Amrit, Alain Bernard, Joss Brooks, Frederick Buxloh, Prudence Carlson, Roy Chvat, Michel Danino, Philippe De Craene, Nicole Elfi, Robert Lawlor, Judith Murray, Francis Neemberry, Jocelyn Shupak, Shyama, B. Sullivan, Sundaram and Amudha, Roger Toll, Jaime Urrutia, Luc Venet, and Robert Yasuda. Special thanks to Larry Nagel—father and grandfather (and father-in-law) extraordinaire. We are all so grateful to have you in our lives.

For reading and commenting on early drafts, I am indebted to Nell Freudenberger, Peter Heehs, Peter Hessler, Larissa MacFarquhar, and Cindy Spiegel. At the *New Yorker*, I am grateful to Henry Finder and David Remnick for letting me tease out some early ideas on utopia, and more generally for allowing me to write for them over the years. I am also grateful to Rozina Ali, Clare Sestanovich, Nick Thompson, and Hélène Werner.

Thanks to the Whiting Foundation, the Portsmouth Abbey, the National Gallery of Art, and Bodhi Zendo for space and financial support. Huge appreciation, too, for the Auroville Archives, which, under the able leadership of Gilles Guigan, is such a nurturing, welcoming, and undogmatic place and offers a repository of information and insight for anyone writing about Auroville. Future generations will be grateful, as they will be for General Krishna Tewari's foresight in initiating and nurturing the archives during its early years.

Callum Crowe and Lhamu Tsering provided vital research support. And thanks, for various reasons, to Anthony Appiah, Afsaneh Bader, Roy Bahat,

Vlatko Balic, Auroson Bystrom, Vishakha Desai, S. Dhananchezian, Yeshe Dolma, Naresh Fernandes, Luk Gastmans, Ingrid Graft, Jane Guttridge, Kiran Kakkad, Jacqueline Kapur, Benjamin Laroquette, Jean Laroquette, V. Laxmi (RIP), Denise Maes, Guiseppe Marchese, Albert Maysles, Philip Maysles, Rebekah Maysles, Sara Maysles, Pankaj Mishra, Mary Mount, Poonga, Muniandi Radhakrishna, Rajlakshmi, R. Sathyanarayanan, E. Sekar, Ruth Sequeira, Aurovici Sercomanens, Pattie Sullivan, T. Vasantha, and Stefaan Verhulst.

I want to thank Auralice again—she was not only an accomplice in shaping the book but also a patient and loving partner in life who, along with Aman and Emil, put up with so much. I am blessed to have them in my life and, now that I know the full dimensions of the story, in awe more than ever of what Auralice has come through. Her strength, balance, and graciousness are a source of inspiration for me (and many others). Thanks, also, to my siblings, Vikas, Ayesha, and Milan, who shared the journey with me.

And finally: Gratitude does not begin to sum up my feelings toward Auroville—this astonishing, mysterious project, so human and full of human frailty, yet also aiming at perfection in a way unlike any other place I know. Wherever I go, whatever I do, however much I may buck and protest, I am privileged, humbled, and blessed to call Auroville my home in the world.

AUTHOR'S NOTE

THE NARRATIVE CONTAINED IN THIS book is constructed primarily from hundreds of hours of oral interviews and conversations, as well as a number of documentary sources. Memory is fickle, and recollections among those I interviewed often varied; sometimes the same person's memories changed over time. I have tried to verify information where possible, and in some cases followed a version of events that seemed most plausible. Of course, any errors—and there will, inevitably, be some—are my responsibility.

The documentary sources I relied on include both published and unpublished materials. I am grateful to Gillian Walker (and her family) for sharing John's letters and diaries with me; these materials represent the inspiration for this project. I have also used materials from the Auroville Archives, the Sri Aurobindo Ashram Archives, and the National Gallery of Art in Washington, DC.

In addition, I drew from a number of published sources. Special mention is due to Jocelyn Shupak's *The Antithesis of Yoga*, which includes a (fictionalized) version of some of the events included in this book. John Walker also features in Jean Stein's *Edie: An American Girl*. For Auroville's history, I drew from, among other sources, *Children of Change: A Spiritual Pilgrimage* by Amrit; *Genesis of the Auroville Foundation Act* by Alain Bernard; *A House for the Third Millennium* by Ruud Lohman; *Auroville: A City for the Future* by Anu Majumdar; *The Religious, the Spiritual, and the Secular: Auroville and Secular India* by Robert N. Minor; *Auroville: The First Six Years* and *Auroville, Sun-Word Rising: A Trust for the Earth* by Savitra; *The Dawning of Auroville* by W. M. Sullivan; and *Economics for People and Earth: The Auroville Case, 1968–2008* by Henk Thomas and Manuel Thomas.

For background on the Ashram, Sri Aurobindo, and the Mother, I drew from *The Lives of Sri Aurobindo* by Peter Heehs; *On the Mother* by Srinivasa Iyengar; *The Mother's Agenda* and *Notes on the Way*; *The Mother Trilogy* by Satprem; *Homage to the Service Tree* and *The Story of the Main Building* by the Sri Aurobindo Ashram; and *The Mother* and *Beyond Man* by Georges Van Vrekhem.

Other works I have turned to include *The Bernard Berenson Treasury* by Bernard Berenson; *I Remember* by Pranab Kumar Bhattacharya; *History and Utopia* by E. M. Cioran; *Bernard Berenson: A Life in the Picture Trade* by Rachel Cohen; *Mona Lisa in Camelot* by Margaret Leslie Davis; *Satprem: Par un Fil de Lumière* by Nicole Elfi; *India After Gandhi* by Ramachandra Guha; *Paradise Now: The Story of American Utopianism* by Chris Jennings; *Capital Culture: J. Carter Brown, the National Gallery of Art, and the Reinvention of the Museum Experience* by Neil Harris; *The Georgetown Set: Friends and Rivals in Cold War Washington* by Gregg Herken; *Down Memory Lane* by SS (Shyam Sunder) Jhunjhunwala; and *Notebooks of an Apocalypse* and *My Burning Heart* by Satprem.

I am grateful to the Sri Aurobindo Ashram Trust for allowing me to quote certain longer passages; to Roger Toll and Divakar for permission to quote from their diaries; and to Akash Heimlich for permission to quote from Ruud Lohman's Matrimandir diaries. I am also grateful to Robert Lawlor for permission to quote from his letters.

The line "stepson of the age"—from the Epilogue—is borrowed from Vasily Grossman's magnificent *Life and Fate*, which got me through some of the darker days of this project.

This is a work of nonfiction. To the best of my abilities, I have recounted events as they actually occurred. There are no invented or composite characters or places. I have in some instances changed identifying details, including the names of individuals, places, and organizations. I have also moved certain events in time, and edited and concatenated some passages from John's writings in the interests of narrative concision and cohesiveness.

Finally, I am grateful to the many photographers, artists, and archivists who have allowed me to use the included images, helping to bring to life some of the scenes, events, and people I describe. The image credits are as follows:

Pages vi–vii: The Drone Project, Auroville

Pages 8–9: Anita Reichle

Pages 12, 44, 93, 164, 226–27, 240, 249, 262, 264, 268: courtesy of Gillian Walker

Page 13: courtesy of National Gallery of Art, Washington, DC, Gallery Archives

Pages 17, 47, 192, 196, 242, 293: courtesy of Auralice Graft

Pages 27, 63 bottom row, 71, 122, 213: courtesy of Sri Aurobindo Ashram Archives

Page 35: courtesy of INTACH, Pondicherry

Page 40: Muniandi Radhakrishna

Page 48: André Hababou

Page 50: Camilla Smith

Page 55: Nadia Loury

Page 58: courtesy of Robert Lawlor

Pages 63 top and middle row, 80, 99, 108, 152, 169: courtesy of Auroville Archives

Page 83: Dale Beldin

Pages 31, 36, 104: courtesy of Sri Aurobindo Ashram

Pages 132–33, 186, 209: Rakhal Venet

Page 137: Eccles/Shutterstock.com

Page 144: Lisbeth Nusselein

Author's Note

Page 158: Bruce Davidson

Page 167: Roger Toll

Page 214: courtesy of Amrit

Pages 219, 253, 320: Michel Danino and Nicole Elfi

Page 231: Ermess/Shutterstock.com

Page 289: courtesy of the author

Pages 306, 308: Emil Kapur

Page 331: Oliver Barot

Page 335: Ireno Guerci

ABOUT THE AUTHOR

Akash Kapur is the author of *India Becoming: A Portrait of Life in Modern India* and the editor of an anthology, *Auroville: Dream and Reality*. He is the former Letter from India columnist for the international *New York Times*, the recipient of a Whiting Grant, and has written for various leading publications. He grew up in Auroville and returned there to live with his family after boarding school and college in America.